A Concise History of Ireland

PREFACE

THE first part of this little book is an abridgment of my larger work, "A Short History of Ireland," of which the very words are used here as far as possible. The whole book is of necessity greatly condensed, containing much matter in little space: but it is not a cram book. It is a connected intelligible narrative, into which I have tried to infuse some life and human interest.

The series of short Chapters forming Part I., on the Literature, Art, and Institutions of ancient Ireland, will, I hope, prove useful; and perhaps they may be found interesting. In four of them I have given, in language as simple and clear as I could command, a popular exposition of a subject not easy to deal with—the Brehon Laws, including those relating to land.

I have, I hope, written soberly and moderately, avoiding exaggeration and bitterness, and showing fair play all round. A writer may accomplish all this while sympathising heartily, as I do, with Ireland and her people.

P. W. J.
DUBLIN
1909

PART I. THE MANNERS, CUSTOMS, AND INSTITUTIONS OF THE ANCIENT IRISH.

IN WRITING the history of a country it is desirable to begin with some account of the early inhabitants and their modes of life. The following chapters, forming the first Part of this book, have been written with the object of giving, in a popular form, some trustworthy information on the institutions, literature, laws, and customs of the ancient Irish people.

THE IRISH LANGUAGE

1. Dialects of Celtic. There are two main branches of the Ancient Celtic Language: The Goidelic, or Gaelic, or Irish; and the British; corresponding with the two main divisions of the Celtic people of the British Islands.

Each of these has branched into three dialects. Those of Gaelic are:—The Irish proper; the Gaelic of Scotland, differing only slightly from the Irish; and the Manx. The dialects of British are: Welsh, Cornish, and Breton or Armoric. Of the whole six dialects, five are still spoken; the Cornish became extinct in the last century; and Manx is nearly extinct.

2. Three Divisions of Irish. It is usual to divide Irish, as we find it written, into three stages: I. Old Irish, from the eighth to the twelfth century. This is the language of the Irish found in the Book of Armagh, and of some few passages in the Book of the Dun Cow. II. Middle Irish, from the twelfth to the fifteenth century, marked by many departures from the pure Old Irish forms. This is the language of most of our important manuscripts, described in next Chapter; such as the Book of the Dun Cow, the Book of Leinster, the Lebar Brecc, and the Book of Ballymote. III. Modern Irish, from the fifteenth century to the present day. This is the language of most of the Ossianic tales. The purest specimens are the writings of Keating. There is a vast amount of manuscript literature in Modern Irish.

3. Ogham was a species of writing in use in early ages, the letters of which were formed by combinations of short lines and points on and at both sides of a middle or stem line called a flesc. Scraps of Ogham are sometimes found in manuscripts, but it was almost always used for stone inscriptions, the groups of lines and points generally running along two adjacent sides of the stone, with the angle for a flesc. Upwards of 200 Ogham monuments have been found in various parts of the four provinces of Ireland; but they are far more numerous in the south and south-west than elsewhere.

Nearly all the Oghams hitherto found are sepulchral inscriptions. Where inscriptions have not been injured or defaced, they can in general be deciphered, so that many have been made out beyond all question. But as the greatest number of Ogham stones are more or less worn or chipped or broken, there is in the interpretation of the majority of the inscriptions some conjecture and uncertainty.

As to the antiquity of Ogham writing, the best authorities now agree that it is a survival from the far distant ages of paganism, and that it was developed before Christianity was heard of in Ireland. But the custom of engraving Ogham on stones, and of—occasionally—writing in Ogham characters in vellum books, continued far into Christian times. In the ancient tales we find it often stated that Oghams were cut on rods of yew or oak, and that such rods were used as a mode of communication between individuals, serving the same purpose among them as letter-writing serves now.

IRISH LITERATURE

4. There are many passages in ancient writings proving beyond question

that there was some form of written literature in Ireland before the advent of Christianity. In the oldest native literature it is expressly stated that the pagan Irish had books, and the statement is corroborated by an extern writer, a Christian philosopher and traveller of the fourth century named Ethicus of Istria; who, in a work he calls his "Topography," tells us that in the course of his travels he crossed over from Spain to Ireland, where he spent some time examining the books written by the native Irish scholars. This was at least a century before the arrival of St. Patrick.

Several circumstances indicate a state of literary activity at the time of St. Patrick, who, on his arrival in the country, found literary and professional men:—Druids, poets, and antiquarians.

5. After the time of St. Patrick, as everything seems to have been written down that was considered worth preserving, manuscripts accumulated in the course of time, which were kept either in monasteries or in the houses of hereditary professors of learning. In the dark time of the Danish ravages and during the troubled centuries that followed the Anglo-Norman invasion, the manuscript collections were gradually dispersed, and a large proportion lost or destroyed. Yet we have remaining—rescued by good fortune from the general wreck—a great body of manuscript literature. The two most important collections are those in Trinity College and in the Royal Irish Academy, Dublin, where there are manuscripts of various ages, from the fifth down to the present century. In the Franciscan monastery of Adam and Eve in Dublin are a number of valuable manuscripts which were sent from Rome a few years ago. There are also many important manuscripts in Maynooth College, in the British Museum in London, and in the Bodleian Library at Oxford.

6. Before the invention of printing it was customary in Ireland for individuals, or families, or religious communities, to keep large manuscript books of miscellaneous literature. In these were written suck literary pieces as were considered worthy of being preserved in writing—tales, poems, biographies, genealogies, histories, annals, and so forth—all mixed up in one volume, and almost always copied from older books. The value set on these books may be estimated from the fact that one of them was sometimes given as ransom for a captive chief.

7. The oldest of all these books of miscellaneous literature is the Lebar-na-Heera, or the Book of the Dun Cow, now in the Royal Irish Academy. It was written by Mailmurri Mac Kelleher, a learned scribe, who died in Clonmacnoise in the year 1106. As it now stands it consists of only 134 folio pages, a mere fragment of the original work. It contains 65 pieces of various kinds, several of which are imperfect on account of missing leaves. There are a number of romantic tales in prose; a copy of the celebrated Amra or elegy on St. Columkille, composed by Dallan Forgaill about the year 592, which no one can yet wholly understand, the language is so

ancient and difficult; an imperfect copy of the Voyage of Maildun; and an imperfect copy of the Tain-bo-Quelna with several of the minor tales connected with it.

8. The Book of Leinster, the next in order of age, now in Trinity College, Dublin, was written in 1160 and in the years before and after. The part of the original book remaining—for it is only a part—consists of 410 folio pages, and contains nearly 1,000 pieces of various kinds—prose and poetry—historical sketches, romantic tales (among which is a perfect copy of the Tain-bo-Quelna), topographical tracts, genealogies, etc.—a vast collection of ancient Irish lore.

9. The Lebar Brecc, or Speckled Book of Mac Egan, also called the Great Book of Duniry, is in the Royal Irish Academy. It is a large folio volume, now consisting of 280 pages, but originally containing many more, written in a small, uniform, beautiful hand, toward the end of the fourteenth century, by the Mac Egans, a family of learned professors and teachers. The book, which contains 226 pieces, was copied from various older books, most of them now lost. All, both text and notes, with a few exceptions, are on religious subjects; there is a good deal of Latin mixed with the Irish.

10. The Book of Ballymote, in the Royal Irish Academy, is a large folio volume of 501 pages. It was written by several scribes about the year 1391, at Ballymote in Sligo, from older books; and contains a great number of pieces in prose and verse. Among them is a copy of the Book of Invasions, i.e., a history of the Conquests of Ireland by the several ancient colonists. There are genealogies of almost all the principal Irish families; several historical and romantic tales of the early Irish kings; a copy of the Dinnsenchus; a translation of the Argonautic Expedition and of the War of Troy.

11. The Yellow Book of Lecan [Leckan] in Trinity College, is a large quarto volume of about 500 pages. It was written at Lecan in the County Sligo in and about the year 1390, and contains a great number of pieces in prose and verse, historical, biographical, topographical, &c.

12. The five books above described have been published in facsimile without translations by the Royal Irish Academy, page for page, line for line, letter for letter, so that scholars in all parts of the world can now study them without coming to Dublin.

13. The Book of Lecan, in the Royal Irish Academy, about 600 pages, was written in 1416, chiefly by Gilla Isa More Mac Firbis. The contents resemble in a general way those of the Book of Ballymote.

There are many other books of miscellaneous Gaelic literature in the Royal Irish Academy and in Trinity College, such as the Book of Lismore, the Book of Fermoy, the Book of Hy Many; besides numerous volumes without special names.

Ancient Irish literature, so far as it has been preserved, may be classed as follows:

I. Ecclesiastical and Religious writings.
II. Annals, History, and Genealogy.
III. Tales, historical and romantic.
IV. Law, Medicine, and Science.
V. Translations of Pieces from other languages.

IRISH ECCLESIASTICAL WRITINGS

14. Copies of the Gospels or of other portions of Scripture, that were either written or owned by eminent saints of the early Irish Church, were treasured with great veneration by succeeding generations; and it became a common practice to enclose them, for better preservation, in ornamental boxes or shrines, which are generally of exquisite workmanship in gold, silver, or other metals, precious stones, and enamel. Books of this kind are the oldest we possess.

15. The Domnach Airgid, or Silver Shrine, which is in the National Museum, Dublin, is a box containing a Latin copy of the Gospels written on vellum. It was once thought the enclosed book was the identical copy of the Gospels presented by St. Patrick to his disciple St. Mac Carthenn, the founder of the see of Clogher: but recent investigations go to show that it is not so old as the time of the great apostle.

16. The Book of Kells is the most remarkable book of this class, though not the oldest. It is a Latin copy in vellum, of the four Gospels, now in Trinity College, Dublin, and received its name from having been kept for many centuries at Kells in Meath. Its exact age is unknown, but it was probably written in the seventh or eighth century. At the present day this is the best known of all the old Irish books, on account of its elaborate and beautiful ornamentation, of which a description will be found in the Chapter on Art.

17. The Cathach [Caha] of the O'Donnells. According to a very old tradition this book was written by St. Columkille; and at any rate it has been in the family of his kindred, the O'Donnells, since his time. They always brought it with them to battle; and it was their custom to have it carried three times round their army before fighting, in the belief that this would insure victory; hence it name, Cathach, which means Battle-book. This venerable relic, covered with a beautifully wrought case of silver gilt and precious stones, may be seen in the National Museum, Dublin.

18. In Trinity College, Dublin, are two beautiful shrines enclosing two illuminated Gospel manuscripts, the Book of Dimma and the Book of St. Moling, both written in the seventh or eighth century.

19. The Book of Armagh, now in Trinity College, is almost as beautifully written as the Book of Kells. The accomplished scribe was Ferdomnach of Armagh, who finished the book in 807. It is chiefly in Latin, with a good

deal of Old Irish interspersed. It contains a life of St. Patrick; a number of Notes on his life, by Bishop Tirechan; a complete copy of the New Testament; and St. Patrick's Confession, in which the saint gives a brief account, in simple, unaffected Latin, of his mission in Ireland, The Confession was copied by Ferdomnach from the very handwriting of St. Patrick.

In the year 1004, a highly interesting and important entry was made in this book. In that year the great King Brian Boru, arriving at Armagh, made an offering of twenty ounces of gold on the altar of St. Patrick. He confirmed the ancient ecclesiastical supremacy of Armagh, and caused his secretary, Mailsuthain, to enter in the Book of Armagh this decree, which is as plain now as the day it was written.

20. We have a vast body of original ecclesiastical and religious writings. Among them are the Lives of a great many of the most distinguished Irish saints, mostly in Irish, some few in Latin; of various ages, from the eighth century, the period of the Book of Armagh, down to the last century. The Lives of Saints Patrick, Brigit, and Columkille are more numerous than those of the others. Of these the best known is the "Tripartite Life of St. Patrick," so called because it is divided into three parts.

Besides the Irish Lives of St, Columkille, there is one in Latin, written by Adamnan, who died in the year 703. He was a native of Donegal, and ninth abbot of Iona; and his memoir is one of the most graceful pieces of Latin composition of the Middle Ages. It has been published.

21. Another class of Irish ecclesiastical writings are the Calendars or Martyrologies, or Festilogies — Irish Feilire [Fail'ira], a festival list. The Feilire is a catalogue of saints arranged according to their festival days, with usually a few facts about each, briefly stated. There are several of these Martyrologies. One is the Calendar or Martyrology of Donegal, written by Michael O'Clery the chief of the Four Masters, which has been published. The only other one I will notice is the Feilire of Aengus the Culdee, which is in verse, and which has been translated and printed.

22. The Book of Hymns is one of the manuscripts of Trinity College, Dublin, copied at some time not later than the ninth or tenth century. It consists of a number of hymns—some in Latin, some in Irish—composed by the primitive saints of Ireland.

23. There are manuscripts on various other ecclesiastical subjects, scattered through our libraries; canons and rules of monastic life, prayers and litanies, hymns, sermons, explanations of the Christian mysteries, commentaries on the Scriptures, &c.—many very ancient.

ANNALS, HISTORIES, GENEALOGIES

24. Annals. The Irish chroniclers were very careful to record in their annals remarkable occurrences of their own time, or past events as handed down to them by former chroniclers. The annals are among the most

important of the ancient manuscript writings for the study of Irish history.

The following are the principal books of Irish Annals remaining. The Synchronisms of Flann, who was a layman, Ferleginn or chief professor of the school of Monasterboice; died in 1056. He compares the chronology of Ireland with that of other countries, and gives the names of the monarchs that reigned in them, with lists of the Irish kings who reigned contemporaneously. Copies of this tract are preserved in the Books of Lecan and Ballymote.

25. The Annals of Tighernach [Teerna]. Tighernach O'Breen, the compiler of these annals, one of the greatest scholars of his time, was abbot of the two monasteries of Clonmacnoise and Roscommon. He was acquainted with the chief historical writers of the world known in his day, and made use of Flann's Synchronisms, and of most other ancient Irish historical writings of importance. He states that authentic Irish history begins at the foundation of Emania, and that all preceding accounts are uncertain. He died 1088.

26. The Annals of Innisfallen were compiled about the year 1215 by some scholars of the monastery of Innisfallen in the Lower Lake of Killarney.

The Annals of Ulster, also called the Annals of Senait Mac Manus, now called Belle Isle, in upper Lough Erne. The original compiler was Cathal [Cahal] Maguire, who died of small-pox in 1498. They have been published with translation.

The Annals of Loch Ce [Key] were copied in 1588 for Brian Mac Dermot, who had his residence in an island in Lough Key, in Roscommon. They have been translated and edited in two volumes.

The Annals of Connaught from 1224 to 1562.

27. The Chronicon Scotorum (Chronicle of the Scots or Irish), down to A.D. 1135, was compiled about 1650 by the great Irish antiquary Duald Mac Firbis. These annals have been printed with translation.

The Annals of Boyle, from the earliest time to 1253, are written in Irish mixed with Latin; and the entries throughout are very meagre.

The Annals of Clonmacnoise from the earliest period to 1408. The original Irish of these is lost; but we have an English translation by Connell Mac Geoghegan of Westmeath, which he completed in 1627.

28. The Annals of the Four Masters, also called the Annals of Donegal, are the most important of all. They were compiled in the Franciscan monastery of Donegal, by three of the O'Clerys, Michael, Conary, and Cucogry, and by Ferfesa O'Mulconry, who are now commonly known as the Four Masters. They began in 1632, and completed the work in 1636. "The Annals of the Four Masters" was translated with most elaborate and learned annotations by Dr. John O'Donovan; and it was published—Irish text, translation, and notes—in seven large volumes.

A book of annals called the Psalter of Cashel was compiled by Cormac Mac Cullenan, but this has been lost. He also wrote "Cormac's Glossary," an explanation of many old Irish words. This work still exists and has been translated and printed. Besides annals in the Irish language, there are also Annals of Ireland in Latin; such as those of Clyn, Dowling, Pembridge, of Multifarnham, &c., most of which have been published.

29. Histories. None of the writers of old times conceived the plan of writing a general history of Ireland. The first history of the whole country was the Forus Feasa ar Erinn, or History of Ireland, from the most ancient times to the Anglo-Norman invasion, written by Dr. Geoffrey Keating of Tubbrid in Tipperary, who died in 1644. Keating was deeply versed in the ancient language and literature of Ireland; and his history, though containing much that is legendary, is very interesting and valuable.

30. Genealogies. The genealogies of the principal families were most faithfully preserved in ancient Ireland. Each king and chief had in his household a Shanachy or historian, whose duty it was to keep a written record or all the ancestors and of the several branches of the family.

Many of the ancient genealogies are preserved in the Books of Leinster, Lecan, Ballymote, &c. But the most important collection of all is the great Book of Genealogies compiled in the years 1650 to 1666 in the College of St. Nicholas in Galway, by Duald Mac Firbis.

31. In this place may be mentioned the Dinnsenchus [Din-Shan'ahus], a topographical tract giving the legendary history and the etymology of the names of remarkable hills, mounds, caves, cairns, cromlechs, raths, duns, and so forth. Copies of this tract are found in several of the old Irish books of miscellaneous literature, as already mentioned in Chapter II. The Coir Anmann ("Fitness of Names") is another work explaining the names of remarkable Irish historical persons. It has been published with translation.

HISTORICAL AND ROMANTIC TALES

32. Of all our manuscript remains, romantic literature is the most abundant. In course of time a great body of such literature accumulated, consisting chiefly of prose tales. In the Book of Leinster there is a very interesting list of ancient historical tales, to the number of 187, which are classified into Battles, Voyages, Tragedies, Military Expeditions, Cattle-raids, Courtships, Pursuits, Adventures, Caves (i.e. adventures in caves), Visions, Sieges, Feasts, Slaughters, Exiles, and Lake eruptions. We have in our old books stories belonging to every one of these classes.

"Some of the tales are historical, i.e. founded on historical events— history embellished with fiction; while others are altogether fictitious. But it is to be observed that even in the fictitious tales, the main characters are nearly always historical, or such as were considered so. The greater number of the tales are in prose, but some are in verse; and in many of the prose tales the leading characters are often made to express themselves in verse or some striking incident of the story is related in a poetical form." *

33. A large proportion of the tales fall under two main cycles of ancient Irish history, which in all the Irish poetical and romantic literature were kept perfectly distinct:—the cycle of Conor Mac Nessa and his Red Branch Knights, and the cycle of Finn, the son of Cumal and his Fianna [Feena]. Conor Mac Nessa was King of Ulster in the first century, and lived in the palace of Emain or Emania. Under him flourished the Red Branch Knights, a sort of militia for the defence of the throne. The stories of this period form by far the finest part of our ancient romantic literature.

The most celebrated of all the tales is the Tain-bo-Cuailnge [Quel'ne], the epic of Ireland; which celebrates a cattle-raiding invasion of Ulster by Maive Queen of Connaught in the first century. In connexion with it there are about thirty minor tales.

34. Of the cycle of Finn and the Fena of Erin we have a vast collection of tales : commonly known as the Ossianic Tales. Finn the son of Cumal lived in the third century, and had his chief residence on the Hill of Allen in Kildare. He was killed on the Boyne when an old man, A.D. 283; and of all the heroes of ancient Ireland he is most vividly remembered in popular tradition. He was son-in-law of Cormac Mac Art, King of Ireland; and under that monarch he commanded a militia or standing army called the Fianna of Erin.

The tales of the Fena are neither so ancient nor so fine as those of the Red Branch Knights : the greater number are contained in manuscripts not more than 100 or 150 years old. Six volumes of tales, chiefly of the cycle of Finn, have been published with translations. The best of them is "The Pursuit of Dermot and Grania," of which I have given a free English translation in my "Old Celtic Romances."

35. The battle of Moylena and the battle of Moyrath are the subjects of two historic tales, both of which have been published, the former edited by Eugene O'Curry and the latter by O'Donovan. What are called the "Three Tragic Stories of Erin," viz., the Fate of the Children of Lir, the Fate of the Sons of Turenn, and the Fate of the Children of Usna, have been translated and edited by O'Curry. I have myself published in my Old Celtic Romances free translations, without texts, of thirteen ancient tales; among them the Three Tragic Stories of Erin.

The great majority of those old tales still remain unpublished and untranslated.

* Joyce's Old Celtic Romances, Preface.

THE BREHON LAW

36. In Ireland judges were called Brehons; and the law they administered—the ancient law of Ireland—is now commonly known as the Brehon law. To become a brehon, a person had to go through a regular, well defined course of training.

The brehons were a very influential class of men, and those attached to chiefs had free lands for their maintenance. Those not so attached lived simply on the fees of their profession. It generally required great technical skill to decide cases, the legal rules, as set forth in the law-books, were so complicated, and so many circumstances had to be taken into account. The brehon, moreover, had to be very careful, for he was himself liable to damages if he delivered a false or an unjust judgment.

37. The brehons had collections of laws in volumes or tracts, all in the Irish language, by which they regulated their judgments. Many of these have been preserved, and of late years the most important of them have been published, with translations, forming five printed volumes. Of the tracts contained in these volumes, the two largest and most important are the Senchus Mor [Shan'ahus More] and the Book of Acaill [Ack'ill]. The Senchus Mor is chiefly concerned with the Irish civil law, and the Book of Acaill with the criminal law and the law relating to personal injuries.

38. At the request of St. Patrick, Laeghaire [Leary] King of Ireland formed a committee of nine persons to revise the laws:— viz., three kings, of whom Laeghaire himself was one: three ecclesiastics, of whom Patrick was one; and three poets and antiquarians, of whom Duftach, Laeghaire's chief poet was one. These nine having expunged everything that clashed with the Christian faith, produced at the end of three years a revised code which was called Senchus Mor.

39. The very book left by St. Patrick and the others has been long lost. Successive copies were made from time to time, with commentaries and explanations appended, till the manuscripts we now possess were produced.

The language of the laws is extremely archaic and difficult, indicating a very remote antiquity, though probably not the very language of the text left by the revising committee, but a modified version of a later time. The two great Irish scholars—John O'Donovan and Eugene O'Curry—who translated them, were able to do so only after long study; and in numerous instances were, to the last, not quite sure of the meaning. Even the translation is hard enough to understand, and is often unintelligible.

THE LAW OF COMPENSATION

40. The Brehon code forms a great body of civil, military, and criminal law. It regulates the various ranks of society, from the king down to the slave, and enumerates their several rights and privileges. There are minute rules for the management of property, for the several industries—building, brewing, mills, water-courses, fishing-weirs, bees and honey—for distress or seizure of goods, for tithes, trespass, and evidence. The relations of landlord and tenant, the fees of professional men—doctors, judges, teachers, builders, artificers—the mutual duties of father and son, of foster-parents and foster-children, of master and servant, are all carefully

regulated. Contracts are regarded as peculiarly sacred, and are treated in great detail.

In criminal law, the various offences are minutely distinguished:—Murder, manslaughter, wounding, thefts, and every variety of wilful damage; and accidental injuries from flails, sledge-hammers, and all sorts of weapons.

41. Injuries of all kinds as between man and man were atoned for by a compensation payment. Homicide, whether by intent or by misadventure, was atoned for like other injuries, by a money fine.

The fine for homicide or for bodily injury of any kind was called eric [er'rick]: the amount was adjudged by a brehon. The principles on which these awards should be made are laid down in great detail in the Book of Acaill.

In case of homicide the family of the victim were entitled to the eric. If the culprit did not pay, or absconded, leaving no property, his fine [finna] or family were liable. If they wished to avoid this they were required to give up the offender to the family of the victim, who might then if they pleased, kill him: or failing this, his family had to expel him. and to lodge a sum to free themselves from the consequences of his subsequent misconduct.

In the Book of Acaill there is a minute enumeration of bodily injuries, whether by design or accident, with the compensation for each, taking into account the position of the parties and the other numerous circumstances that modified the amount.

42. For homicide and for most injuries to person, property or dignity, the fine consisted of two parts:—first, the payment for the mere injury, which was determined by the severity of the injury, and by other circumstances: second, a sum called Log-enech or Honour-price, which varied according to the rank of the parties: the higher the rank the greater the honour-price. The consideration of honour-price entered into a great number of the provisions of the Brehon law. This principle also existed in the early Teutonic codes.

To make due allowance for all modifying circumstances in cases of trial, called for much legal knowledge and technical skill on the part of the brehon: quite as much as we expect in a lawyer of the present day.

The principle of compensation for murder was not peculiar to Ireland. It existed among the Anglo-Saxons, as well as among the ancient Greeks, Franks, and Germans.

GRADES AND GROUPS OF SOCIETY

43. The people were divided into classes, from the king down to the slave, and the Brehon law took cognisance of all—setting forth their rights, duties and privileges. These classes were not castes; for under certain conditions persons could pass from one to the next above. There were five

main classes:— (1) Kings of various grades from the king of the tuath or cantred up to the King of Ireland; (2) Nobles; (3) Freemen with property: (4) Freemen without property (or with very little); (5) The non-free classes. The first three were the privileged classes: a person belonging to these was an aire [arra] or chief.

44. The nobles were those who had land as their own property, for which they did not pay rent. Part of this land they held in their own hands and tilled by the labour of the non-free classes: part they let to tenants. An aire of this class was called a flaith [flah], i.e. a noble, a chief, a prince.

A person belonging to the third class of Aire, a non-noble rent-paying freeman with property, had no land of his own; his property consisting of cattle and other movable goods; hence he was called a bo-aire, i.e. a cow-aire. A bo-aire rented land from a flaith; thus taking rank as a free tenant; and he grazed his cattle partly on this and partly on the "commons" grazing land. The bo-aires had certain allowances and privileges according to rank. Among their allowances were a share in the mill and in the kiln of the district, and fees for witnessing contracts and for other legal functions.

45. The Brugh-fer or Brugaid [broo-fer: broo-ey] was an interesting official of the bo-aire class. He was a public hospitaller, bound to keep an open house for the reception of strangers. There should be a number of open roads leading to his house; and he had to keep a light burning on the lawn at night to guide travellers. He had free land and large allowances for the support of the expenses of his house; and he was much honoured.

46. The next class, the fourth, the freemen without property, were free tenants; they differed from the bo-aires only in not possessing property in herds—for the bo-aires were themselves rent-payers; and accordingly, a man of the fourth class became a bo-aire if he accumulated property enough. These freemen without property and the non-free classes will be treated of in next Chapter.

47. The people were formed into groups of various sizes from the family upwards. The family was the group consisting of the living parents and all their descendants. The Sept was a larger group descended from common parents long since dead. All the members of a sept were nearly related, and in later times bore the same surname. The Clan or house was still larger. Clann means children, and the word therefore implied descent from one ancestor. The Tribe was made up of several septs or clans, and usually claimed, like the subordinate groups, to be descended from a common ancestor. But as strangers were often adopted into all the groups, there was much admixture; and the theory of common descent became in great measure a fiction.

48. Septs, clans, and tribes were governed by chiefs: the chief of a tribe had jurisdiction over the chiefs of the several clans or septs composing the tribe, and received tribute from them. If the territory occupied by the tribe

was sufficiently extensive, the ruling flaith was a Ri [ree] or king: the tuath or cantred was the smallest territory whose ruler was called a Ri. There were 184 tuaths in all Ireland, but probably all had not kings.

There was a regular gradation of sub-kingdoms from the tuath upwards. Some were very large, such as Tyrone, Tirconnell, Thomond, Desmond, Ossory, &c., each of which comprised several tribes.

49. Each of the five provinces—Ulster, Leinster, Munster, Connaught, Meath—had a king; this is commonly known as the Pentarchy. These five provincial kings had sovereignty over the sub-kings of their several provinces, all of whom owed them tribute and war service.

Lastly there was the Ard-ri or supreme monarch of all Ireland. He had sovereignty over the provincial kings, who were bound to pay him tribute and attend him in war.

50. The following are the main features of the ancient territorial divisions of the country. It was parcelled out into five provinces from the earliest times of which we have any record:— Leinster, Ulster, Connaught, and the two Munsters. Laighin [Layen] or Leinster extended from the Suir to Inver Colpa (the mouth of the Boyne); Ulaid [Ulla] or Ulster from the Boyne round northwards to the little river Drowes between Donegal and Leitrim; Olnegmacht or Connaught from the Drowes to Limerick and the Shannon; The two Munsters, viz., the province of Curoi Mac Dara from Limerick to Cork and westward to the coasts of Cork and Kerry, and the province of Achy Avraroe from Cork to the mouth of the Suir. It is stated that these provinces met at the hill of Ushnagh in Westmeath.

51. This division became modified in course of time. A new province— that of Mide or Meath—was created in the second century by Tuathal the Legitimate king of Ireland, who formed it by cutting off a portion of each of the other provinces round the hill of Ushnagh. Murthemne, now the county Louth, was transferred from Ulster to Leinster; the present county Cavan, which originally belonged to Connaught, was given to Ulster; and the territory now known as the county Clare was wrested from Connaught and annexed to Munster. The two Munsters ceased to be distinguished, and the whole province was known by the name of Muman or Munster. A better known subdivision of Munster was into Thomond or North Munster, which broadly speaking included Tipperary, Clare, and North Limerick; and Desmond or South Munster, comprising Kerry, Cork, Waterford, and South Limerick. In recent times Meath has disappeared as a province; and the original provinces remain:— Leinster, Ulster, Connaught, and Munster.

52. With the object of avoiding the evils of a disputed sucession, the person to succeed a king or chief was often elected by the tribe during the lifetime of the king or chief himself; when elected he was called the Tanist. The person who was generally looked upon as the king's successor, whether actually elected tanist or not—the heir apparent—was commonly

called the Roydamna.

The king or chief was always elected from members of one family, bearing the same surname: but the succession was not hereditary in our sense of the word; it was elective with the above limitation of being confined to one . family. Any freeborn member of the family was eligible: the tanist might be brother, son, nephew, cousin, &c., of the chief. That member was chosen who was considered best able to lead in war, and govern in peace and he should be free from all personal deformities or blemishes.

THE TENURE OF LAND

53. The land was held by individuals in five different ways.

FIRST: The chief, whether of the tribe or of the sept, had a portion as mensal land for his support, for life or for as long as he remained chief.

SECOND: Another portion was held as private property by persons who had come to own the land in various ways. Most of these were flaiths or nobles, of the several ranks; and some were professional men, such as physicians, judges, poets, historians, artificers, &c., who had got their lands as stipends for their professional services to the chief, and in whose families it often remained for generations.

THIRD: Persons held as tenants portions of the lands belonging to those who owned it as private property, or portions of the mensal land of the chief; much like tenants of the present day: these paid what was equivalent to rent—always in kind.

FOURTH: The rest of the arable land, which was called the tribe land, forming by far the largest part of the territory, belonged to the people in general; no part being private property. This was occupied by the free members of the tribe or sept, who were owners for the time being, each of his own farm. Every free man had a right to his share. Those who occupied the tribe land did not hold for any fixed term, for the land of the sept was liable to Gavelkind or redistribution from time to time—once every three or four years. Yet they were not tenants at will, for they could not be disturbed till the time or redistribution; even then each man kept his crops and got compensation for unexhausted improvements; and though he gave up one farm he always got another.

FIFTH: The non-arable or waste land—mountain, forest, bog, &c.—was "commons" land. This was not appropriated by individuals; but every free man had a right to use it for grazing, for procuring fuel, or for the chase.

54. The revenue of the chief was derived from three main sources. First, his mensal land, some of which he cultivated by his own labourers, some he let to tenants: Second, subsidies of various kinds from the tribesmen: Third, payment for stock as described farther on. But in addition to this he might have land as his own personal property.

Every tribesman had to pay to his chief a certain subsidy according to his means. The usual subsidy for commons pasturage was in the proportion of one animal yearly for every seven, which was considerably less than a reasonable rent of the present day. Probably the subsidy for tillage land was in much the same proportion.

A man who takes land must have stock:— cows and sheep for the pasture-land, horses or oxen to carry on the work of tillage. A small proportion of the tenants had stock of their own, but the great majority had not. Where the tenant needed stock it was the custom for the chief to give him as much as he wanted at certain rates of payment. This giving or lending of stock was very general, and from it the chiefs derived a large part of their income.

55. The tenant was called a céile [caila]. Some tenants were saer-céiles, free tenants: some daer-céiles, base or bond tenants. The free tenants were comparatively independent; the bond tenants had to pay heavy subsidies, which always kept them down.

The céiles or tenants hitherto spoken of were all free men. Each had a house of his own, the right to a share of the tribe land and to the use of the commons. In this sense the daer-ceiles were free men, as well as the saer-céiles.

56. The daer-tenants were bound to give the chief refection on visitation, called coinmed [coiney]; that is, the chief was entitled to go with his followers to the house of the tenant, who had to supply the company with food and drink. The number of followers, the time, and the food, were carefully regulated by the Brehon law, according to the amount of stock the tenant borrowed from the chief. But it was a bad and a dangerous custom.

The Anglo Irish lords imitated and abused this regulation by what was called Coyne and Livery. A military leader, when he had no money to pay his soldiers, turned them out with arms in their hands among the colonists to pay themselves in money and food. This was Coyne and Livery. No distinction was made; and the soldiers being under no restraint, plundered and oppressed the people and committed many other crimes. Many severe laws were passed against Coyne and Livery, but notwithstanding these, it continued to be practised by the great lords for generations. Bad as the Irish coiney was, Coyne and Livery was much worse.

57. The non-free people were those who had scarcely any rights—some none at all. They had no claim to any part of the tribe land or to the use of the commons; though the chief might permit them to till land, for which they had to pay ruinous rent. Their standing varied; some being absolute slaves, some little removed from slavery, and others far above it. The most numerous class of the non-free people were those called fudirs; they had no right to any land they tilled, and were in complete dependence—tenants at will, who could be put out at any time.

We know that Slavery pure and simple existed in Ireland in early times:

and that it continued to a comparatively late period is proved by the testimony of Giraldus Cambrensis, who relates that it was a common custom among the English to sell their children and other relatives to the Irish for slaves; Bristol being the great mart for the trade. Slaves in those days formed a recognised item of traffic in Ireland.

58. LAND descended in three ways.

FIRST: As private property, in the usual way from father to children.

SECOND: By tanistry, i.e. the mensal land held by the chief went, not to his heir, but the person who succeeded him in the Chiefship.

THIRD: By Gavelkind. When a céile or free tenant who held a part of the tribe land died, his farm did not go to his children; but all the tribe land belonging to the sept was redivided or gavelled among all the male adult members of the sept including the dead man's adult sons. Gavelkind in a modified form still exists in Kent.

59. It should be remarked that all payments were made in kind: Cows, horses, sheep, or silver. A cow was the unit of value, and as such was called a séd [shade]. A cumal was equal to three séds.

IRISH MUSIC

60. From very early times the Irish were celebrated for their skill in music. Our native literature abounds in references to music and to skilful musicians, who are always spoken of in terms of the utmost respect.

During the long period when learning flourished in Ireland, Irish professors and teachers of music would seem to have been almost as much in request in foreign countries as those of literature and philosophy. In the middle of the seventh century, Gertrude, abbess of Nivelle in Belgium, daughter of Pepin mayor of the palace, engaged SS. Foillan and Ultan, brothers of the Irish saint Fursa, of Peronne, to instruct her nuns in psalmody. In the latter half of the ninth century the cloister schools of St. Gall were conducted by an Irishman, Maengal or Marcellus, under whose teaching the music school there attained its highest fame.

61. The cultivation of music was not materially interrupted by the Danish troubles. Giraldus Cambrensis, who seldom had a good word for anything Irish, speaks of the Irish harpers as follows:—"They are incomparably more skilful than any other nation I have ever seen. For their manner of playing on these instruments, unlike that of the Britons to which I am accustomed, is not slow and harsh, but lively and rapid, while the melody is both sweet and sprightly. It is astonishing that in so complex and rapid a movement of the fingers the musical proportions [as to time] can be preserved; and that throughout the difficult modulations on their various instruments, the harmony is completed with such a sweet rapidity." For centuries after the time of Giraldus music continued to be cultivated uninterruptedly; and there was an unbroken succession of great professional harpers, who maintained their ancient pre-eminence down to

the seventeenth century.

62. It is only when we arrive at the seventeenth century that we begin to be able to identify certain composers as the authors of existing airs. The oldest harper of great eminence coming within this description is Rory Dall (blind) O'Cahan, who was the composer of many fine airs, some of which we still possess. Died 1600.

Thomas O'Connallon was born in the county Sligo early in the seventeenth century. He seems to have been incomparably the greatest harper of his day, and composed many exquisite airs. Died about 1700.

A much better known personage was Turlogh O'Carolan or Carolan: born at Nobber, county Meath, about 1670, died in 1738. He was blind from his youth, and ultimately became the greatest Irish musical composer of modern times. A large part of his musical compositions are preserved.

63. The harp is the earliest musical instrument mentioned in Irish literature. It was called crot or cruit, and was of various sizes from the small portable hand harp to the great bardic instrument six feet high. It was commonly furnished with thirty strings, but sometimes had many more.

The Irish had a small stringed instrument called a timpan, which had only a few strings—from three to eight. It was played with a bow or plectrum.

The bagpipe was known in Ireland from very early times: the form used was that now commonly known as the Highland pipes—slung from the shoulder: the bag inflated by the mouth,. The other form—resting on the lap, the bag inflated by a bellows—which is much the finer instrument, is of modern invention. The bagpipe was in very general use, but it was only the lower classes that played on it: the harp was the instrument of the higher classes.

64. The music of ancient Ireland consisted wholly of short airs, each with two strains or parts, seldom more. But these, though simple in comparison with modern music, were constructed with such exquisite art that of a large proportion of them it may be truly said no modern composer can produce airs of a similar kind to equal them.

65. It was only in the last century that people began to collect Irish airs from singers and players, and to write them down. The principal collections of Irish airs are those of Bunting, Petrie, Joyce, Horncastle, Lynch, and Hoffman. Other collections are mostly copied from these.

The man who did most in modern times to draw attention to Irish music was Thomas Moore. He composed his exquisite songs to old Irish airs. The whole collection of songs and airs—well known as 'Moore's Melodies'—is now published in one small cheap volume.

66. We know the authors of many of the airs composed within the last 200 years: but these form the smallest portion of the whole body of Irish music. All the rest have come down from old times, scattered fragments of exquisite beauty, that remind us of the refined musical culture of our

forefathers. To this last class belong such well known airs as Savourneen Dheelish, Shule Aroon, Molly Asthore, The Boyne Water, Garryowen, Patrick's Day, Eileen Aroon, Langolee, &c. To illustrate what is here said, I may mention that of about 120 Irish airs in all Moore's Melodies, we know the authors of less than a dozen: as to the rest, nothing is known either of the persons who composed them or of the times of their composition.

IRISH ART

67. Penwork. In Ireland art was practised in four different branches:— Ornamentation and illumination of manuscript books; metal work; sculpture; and building. Art of every kind readied its highest perfection in the period between the end of the ninth and the beginning of the twelfth century. All cultivation degenerated after that, on account of the Danish irruptions and the Anglo Norman Invasion.

68. The special style of pen ornamentation was quite peculiar to the Celtic people of Ireland. Its most marked characteristic is interlaced work formed by bands, ribbons, and cords, which are curved and twisted and interwoven in the most intricate way, something like basket work infinitely varied in pattern. These are intermingled and alternated with zigzags, waves, spirals, and lozenges; while here and there among the curves are seen the faces or forms of dragons, serpents, or other strange looking animals, their tails, or ears, or tongues elongated and woven till they become merged and lost in the general design. This ornamentation was chiefly used in the capital letters, which are generally very large. One capital of the Book of Kells covers a whole page. The pattern is often so minute and complicated as to require the aid of a magnifying glass to examine it. The pen work is throughout illuminated in brilliant colours, which in several of the old books are even now very little faded after the lapse of so many centuries.

69. The Book of Kells, written in the seventh or eighth century, is the most beautiful Irish book in existence. Professor Westwood of Oxford, who has examined the best specimens of ancient penwork all over Europe, says:—"It is the most astonishing book of the Four Gospels which exists in the world: there is nothing like it in all the books which were written for Charlemagne and his immediate successors."

Speaking of another Irish book, Mr. Westwood says:—"I have counted [with a magnifying glass] in a small space scarcely three quarters of an inch in length by less than half an inch in width, in the Book of Armagh, no less than 158 interlacements of a slender ribbon pattern formed of white lines edged with black ones." The Book of Durrow and the Book of Armagh, both in Trinity College, Dublin, are splendidly ornamented and illuminated.

Giraldus Cambrensis when in Ireland in 1185, saw a copy of the Four

Gospels in St. Brigit's nunnery in Kildare, which so astonished him that he has recorded a legend that it was written under the direction of an angel.

70. The early Irish missionaries brought their arts of writing and illuminating wherever they went, and taught them to others; and to this day numerous exquisite specimens of their skill and taste are preserved in the libraries of England, France, Germany, and Italy.

71. Metal work. The pagan Irish, like the ancient Britons, practised the art of working in bronze, silver, gold, and enamel. This primitive art was continued into Christian times, and was brought to its highest perfection in the tenth and eleventh centuries.

The ornamental designs of metal work were generally similar to those used in manuscripts, and the execution was distinguished by the same exquisite skill and masterly precision. The principal articles made by the artists were crosses; croziers; chalices; bells; brooches; shrines or boxes to hold books or bells or relics; and book satchels, in which the two materials, metal and leather, were used. Specimens of all these may be seen in the National Museum in Dublin. The three most remarkable as well as the most beautiful objects in the Museum are the Cross of Cong, the Ardagh chalice, and the Tara brooch.

72. The chalice was found a few years ago buried in the ground under a stone in old lis at Ardagh, in the county Limerick. It is elaborately ornamented with designs in metal and enamel; and was probably made some short time before the tenth century.

The Tara brooch is ornamented all over with amber, glass, and enamel, and with the characteristic Irish interlaced work in metal. Many old brooches are preserved, but this is by far the most beautiful and perfect of all.

The cross of Cong, which is 2 feet 6 inches high, is covered with elaborate ornamentation of pure Celtic design; and a series of inscriptions in the Irish language along the sides give its full history. It was made by order of Turlogh O'Connor King of Cannaught. The artist, who finished his work in 1123, was Mailisa Mac Braddan O'Hechan.

73. A great variety of gold ornaments may be seen in the National Museum, many of beautiful workmanship. There are several torques, all pure gold, one of which—found at Tara—is 5 feet 7 inches in length and weighs 27 ½ ounces. The torques were worn round the neck, but of many of the other articles the uses are unknown.

74. Sculpture. Artistic sculpture is chiefly exhibited in the great stone crosses, of which about forty-five still remain in various parts of Ireland. One peculiarity of the Celtic cross is a circular ring round the intersection, binding the arms together. Thirty-two of the forty-five existing crosses are richly ornamented; and eight have inscriptions. The elites of the stone crosses extend from the tenth to the thirteenth century. Besides the

ornamentation, most of the high crosses contain groups of figures representing various subjects of sacred history. The ornamentation is still of the same general Celtic character that we find in metal work and in illuminated manuscripts, and it exhibits the same masterly skill and ease both in design and execution. One of the crosses at Monasterboice is 27 feet high.

DWELLINGS, FORTRESSES, ECCLESIASTICAL BUILDINGS

75. Dwellings and Fortresses. Before the introduction of Christianity, buildings of every kind in Ireland were almost universally round. The quadrangular shape, which was first used in the churches in the time of St. Patrick, came very slowly into use; and round shaped structures finally disappeared only in the thirteenth or fourteenth century. The dwelling houses were almost always of wood. The wall was formed of strong posts, with the intervening spaces filled with wicker-work, plastered, and often whitened or variously coloured.

76. The homesteads had to be fenced in to protect them from robbers and wild animals. This was done by digging a deep circular trench, the clay from which was thrown up on the inside. Thus was formed all round, a high mound or dyke with a trench outside: one opening was left for a door or gate.

These old circular forts are found in every part of Ireland, but more in the south and west than elsewhere, many of them still very perfect—but of course the timber houses are all gone. Almost all are believed in popular superstition to be the haunts of fairies. They are known by various names, Lis, Bath, Brugh [broo], Dun, Cashel, and Caher—the cashels and cahers being usually built of stone. Some forts are very large—300 feet or more across —so as to give ample room for the group of timber houses, or for the cattle at night. The smaller forts were the residences of the farmers. Very often the flat middle space is raised to a higher level than the surrounding land, and sometimes there is a great mound in the centre, with a flat top, on which no doubt the strong house of the chief stood. In the very large forts there are often three or more great circumvallations. Round the forts of kings or chiefs were grouped the timber dwellings of the dependents, forming a sort of village.

In most of the forts both large and small, whether with flat areas or with raised mounds, there are underground chambers, which were probably used as storehouses, and in case of sudden attack, as places of refuge for women and children.

77. Where stone was abundant the surrounding rampart was often built of dry masonry, the stones being fitted with great exactness. In some of these structures the stones are very large, and then the style of building is termed Cyclopean. Many great stone fortresses still remain near the coasts of Sligo, Galway, Clare, and Kerry, and a few in Antrim and Donegal.

78. For greater security dwellings were often constructed on artificial islands made with stakes, trees, and bushes, in shallow lakes: these were called crannoges. Communication with the shore was carried on by means of a rude boat kept on the island. Crannoge dwellings were in very general use in the time of Elizabeth; and the remains of many of them are still to be seen in our lakes.

79. Churches. From the time of St. Patrick downwards, churches were built, the greater number of wood, but many of stone.

The primitive stone churches, erected in the fifth, sixth, and seventh centuries are simple oblongs, small and rude. As Christianity spread, the churches became gradually larger and more ornamental, and a chancel was often added at the east end, which was another oblong, merely a continuation of the larger building. The jambs of both doors and windows inclined so that the bottom of the opening was wider than the top: this shape of door or window is a sure mark of antiquity. The remains of little stone churches of this antique pattern, of ages from the fifth century to the tenth or eleventh, are still to be found all over Ireland.

80. Round Towers. In connection with many of the ancient churches there were round towers of stone from 60 to 150 feet high, and from 13 to 20 feet in external diameter at the base: the top was conical. The interior was divided into six or seven stories, reached by ladders from one to another, and each story was lighted by one window: the top story had usually four large windows. The door was placed 10 or more feet from the ground outside, and was reached by a ladder: both doors and windows had sloping jambs like those of the churches. About 80 round towers still remain, of which about 20 are perfect.

Formerly there was much speculation as to the uses of these round towers; but Dr. George Petrie set the question at rest in his Essay on their Origin and Uses. It is now known that they are of Christian origin, and that they were always built in connection with ecclesiastical establishments. They were erected at various times from about the ninth to the thirteenth century. They had at least a twofold use: as belfries and as keeps to which the inmates of the monastery retired with their valuables in case of sudden attack. They were probably used also, when occasion required, as beacons and watch-towers. These are Dr. Petrie's conclusions, except only that he fixed the date of some few in the fifth century, which recent investigations have shown to be too early.

81. Later Churches. Until about the period of the Anglo Norman invasion all the churches were small, because the congregations were small. Towards the close of the twelfth century, when many of the great English lords had settled in Ireland, they began to indulge their taste for architectural magnificence, and the native Irish chiefs imitated and emulated them; large cruciform churches in the pointed style began to

prevail; and all over the country splendid buildings of every kind sprang up. Then were erected—some by the English, some by the Irish—those splendid abbeys and churches of which the ruins are still to be seen, such as those of Kilmallock and Monasteranenagh in Limerick, Dublin (Christ church and St. Patrick's); Jerpoint in Kilkenny; Grey Abbey in Down: Bective and Newtown in Meath; Sligo; Quin and Corcomroe in Clare; Balintober in Mayo; Knockmoy in Galway; Dunbrody in Wexford; Buttevant; Cashel; and many others.

IRISH CUSTOMS

82. Arms and Armour. The Irish employed two kinds of foot-soldiers: Galloglachs or Galloglasses and Kern. The galloglasses were heavy-armed infantry. They wore a coat of mail and an iron helmet; a long sword hung by the side, and in the hand was carried a broad heavy keen-edged axe. The Irish never took to armour very generally, but preferred to fight in saffron linen tunics, which lost them many a battle. The Kern were light-armed foot-soldiers: they wore head pieces, and fought with a skean, i. e. a dagger or short sword, and with a javelin attached to a thong.

83. "It is curious that bows and arrows are very seldom mentioned in our old writings: and the passages that are supposed to refer to them are so indistinct, that if we had no other evidence it might be difficult to prove that the use of the bow was known at all to the ancient Irish. However the matter is placed beyond dispute by the fact that flint arrow-heads are found in the ground in various parts of the country." *

In prehistoric ages, hammers, axes, spear-heads and arrow-heads were made of flint or other stone. Next came bronze axes, spear-heads, and swords. Lastly, swords, daggers, and spears of iron and steel. Shields were made of wicker-work covered with hides; also of yew and bronze.

84. Chariots and Roads. Our literature affords unquestionable evidence that chariots were used in Ireland from the most remote ages. The war chariots had spikes and scythe-blades like those of the ancient Britons.

That the country was well provided with roads we know, partly from our ancient literature, and partly from the general use of chariots. There were five main roads leading from Tara through the country in different directions; and numerous minor roads—all with distinct names—are mentioned in the annals.

85. Boats. The ancient Irish used three kinds of boats:—small sailing vessels; canoes hollowed out from the trunks of trees; and currachs. The currach was made of wicker-work covered with hides. These boats are constantly mentioned in lay as well as in ecclesiastical literature; and they are used still round the coasts, but tarred canvas is employed instead of skins.

86. Mills. Water-mills were known from very remote ages, and were more common in ancient than in modern times. In most houses there was a

quern or hand-mill, and the use of it was part of the education of every woman of the working class. The quern continued in use until very recently both in Ireland and Scotland.

87. Burial. Three modes of disposing of the dead were practised in ancient Ireland. First mode: the body was buried as at present. Second: sometimes the body of a king or warrior was placed standing up in the grave, fully accoutred and armed. Third: the body was burned and the ashes were deposited in the grave in an ornamental urn of baked clay.

88. Often that sort of stone monument now known as a cromlech was constructed, formed of one great flat stone lying on the tops of several large standing stones, thus enclosing a rude chamber in which one or more bodies or urns were placed. These cromlechs—which are sometimes wrongly called druids' altars—remain in every part of Ireland; and skeletons, and urns containing burnt bones, have been found under many of them.

A mound of stones raised over a grave is called a cairn. In old times people had a fancy to bury on the tops of hills; and the summits of very many hills in Ireland are crowned with cairns, under every one of which—in a stone coffin—reposes some chief renowned in the olden time. Sometimes these mounds were of clay. All contain chambers. The greatest mounds in Ireland are those of Newgrange, Dowth, and Knowth, on the Boyne, five miles above Drogheda.

At the burial of important persons funeral games were celebrated: these gave origin to many of the Aenachs or fairs.

89. Fosterage. One of the leading features of Irish social life was fosterage, which prevailed from the remotest period. It was practised by persons of all classes, but more especially by those in the higher ranks. A man sent his child to be reared and educated in the home and with the family of another member of the tribe, who then became foster father, and his children the foster brothers and foster sisters of the child. Fosterage, which was the closest tie between families, was subject to stringent regulations, which were carefully set forth in the Brehon Law.

90. Gossipred. When a man stood sponsor for a child at baptism he became the child's godfather and gossip to the parents. Gossipred was regarded as a sort of religious relationship between families, and created mutual obligations of regard and friendship.

91. Public assemblies. In early times when means of intercommunication were very limited, it was important that the people should hold meetings to discuss divers affairs affecting the public weal, and for other business of importance. In Ireland popular assemblies and meetings of representatives were very common, and were called by various names—Fes, Dal, Mordal, Aenach, etc. They were continued to a late period.

The Aenach or Fair was an assembly of the people of every class belonging to a district or province. Some fairs were annual; some triennial. According to the most ancient traditions, many of these Aenachs—perhaps all —had their origin in funeral games; and we know as a fact that the most important of them were held at ancient cemeteries, where kings or renowned heroes or other noted personages of history or legend were buried. Fairs were held at Tlachtga, now the hill of Ward near Athboy in Meath; Tailltenn, now Teltown midway between Navan and Kells; and at many other places. At all these meetings national games were celebrated.

92. The most celebrated of all the ancient meetings was the Fes or Convention of Tara. The old tradition states, that it was instituted by Ollamh Fodla [Ollav Fola]. It was originally held, or intended to be held, every third year; but since the fourth or fifth century, it was generally convened only once by each king, namely at the beginning of his reign.

This Fes was a convention of the leading people, not an aenach for the masses; and it represented all Ireland. The provincial kings, the minor kings and chiefs, and the most distinguished representatives of the learned professions—the ollaves of history, law, poetry, etc.—attended. It lasted for seven days, from the third day before Samin (1st November) to the third day after it. The delegates met to consider the Government of the country. The King of Ireland feasted the company every day: there was a separate compartment for the representatives of each province with their numerous attendants; and each guest had his special place assigned according to rank. The last convention was held here by King Dermot the son of Fergus, A. D. 560.

At the Fes of Tara, as well indeed as at all other important meetings, elaborate precautions were taken to prevent quarrels or unpleasantness of any kind. Any one who struck or wounded another, used insulting words, or stole anything, was punished with death; and all persons who attended were free for the time from prosecution and from legal proceedings of every kind.

* See my Irish Names of Places, Vol. II., Chap. XI.

PART II. IRELAND UNDER NATIVE RULERS.

(From the most ancient times to 1172.)

IN the beginning of this Second Part the narrative is legendary, like the early accounts of all other nations.

This period includes the Danish invasions, which never broke the continuity of the monarchy in Ireland as they did in England. It ended about 1172; for after that time there was no longer a supreme native king over Ireland.

THE LEGENDS OF THE EARLY COLONIES

[The whole of this Chapter is legendary, and the dates are quite fanciful].

93. Besides some fables about the landing of the lady Ceasair [Kasser]

and her people forty days before the flood, our manuscripts have legends of five ancient colonies.

The Parthalonians: the first colony, A. M. 2520. The first man that led a colony to Ireland after the flood was a chief named Parthalon, who came hither from Greece, with his wife, his three sons, and 1,000 followers. He took up his abode first on the little island of Inish-Samer in the river Erne just below the waterfall of Assaroe at Ballyshannon; and afterwards on Moy-Elta, the level district between Dublin and Ben-Edar or Howth. At the end of 300 years the people of this colony were destroyed by a plague, which carried off 9,000 of them in one week on Moy-Elta.

94. The Nemedians: the second colony, A. M. 2850. After the destruction of the Parthalonians Nemed came from Scythia with his followers. These Nemedians were harassed by the Fomorian pirates, but Nemed defeated them in several battles. After some years he and 3,000 of his followers died of the plague.

The Fomorians were a race of sea-robbers, who, after the death of Nemed, oppressed his people and made them pay an intolerable yearly tribute. So the Nemedians, unable to bear their miserable state any longer, rose up in a fury; and a dreadful battle was fought on the sea beach near Tory Island, in which nearly all the combatants fell. And those who were not killed in battle were drowned, lor the combatants fought so furiously that they gave no heed to the advancing tide-wave which rose and overwhelmed them.

95. The Firbolgs: the third colony, A. M. 3266, came from Greece under the leadership of the five sons of Dela, who led them to Ireland. These brothers partitioned the country into five provinces, Ulster, Leinster, Connaught, and the two Munsters.

The Dedannans: the fourth colony, A. M. 3303, also came from Greece, and were celebrated for their skill in magic. As soon as they had landed in Ireland they burned their ships; and shrouding themselves in a magic mist, so that the Firbolgs could not see them, they marched unperceived to Slieve an-Ierin mountain in the present county Leitrim. Soon afterwards a battle was fought which lasted for four days, till the Firbolgs were defeated, and the Dedannans remained masters of the island. These Dedannans were in subsequent ages deified and became Side [Shee] or fairies, whom the ancient Irish worshipped.

96. The Milesians: the fifth colony, A. M. 3500. From Scythia their original home they began their long pilgrimage. Their first migration was to Egypt, where they were sojourning at the time that Pharaoh and his host were drowned in the Red Sea; and after wandering through Europe for many generations they arrived in Spain. Here they abode for a long time; and at last they came to Ireland with a fleet of thirty ships under the command of the eight sons of the hero Miled or Milesius.

The Dedannans, by their magical incantations, raised a furious tempest which scattered and wrecked the fleet along the rocky coasts. Five of the eight brothers perished; and the remaining three, Eremon, Eber-Finn, and Amergin, landed with the remnant of their people. Soon afterwards two battles were fought, in which the Dedannans were defeated; and the Milesians took possession of the country.

The two brothers Eber-Finn and Eremon now divided Ireland, Eber-Finn taking the two Munsters and Eremon Leinster and Connaught. They gave Ulster to their nephew Eber, and made Amergin chief poet and brehon of the kingdom.

THE KINGS OF PAGAN IRELAND

[In the beginning this Chapter is legendary and the dates are still little more than guesses. After the foundation of Emania we begin to have a mixture of real history. As we approach the reign of Laeghaire there is a constantly increasing proportion of fact: and the dates are approximately correct].

97. The brothers Eber-Finn and Eremon had no sooner settled down in their new kingdoms than they quarrelled and fought a battle (A. M. 3501), in which Eber was defeated and slain, and Eremon became sole king.

By far the greater number of the Irish Pagan kings after Eremon fell in battle or by assassination: a few only of the most distinguished need be noticed here.

98. Tighernmas [Teernmas], who began his reign A. M. 3581, was the first of the Irish kings to work gold. He distinguished the various classes of his people by the numbers of hues in their garments.

99. This king, we are told, was miraculously destroyed, with a multitude of his people, while they were worshipping the great national idol Crom Cruach on the plain of Moy Slecht in Brefney, on the eve of the pagan festival of Samin (1st November).

The mighty King Ollamh Fodla [Ollav Fola] — A. M. 3922—established the Fes or meeting of Tara; the proceedings of which were entered in the great national record called the Psalter of Tara. And he made laws for the whole country.

100. About 300 years before the Christian era, Macha of the Golden Hair, the Queen of Cimbaeth [Kimbay] King of Ulster, built the palace of Emain or Emania, which for more than 600 years continued to be the residence of the Ulster kings. Here in after ages, the Red Branch Knights were trained in military accomplishments and deeds of arms. The remains of this palace are still to be seen two miles west of Armagh: it is now called Navan Fort, Navan being the pronunciation of the old Irish name N-Emain.

100a. Achy Feidlech [Fealagh], who ascended the throne a little before the Christian era, built the palace of Croghan for his daughter, the celebrated Medb [Maive] Queen of Connaught, where the kings of that province afterwards resided. This old fort is in the north of Roscommon, and still retains the original name.

The king who reigned at the time of the Incarnation was Conary I., or Conary the Great. In his time occurred the seven years' war between Maive Queen of Connaught and Conor Mac Nessa king of Ulster.

101. Some time in the first century of the Christian era the Attacottic or plebeian races, i.e. the Firbolgs, Dedannans, and Fomorians whom the Milesians had enslaved, rose up in rebellion, wrested the sovereignty from their masters, and almost exterminated the Milesian princes and nobles: after which they chose Carbery Kinncat for their king. But the Milesian Monarchy was after some time restored in the person of Tuathal [Toohal] the Legitimate, who ascended the throne early in the second century.

This King Tuathal took measures to consolidate the monarchy. Before his time the over-kings had for their personal estate only a small tract round Tara. But he cut off a portion from each of the provinces, and formed therewith the province of Meath, to be the special demesne or estate of the supreme kings of Ireland. He imposed on Leinster an enormous tribute called the Boruma or Boru to be paid to the kings of Ireland every second year. This tribute was never yielded without resistance more or less, and for many centuries it was the cause of constant bloodshed.

102. The renowned Conn Ced-Cathach [Kead-Caha], or Conn the Hundred-fighter, became king late in the second century (A. D. 177). His most formidable antagonist was the great hero Eoghan-Mor [Owen More], otherwise called Mogh-Nuadhat [Mow-Nooat] king of Munster, who having defeated him in ten battles, forced him at last to divide Ireland between them. For a line of demarcation they fixed on a natural ridge of sandhills called Esker-Riada, which can still be traced running across Ireland with little interruption from Dublin to Galway. This division is perpetually referred to in Irish literature: the northern half, which belonged to Conn was called Leth-Chuinn [Leh-Conn] or Conn's half; and the southern Leth-Mogha [Leh-Mow], that is Mogh's half. Conn was succeeded by his son-in-law Conary II, (A. D. 212).

103. From the earliest ages the Irish of Ulster were in the habit of crossing the narrow sea to Alban or Scotland, where colonies were settled from time to time. The first regular colony of which we have any reliable account was conducted by Carbery Riada, the son of King Conary. Hence that part of Scotland in which he settled got the name of Dalriada, i.e. Riada's portion. There was also a Dalriada in the north of Antrim, which still retains the old name in the form of Route.

104. Cormac Mac Art, or Cormac Ulfada (A. D. 254), the grandson of Conn the Hundred-fighter, was the most illustrious of all the pagan kings

of Ireland. He founded three colleges at Tara, one for the study of military science, one for history and literature, and one for law.

After a prosperous reign, Cormac abdicated on account of the accidental loss of an eye, for no king with a personal blemish was allowed to reign at Tara. He retired to his kingly cottage, called Cletta, on the shore of the river Boyne; where he composed the book called Tegasg Righ [Ree] or Instructions for a king, and other law tracts, of which we have copies in our old manuscript Volumes: and here he died in the year 277.

In the time of Cormac flourished the Fianna [Feena] of Erin, a sort of militia, like the Red Branch Knights, in the service of the monarch. They were commanded by Cormac's son-in-law, the renowned Finn Mac Cumhail [Cool] who is remembered in tradition all over Ireland to this day. Finn's son was Oisin or Ossian the poet; the brave and gentle hero Oscar was the son of Oisin.

Cormac was succeeded (A.D. 279) by his son Carbery of the Liffey; who defeated the rebellious Fena in the battle of Gavra near Skreen in Meath, and dispersed them for evermore.

105. During the reign of Muredach (A.D. 881) his three cousins, Colla Huas, Colla Menn, and Colla Da-Crich [Cree]—commonly called the Three Collas—invaded and conquered Ulster, destroyed the Palace of Emania, and took possession of that part of the province lying west of the Newry river.

Niall of the Nine Hostages (A.D. 879) was one of the greatest, most warlike, and most famous of all the ancient Irish kings. Four of his sons settled in Meath, and four others conquered for themselves a territory in Ulster, where they settled. The posterity of Niall are called Hy Neill; the southern Hy Neill being descended from those that settled in Meath, the northern Hy Neill from those that went to Ulster. By far the greatest number of the Irish kings, from this period till the Anglo-Norman invasion, were descended from Niall through one or the other of these two branches.

106. At this time the "Picts and Scots" gave great trouble to the Britons and Romans in Britain. The Picts were the people of Scotland—a branch of the Goidels or Gaels: the Scots were Irish Gaels. In those times the Scots often went from Ireland on plundering excursions to the coasts of Britain and Gaul, and seem to have been almost as much dreaded then as the Danes were in later ages.

During the whole time of the Roman occupation of Britain we constantly hear—both from native and Roman sources—of the excursions of the Scots to Britain; and when the Roman power began to wane they became still more frequent. The most formidable invasions of all were led by Niall. He collected a great fleet and landing in Wales carried off immense plunder, but was forced to retreat by the valiant Roman general Stilicho. In one of Niall's excursions St. Patrick was brought captive to Ireland, as related in next Chapter.

It was in one of his expeditions to the coast of Gaul that Niall, while marching at the head of his army, was assassinated (A. D. 405) on the shore of the river Loire by the King of Leinster, who shot him with an arrow beside the river.

107. Dathi [Dauhy] Niall's successor (A. D. 405), was the last king of pagan Ireland. He too made inroads into foreign lands; and he was killed by a flash of lightning at the foot of the Alps. His soldiers brought his body home and buried it at Croghan under a red pillar stone which remains in the old pagan cemetery to this day.

108. Laeghaire [Leary] the son of Niall succeeded in 428. In the fifth year of his reign St. Patrick came to Ireland on his great mission. This king like many of his predecessors waged war against the Leinstermen to exact the Boru tribute; but they defeated him and took him prisoner. Then they made him swear by the sun and wind and all the elements that he would never again demand the tribute; and when he had sworn they set him free. But the very next year, A. D. 463, he invaded Leinster again; whereupon—so says the legend—he was killed while on his march by the sun and wind for having broken his oath.

SAINT PATRICK

109. It is commonly supposed that the druidic religion prevailed in pagan Ireland; but we know very little of the nature and ceremonials of this Irish druidism.

In the oldest Irish traditions the druids figure conspicuously. All the early colonists had their druids, who are mentioned as holding high rank among kings and chiefs. They are often called men of science to indicate their superior knowledge. Many worshipped idols of some kind: some worshipped water; some, fire; some, the sun.

They were skilled in magic—indeed they figure more conspicuously as magicians than in any other capacity—and were believed to be possessed of tremendous preternatural powers. They practised divination, and foretold future events from dreams and visions, from sneezing and casting lots; from the croaking of ravens and the chirping of wrens. They bitterly opposed Christianity; and we know that there were druids in the country long after St. Patrick's time, who continued to exercise powerful influence.

110. Our most ancient secular and ecclesiastical literature attests the universal belief in the side [Shee] or fairies, who, as we are told, were worshipped by the Irish. These were local deities who were supposed to live in the interior of pleasant green hills or under great rocks or sepulchral cairns, where they had splendid palaces. Many of these fairy hills are still known all over the country, each with its tutelary deity; and they are held in much superstitious awe by the peasantry.

The fairies were also believed to inhabit the old raths and lisses, so numerous through the country, a superstition that still lingers everywhere among the people.

111. In some places idols were worshipped. There was a great idol, called Crom Cruach, covered all over with gold, on Moy-Slecht (the plain of adoration) in the present county of Cavan, surrounded by twelve lesser idols, all of which were destroyed by St. Patrick. These thirteen idols were all pillar-stones; and according to our ancient authorities pillar-stone idols were worshipped in many other parts of Ireland as well as at Moy-Slecht.

112. We know that there were Christians in Ireland long before the time of St. Patrick, but we have no evidence to show how Christianity was introduced in those early ages. In the year 431, Pope Celestine sent Palladius "to the Scots believing in Christ" to be their first bishop. There must have been Christians in considerable numbers when the Pope thought this measure necessary; and such numbers could not have grown up in a short time. Palladius landed in Wicklow, from which he was expelled by the local chief; and he died soon afterwards in Scotland.

113. The next mission had very different results. "Although Christianity was not propagated in Ireland by the blood of martyrs, there is no instance of any other nation that universally received it in as short a space of time as the Irish did;" and in the whole history of Christianity we do not find a missionary more successful than St. Patrick.

114. It is pretty certain that Patrick was born either in Scotland or in Armoric Gaul: the weight of authority tends to Dumbarton in Scotland. His parents were Christians: his father Calpurnius was a deacon, and also a decurion or magistrate in a Roman colony. When Patrick was a boy of sixteen he was taken captive with many others and brought to Ireland about the year 403, in one of these predatory excursions, already spoken of, by Niall of the Nine Hostages. He was sold as a slave and spent six years of his life herding sheep on the bleak slopes of Slemish mountain in Antrim. Here in his solitude his mind was turned to God, and while carefully doing the work of his hard master Milcho, he employed his leisure hours in devotions. We know this from his own words in the Confession:—"I was daily tending the flocks and praying frequently every day that the love of God might be more enkindled in my heart; so much so that in one day I poured out my prayers a hundred times and as often in the night: nay, even in woods and mountains I remained and rose before the light to my prayers, in frost and snow and rain, and suffered no inconvenience, nor yielded to any slothfulness, for the Spirit of the Lord was fervent within me."

115. At the end of six years he escaped and made his way through many hardships and dangers to his native country. During his residence in Ireland he had learned the language of the people; and brooding continually on the state of pagan darkness in which they lived, he formed the resolution to

devote his life to their conversion. He set about his preparation very deliberately. He first studied under St. Martin in his monastic school at Tours, and spent some time subsequently with St. Germain of Auxerre.

During all this time he applied himself fervently to works of piety; and he had visions and dreams in which he heard the Irish people calling to him to return to Ireland and walk among them with the light of faith. At length the time came to begin the great work of his life; and he repaired to Rome with a letter from St. Germain recommending him to Pope Celestine as a suitable person to attempt the conversion of the Irish nation.

116. Having received authority and benediction from the Pope he set out for Ireland. On his way through Gaul news came of the death of Palladius, and as this left Ireland without a bishop, Patrick was consecrated bishop by a certain holy prelate named Amator. Embarking for Ireland he landed, in the year 432, on the Coast of Wicklow, at the mouth of the Vartry river, the spot where the town of Wicklow now stands, He was then about forty-five years of age. Soon after landing he was expelled from Wicklow like his predecessor; and coasting northwards and resting for a time at the little island of Holmpatrick on the Dublin Coast near Skerries, he and his companions finally landed at Lecale in Down. Dicho, the chief of the district, instantly sallied forth with his people to drive them back; but when he caught sight of them he was so struck by their calm and dignified aspect that he saluted them respectfully and invited them to his house.

Here the saint announced his mission and explained his doctrine; and Dicho and his whole family became Christians and were baptized: the first of the Irish converted by St. Patrick. He celebrated Mass in a sabhall [saval] or bam presented to him by the chief, on the site of which a monastery was subsequently erected, which for many ages was held in great veneration. And the memory of the auspicious event was preserved in the name by which the place was subsequently known, Saval-Patrick or Patrick's Barn, now shortened to Saul.

117. During the whole of St. Patrick's mission his invariable plan was to address himself in the first instance to the kings and chiefs. He now resolved to go straightway to Tara, where king Laeghaire and his nobles happened at this time to be celebrating a festival of some kind. Bidding farewell to his friend Dicho, he sailed southwards to the mouth of the Boyne, from which he set out on foot with his companions for Tara, and arrived at Slane on Saturday, Easter eve, A. D. 433. Here he prepared to celebrate the Easter festival, and towards nightfall, as was then the custom, lighted the Paschal fire on the hill of Slane.

118. At this very time it happened that the king's people were about to light the festival fire at Tara, which was a part of their ceremonial; and there was a law that while this fire was burning no other should be kindled in the country all round, on pain of death. The king and his courtiers were

much astonished when they saw the fire ablaze upon the hill of Slane, nine miles off; and when the monarch inquired about it his diuids said:—"If that fire which we see be not extinguished to-night it will never be extinguished, but will over-top all our fires: and he that has kindled it will overturn thy kingdom." Whereupon the king, in great wrath, instantly set out in his chariot with a small retinue; and having arrived near Slane, he summoned the strangers to his presence. He had commanded that none should rise up to show them respect; but when they presented themselves, one of the courtiers, Erc the son of Dego, struck with the saint's commanding appearance, rose from his seat and saluted him. This Erc was converted and became afterwards bishop of Slane. The result of this interview was what St, Patrick most earnestly desired; he was commanded to appear next day at Tara and give an account of his proceedings before the assembled court.

119. The next day was Easter Sunday. Patrick and his companions set out for the palace, and on their way they chanted a hymn in the native tongue—an invocation for protection against the dangers and treachery by which they were beset; for they had heard that persons were lying in wait to slay them. This hymn was long held in great veneration by the people of this country, and we still possess copies of it in a very old dialect of the Irish language.

In the history of the spread of Christianity, it would be perhaps difficult to find a more singular and impressive scene than was presented at the court of King Laeghaire on that memorable Easter morning. The saint was robed in white, as were also his companions; he wore his mitre, and carried his crozier in his hand; and when he presented himself before the assembly, Dubhthach [Duffa] the chief poet, rose to welcome him, contrary to the express commands of the king. In presence of the monarch and his nobles, the saint explained the leading points of the Christian doctrine, and silenced the king's druids in argument.

120. The proceedings of this auspicious day were a type of St. Patrick's future career. Dubhthach became a convert and thenceforward devoted his poetical talents to the service of God; and Laeghaire gave permission to the strange missionaries to preach their doctrines throughout his dominions. Patrick next proceeded to Tailltenn, where during the celebration of the national games he preached for a week to the assembled multitudes, making many converts, among whom was Conall Gulban, brother to King Laeghaire, the ancestor of the O'Donnells of Tirconnell.

We find him soon after making straight for Moy Slecht, where stood the great national idol Crom Cruach, surrounded by twelve lesser idols. These he destroyed, and thus terminated for ever the abominations enacted for so many ages at that ancient haunt of gloomy superstition.

121. In his journey through Connaught he and his companions met the

two daughters of King Laeghaire—Ethnea the fair and Fedelma the ruddy—near the royal palace of Croghan. The virgins inquired whence they came, and Patrick answered them, "It were better for you to confess to our true God than to inquire concerning our race." They eagerly asked about God, his attributes, his dwelling-place—whether in the sea, in rivers, in mountainous places, or in valleys—how knowledge of him was to be obtained, how he was to be found, seen, and loved, with other inquiries of a like nature. The Saint answered their questions, and explained the leading points of the faith; and the virgins were immediately baptized and consecrated to the service of religion.

122. On the approach of Lent he retired to the mountain which has since borne his name—Croagh Patrick or Patrick's hill—where he spent some time in fasting and prayer. At this time, A.D. 449, the seven sons of Amalgaidh [Awley] King of Connaught had convened a great assembly, to which Patrick repaired. He expounded his doctrines to the wondering assembly; and the seven princes with twelve thousand persons were baptized.

123. After spending seven years in Connaught, he visited successively Ulster, Leinster, and Munster. Soon after entering Leinster, he converted at Naas—then the residence of the Leinster kings—the two princes Ilann and Olioll, sons of the King of Leinster, who both afterwards succeeded to the throne of their father. And at Cashel, the seat of the kings of Munster, he was met by the king, Aengus the son of Natfree, who conducted him into the palace with the highest reverence and was at once baptized.

124. Wherever he went he founded churches, and left them in charge of his disciples. In his various journeys, he encountered many dangers and met with numerous repulses; but his failures were few and unimportant, and success attended his efforts in every part of his wonderful career. He founded the see of Armagh about the year 455, and constituted it the metropolitan see of all Ireland.

The greater part of the country was now filled with Christians and with churches; and the mission of the venerable apostle was drawing to a close. He was seized with his last illness in Saul, the scene of his first spiritual triumph; and he breathed his last on the seventeenth of March, in or about the year 465, in the seventy-eighth year of his age.[2]

The news of his death was the signal for universal mourning. From the remotest districts of the island, the clergy turned their steps towards the little village of Saul —bishops, priests, abbots and monks—all came to pay the last tribute of love and respect to their great master. They celebrated the obsequies for twelve days and nights without interruption, joining in the solemnities as they arrived in succession; and in the language of one of his biographers, the blaze of myriads of torches made the whole time appear like one continuous day. He was buried with great solemnity at Dun-daleth-glas, the old residence of the princes of Ulidia; and the name, in the altered form of Downpatrick, commemorates to all time the saint's place of interment.

125. It must not be supposed that Ireland was completely Christianized by St. Patrick. There still remained large districts never visited by him or his companions; and in many others the Christianity of the people was merely on the surface. Much Pagan superstition remained, even among the professing Christians, and the druids still and for long after retained great influence; so that there was ample room for the missionary zeal of St. Patrick's successors.

[1] Some dispute his mission from the Pope.

[2] There is much uncertainty both as to St Patrick's age and as to the year of his death. I have given the age and the year that seem to me most probable.

EARLY CHRISTIAN IRELAND

126. Lewy the son of Laeghaire was too young at the time of his father's death to claim the throne, which was seized by Olioll Molt King of Connaught, son of Dathi, A.D. 463. But Lewy when he came of age raised a great army and defeated and slew King Olioll in the terrible battle of Ocha in Meath and took possession of the throne. This battle, which was fought in 483, was a sort of revolution. Olioll Molt did not belong to the Hy Neill. Lewy was of the Southern Hy Neill; and from this date, for 500 years without a break, the Hy Neill held the throne of Ireland.

During this king's reign (in 503) a colony was led to Scotland, the greatest colony of all, by three brothers, Fergus, Angus, and Lome, sons of an Irish chief named Erc. Fergus, commonly called Fergus Mac Erc, became king of the Scottish Gaelic colony, which before long mastered the whole country and ultimately gave it the name of Scotland (from the Scots or Irish).

127. Dermot the son of Fergus Kervall became king of Ireland in 544. In his reign Tara was deserted as a royal residence on account of a curse pronounced against it by St. Rodan of Lorrha in Tipperary. From that time forth the kings of Ireland lived elsewhere—each in his own province: and the place gradually fell into decay.

128. Aed or Hugh the son of Ainmire reigned from 572 to 598. By him was summoned in 574 the celebrated convention of Druim-cete [Drum-Ketta], now called the Mullagh or Daisy Hill, on the river Roe, near Limavady, which was attended by the chief men of Ireland both lay and clerical. St. Columba also and a number of his clergy came from Iona to take part in the proceedings, as well as the king and chiefs of the Scottish Dalriada. At this meeting two important questions were settled. The bards had become so numerous and so oppressive on the people by their insolence and exactions that King Hugh proposed that the order should be

abolished and the bards banished. But at St. Columkille's intercession a middle course was adopted. Their number was greatly reduced, and strict rules were laid down for the regulation of their conduct for the future. The principal bards, or ollaves, had to employ themselves in teaching schools. The second question had reference to the colony in Scotland. Up to this it had been subject to the kings of Ireland: but at the intercession of St, Columkille it was now made independent.

King Aed, attempting to exact the Borumean tribute, was defeated and slain by Branduff King of Leinster at the battle of Dunbolg, near Dunlavin, in the county Wicklow.

129. Donall the son of King Aed Mac Ainmire ascended the throne, A.D. 627. A powerful Ulster prince named Congal Claen, who had been banished by Donall, landed on the coast of Down, after an exile of nine years, with a great army of auxiliaries—Britons, Saxons, Alban Scots, and Picts—and was immediately joined by his Ulster partisans.

Donall had been fully aware of Congal's projected invasion, and had made preparations to meet it. He marched northwards at the head of his army to Moyrath, now Moira in the county of Down, where was fought, in 637, one of the most sanguinary battles recorded in Irish history. It lasted for six successive days, and terminated in the total defeat of the invaders. Congal fell fiercely fighting at the head of his forces; and his army was almost annihilated.

130. The Irish kings had continued to exact the Boru tribute from the Leinstermen, who struggled manfully against it to the last. But at the earnest solicitation of St. Moling, Finaghta the Festive, who became king in 674, solemnly renounced the Boru for himself and his successors.

The generous action of Finaghta did not end the trouble. After the lapse of two reigns, the monarch Fergal demanded the tribute; and on refusal a battle was fought in 722 at the historic hill of Allen in Kildare, in which the royal forces were utterly defeated, and King Fergal himself and 7,000 of his men were slain.

But when Aed (or Hugh) Allen, the son of Fergal, became king, he engaged the Leinster army at Ballyshannon in Kildare, and nearly exterminated them; A.D. 738.

RELIGION AND LEARNING

131. The spread of the faith suffered no check by the death of St. Patrick; for churches, monasteries, and convents continued to be founded all over the country. The founders of monasteries in Ireland may be said to have been of two classes. Those of the one class settled in the inhabited districts, and took on themselves functions of education and religious ministration. Those of the other class gave themselves up to a life of prayer and contemplation; and these took up their abode in remote islands or mountain valleys, places generally hard to reach, and often almost inaccessible. Here

they lived with their little communities in cells, one for each individual, poor little places, mostly built by the monks themselves. They supported themselves by the work of their hands, lived on hard fare, slept on the bare floor, and occupied their spare time in devotions. There was a very pronounced tendency to this solitary monastic life in the early Christian ages; and on almost all the islands round the coast, as well as on those in the lakes and rivers, the remains of churches and primitive eremitical establishments are found to this day.

132. The three patron saints of Ireland are Patrick, Brigit, and Columba or Columkille.

St. Brigit of Kildare was born about the year 455 at Faughart near Dundalk, where her father, who was a Leinster chief, then lived. She became a nun when very young; and soon the fame of her sanctity spread through the whole country. Having founded convents in various parts of Ireland, she finally settled—about the year 480—at a place in Leinster, where she built her first cell under the shade of a great oak-tree, whence it got the name of Kill-dara, the church of the oak, now Kildare. This became the greatest and most famous nunnery ever established in Ireland. She died on the 1st of February, 523. St. Brigit is venerated in Ireland beyond all other Irishwomen; and there are places all through the country still called Kilbride, and Kilbreedy (Brigit's church) which received their names from churches founded by or in commemoration of her.

133. St. Columba or Columkille of Iona was born in 521 at Gartan in Donegal. He belonged to the Northern Hy Neill, his father being grandson of Conall Gulban son of Niall of the Nine Hostages; but he gave up all the worldly advantages of his high birth for religion. In the year 546 he built the monastery of Derry; after which, during the next fifteen years, he founded a great number of churches and monasteries all over the country, among others those of Kells, Swords, Tory Island, Lambay near Dublin, and Durrow in King's county, the last of which was his chief establishment in Ireland.

In the year 563 he went with twelve companions to the little Island of Iona on the west coast of Scotland, which had been granted to him by his relative the king of that part of Scotland. Here he settled, and founded the monastery which afterwards became so illustrious. He converted the Picts, and he traversed the Hebrides, preaching to the people and founding churches wherever he went. After a life of incessant activity in the service of religion, he died kneeling before the altar of his own church of Iona, in the year 597, in the seventy-sixth year of his age, and was buried within the monastery.

134. Besides the three Patrons, the following are a few of the most eminent of the Irish Saints: St. Ailbè of Emly in Limerick, who was ordained bishop by St. Patrick.

St. Enna or Endeus of Aran in Galway Bay; died about 542, This island was afterwards called Ara-na-Naemh [naive], Aran of the saints, from the number of holy men who lived in it.

St. Ciaran or Kieran, the patron of Ossory: born in the island of Cape Clear: died about 550.

St. Finnen of Clonard, the founder of the great school there: died 549.

St. Ciaran [Kieran] of Clonmacnoise, which became one of the greatest of all the Irish monasteries: died 549.

St. Ita, Ida or Mida, virgin saint, of Killeedy in Limerick; often called the Brigit of Munster: died 569.

St. Brendan of Clonfert in Galway, or Brendan the Navigator: born in Kerry: died 577.

St. Senan of Scattery island in the Shannon: died about 560.

St. Comgall of Bangor in Down, the founder of the celebrated school, which rivalled Clonard: died 602.

St. Kevin, the founder of Glendalough in Wicklow: died 618.

St. Carrthach or Mochuda of Lismore, where he founded one of Ireland's greatest schools: died 637.

St. Adamnan the biographer of St. Columkille; ninth abbot of Iona: died 703.

135. Among the vast number of Irishmen who became illustrious on the continent, the following may be named:—

St. Fursa of Peronne and his brothers Foillan and Ultan; Fursa died about 650.

St. Dympna or Domnat of Gheel, virgin martyr, to whom the great sanatorium for lunatics at Gheel in Belgium is dedicated: martyred in the seventh century.

St. Columbanus of Bobbio in Italy, a pupil of Bangor, founded the two monasteries of Luxeuil and Fontaines: expelled from Burgundy for denouncing the vices of King Theodoric; preached successfully to the Gauls; wrote learned letters; finally settled at Bobbio, where he died 615.

St. Gall, a disciple of Columbanus, patron of St. Gall (in Switzerland) which was named from him.

Virgil or Virgilius bishop of Salzburg, called Virgil the Geometer from his eminence in science: taught, probably for the first time, the rotundity of the earth: died 785.

St. Fridolin the Traveller of Seckingen on the Rhine: died sixth century.

St. Kilian the apostle of Franconia: martyred 689.

St. Cataldus of Tarentum, from the school of Lismore; seventh century.

Clement and Albinus, placed by Charlemagne at the head of two great seminaries.

John Scotus Erigena, celebrated for his knowledge of Greek: the most distinguished scholar of his day: died about 870.

136. In ancient Ireland education and religion went hand in hand, so that in tracing their history it is impossible to separate them. By far the greatest part of the education of the country was carried on by, or under the direction of, priests and monks of the various orders, who combined religious with secular teaching.

137. From the middle of the sixth century schools rapidly arose all over the country, most of them in connection with monasteries. The most celebrated were those of Clonard (in Meath), Armagh, Bangor (in Down), Cashel, Downpatrick, Ross Ailithir now Rosscarbery in Cork, Lismore, Glendalough, Clonmacnoise, Monasterboice near Drogheda, Clonfert in Galway, Glasnevin, and Begerin a little below Wexford. But almost all the monasteries—and convents as well—carried on the function of teaching. Some had very large numbers of students; for instance we are told that at one time there were 3,000 under St. Finnen at Clonard; and some other schools, such as Bangor, had as many. In those great seminaries every branch of knowledge then known was taught; they were in fact the prototypes of our modern universities.

In all the more important schools there were students from foreign lands; the greatest number came from Great Britain—they came in fleet-loads, as Aldhelm bishop of Sherborne (A.D. 705 to 709) expresses it. Many also were from the Continent.

138. Among the foreign visitors were many princes: Aldfrid King of Northumbria, and Dagobert II. King of France, were both, when in exile in the seventh century, educated in Ireland. We get some idea of the numbers of foreigners from the ancient Litany of Aengus the Culdee, in which we find invoked many Romans, Gauls, Germans, Britons, and even Egyptians, all of whom died in Ireland. Venerable Bede, describing the ravages of the yellow plague in 664, says:—"This pestilence did no less harm in the island of Ireland. Many of the nobility and of the lower ranks of the English nation were there at that time: and some of them devoted themselves to a monastic life: others chose to apply themselves to study. The Scots [i.e. the Irish] willingly received them all, and took care to supply them with food, as also to furnish them with books to read, and their teaching, all gratis."

139. In the course of three or four centuries from the time of St. Patrick, Ireland became the most learned country in Europe: and it came to be known by the name now so familiar to us—Insula sanctorum et doctorum, the Island of saints and scholars.

The greatest number of the schools were in monasteries; in these the teaching was not exclusively ecclesiastical; and young persons attended them to get a good general education. Some few schools were purely lay and professional:—for Law, Medicine, Poetry, or Literature. These were taught by laymen.

The highest degree of scholarship was that of Ollave or Doctor: there were Ollaves of the several professions: just as we have doctors of Law, Medicine, Philosophy, Literature, etc. The full course for an Ollave was twelve years: the subordinate degrees had shorter periods.

Men of learning were held in great estimation. They had many valuable allowances and privileges; and an Ollave sat at table next to the king or chief.

140. Great numbers of Irishmen went to teach and to preach the gospel in Great Britain, Wales, and Scotland.

On every side we meet with evidences of the activity of the Irish in Great Britain. Scotland was evangelized by St. Columba and his monks from Iona; and the whole western coasts of England and Wales abound in memorials of Irish missionaries. In the words of Mr. Lecky:—"England owed a great part of her Christianity to Irish monks."

Whole crowds of ardent and learned Irishmen travelled to the Continent, spreading Christianity and secular knowledge among people ten times more rude and dangerous in those ages than the inhabitants of these islands. Irish professors and teachers were in those times held in such estimation that they were employed in most of the schools and colleges of Great Britain, France, Germany, and Italy. To this day in many towns of France, Germany, Switzerland, and Italy, Irishmen are venerated as patron saints. Nay, they found their way even to Iceland; for we have the best authority for the statement that when the Norwegians first arrived at that island, they found there Irish books, bells, croziers, and other traces of Irish missionaries.

141. The term Comorba or Coarb was applied to the inheritor of a bishopric or other ecclesiastical dignity: the archbishop of Armagh is the coarb of St. Patrick: the archbishop of Dublin is the coarb of St. Lawrence O'Toole.

The land belonging to a church was called Termon land; it had the privilege of sanctuary. The manager of church lands was called an Erenach: a sort of steward, usually a layman.

142. For three or four hundred years after the time of St. Patrick the monasteries were unmolested; and learning was cultivated within their walls. In the ninth and tenth and the beginning of the eleventh century, science and art, the Gaelic language, and learning of every kind, were brought to their highest state of perfection But after this came a change for the worse. The Danish inroads broke up most of the schools and disorganized all society. Then the monasteries were no longer the quiet and safe asylums they had been—they became indeed rather more dangerous than other places—learning and art gradually declined, and Ireland ultimately lost her intellectual supremacy.

THE DANISH WARS

143. Towards the close of the eighth century the Danes began to make descents on the coasts of Europe. They came from Norway, Sweden, Jutland, and in general from the islands and coasts of the Baltic. They deemed piracy the noblest career that a chief could engage in; and they sent forth swarms of daring and desperate marauders, who for two centuries kept the whole of Western Europe in a state of continual terror.

144. Our records make mention of two distinct races of Galls or Northmen: the Lochlanns, i.e. Norwegians and Swedes, who, as they were fair-haired, were called Finn-Galls or White strangers; and the Danars or Danes of Denmark, who were called Duv-Galls, Black strangers, because they were dark-haired and swarthy. In modern Irish histories the term "Danes" is applied to both indifferently.

The Finn-Galls or Norwegians were the first to arrive. They appeared on the Irish coast for the first time in 795, when they plundered Lambay Island near Dublin, then called Rechru.

145. From that time forward they continued to send detached parties to Ireland, who plundered and ravaged wherever they came, both islands and mainland, and destroyed many of the great monasteries.

At first they came as mere robbers: then they began to make permanent settlements on several points of the coast, from which they penetrated inland in all directions; and wherever there was a religious establishment likely to afford plunder, there they were sure to appear.

About the middle of the ninth century they established themselves permanently in Dublin, Limerick, and Waterford, where they built fortresses.

146. Hitherto there was little combination among the Norsemen; but now appeared the most renowned of all their leaders—Turgesius or Thorgils—who, coming with a fleet in 832, united the whole of their scattered forces. Soon afterwards three other fleets arrived, one of which, sailing up the lower Bann, took possession of Lough Neagh; another anchored in Dundalk Bay; while the third occupied Lough Ree on the Shannon.

Tergesius established himself for a time in Armagh which he sacked three times in one month; and he posted parties at important points on the coast, such as Dublin, Limerick, Dundalk and Carlingford. After committing great ravages in the north, he placed himself at the head of the fleet in Lough Ree; and from this central station he commanded a large part of Leinster and Connaught, and plundered those of the ecclesiastical establishments that lay within reach—Clonmacnoise, Lorrha and Terryglass in Tipperary, and the churches of Iniscaltra in Lough Derg.

147. Although the Irish made no combined effort to resist the robbers, yet the local chiefs often successfully intercepted them in their murderous raids, and slaughtered them mercilessly. In 838 they were defeated by the Kinel Connell at Assaroe, by the Dalcassians in Clare, and by the Southern

Hy Neill in Meath. During the Fair of Roscrea in 845, a great body of the Norsemen marched suddenly on the town, expecting little resistance and plenty of booty. But the people, meeting them as they entered, killed their leader with a great number of the rank and file, and put the party to the rout. But the whole sea continued—as the Irish record expresses it—to vomit floods of foreigners into Erin; they still held their grip on the main strongholds of the coast, from which they swept like a whirlwind through the country; and wherever they went the track they left after them was a belt of desert.

The career of Turgesius was at last suddenly cut short by the valour of one of the provincial kings. He was taken prisoner in 845 by Malachi King of Meath, who caused him to be drowned in Lough Owel in Westmeath.

This brave prince succeeded to the throne of Ireland in 846, as Malachi I. He followed up his success with great determination; and the Danes now suffered many disastrous defeats, not only by this king, but by several of the provincial rulers.

148. Aed or Hugh Finnliath, who succeeded Malachi in 863, routed the Danes in several battles. He was succeeded by Malachy's son Flann Sinna. For 40 years—from 875 to 915—a period nearly coincident with Flann's reign, the Danes sent no new swarms to Ireland, and the land was comparatively free from their ravages; though those already in the country held their ground in their fortresses along the coast, such as Dublin, Waterford, Limerick, and Lough Foyle. But during this time there were serious wars among the Irish themselves.

149. In the time of Flann Sinna flourished archbishop Cormac Mac Cullenan King of Munster. Very soon after he was crowned king, Munster was invaded and plundered from Gowran to Limerick—in 906—by the monarch Flann and the King of Leinster. Cormac attended by Flahertagh the warlike abbot of Scattery, followed the invaders and defeated the monarch in two battles. But in the year 908 he was defeated and slain in the great battle of Ballaghmoon near Carlow, where 6,000 of the Munstermen fell.

Cormac Mac Cullenan was the most learned Irishman of his time, and was deeply versed in the history, literature, and antiquities of his country. The works written by him have already been mentioned.

150. The heroic King Niall Glunduff who succeeded Flann in 916, routed the Danes in several battles. But he was at last defeated by them in a terrible battle fought in 919 at Kilmashoge near Dublin, where fell the king himself with twelve princes and a great part of the nobles of the north of Ireland.

151. Donogh the son of Flann Sinna succeeded Niall, and in the second year of his reign—in 920—he avenged the battle of Kilmashoge by defeating and slaughtering the Danes on the plain of Bregia north of

Dublin.

During the reign of this king flourished Murkertagh of the Leather Cloaks, son of Niall Glunduff. He was one of the most valiant princes commemorated in Irish history, and waged incessant war against the foreigners.

In order to silence all opposition to his succession, he made a circuit of Ireland with a thousand picked men in the depth of winter, A.D. 941, when he knew that his opponents were unprepared to resist. For protection against the wintry weather each man was furnished with a large loose mantle of leather; and hence this prince has ever since been known by the name of Murkertagh of the Leather Cloaks. In this expedition he was entirely successful. He brought away the provincial kings or their sons to his palace at Ailech, where he kept them captive for five months, after which he sent them to king Donogh as a testimony of loyalty.

But Murkertagh was not destined to be king of Ireland. He was killed in 943 in an obscure skirmish at Ardee by Blacar the Dane, dying as he had lived, in conflict with the enemies of his country.

152. Malachi II., or Malachi the Great, as he is often called, the most distinguished king that had reigned for many generations, became king in 980. The year before his accession he defeated the Danes in a great battle at Tara where vast numbers of them were slain. Following up his success he marched straight on Dublin, which he captured after a siege of three days, took immense booty, and liberated 2,000 captives.

We shall now interrupt the regular course of our narrative in order to trace the career of the man who was destined to crush the power of the Danes for ever.

BRIAN BORU

153. Brian Boru the son of Kennedy, of the Dalgas race was born in Kincora in 941. In 964 his brother Mahon became king of all Munster. At this time the Danes held the chief fortresses of the province, including Limerick, Cork and Waterford, from which their marauding parties swept continually over the country, murdering and destroying wherever they came. King Mahon and his brother Brian, finding that they were not strong enough to withstand them openly, crossed the Shannon with those of their people who abode on the open plains, and took refuge among the forests and mountain solitudes of Clare. From these retreats they carried on a relentless desultory warfare with the foreigners, during which no quarter was given on either side.

154. After a time both parties grew tired of these destructive conflicts; and a truce was agreed on between Mahon and the Danish leaders. But young Brian would have no truce: and he maintained the war on his own account against fearful odds, till at last he was left with only fifteen followers.

And now the king, Mahon, hearing how matters stood, and fearing for his brother's safety, visited him in his wild retreat, and tried to persuade him to abandon further resistance as hopeless. But all in vain: the young chief was not to be moved from his purpose. And he at length persuaded his brother the king to resume hostilities; and the two brave brothers collecting all their forces, formed an encampment at Cashel, from which they sent expeditions to ravage the Danish settlements all round.

155. Now when Ivar of Limerick, king of the Munster Danes, heard of this uprising, he was infuriated to madness; and making a mighty gathering of all the Danes of Munster he determined to march into Thomond and exterminate the whole Dalcassian race root and branch. Molloy King of Desmond and Donovan King of Hy Carbery (in the present Co. Limerick) basely joined and encouraged him; and bent on vengeance he set out from Limerick with his whole army for the encampment at Cashel.

156. When the Dalcassian chiefs heard of this they marched west, and met the enemy half way at Sulcoit, now Sollohod, a level district near the present Limerick junction, twenty miles from Limerick city. The battle of Sulcoit began at sunrise on a summer morning of the year 968, and lasted till mid-day, when the foreigners gave way and fled—"fled to the hedges and to the valleys and to the solitudes of the great flowered-covered plain." They were pursued and slaughtered all the way to Limerick, which now was taken possession of by the victorious Irish. After this decisive battle Mahon defeated the Danes in seven other battles, till at last he became King of all Munster.

157. It is necessary to observe that at this time there were two ruling families in Munster. The Owenaghts or Eugenians who ruled Desmond were now represented by Molloy, and afterwards by the Mac Carthys: the Dalgas or Dalcassians now represented by Mahon and Brian, and afterwards by the O'Briens, ruled over Thomond. It had been for many centuries the custom that the kings of the Eugenian and Dalcassian families should be alternately kings of all Munster.

158. Mahon's uninterrupted success excited the envy and deepened the hatred of Donovan, Molloy, and Ivar the Dane; and they laid a base plot for his destruction. In 976 he was invited to a friendly conference to Bruree, the residence of Donovan, who on his arrival seized him and sent him to be delivered up to Molloy and his Danish associates.

Molloy sent forward an escort to meet him in the pass of Barnaderg, near Ballyorgan, between the counties of Cork and Limerick, with secret instructions to kill him, while Molloy himself remained behind within view of the pass, but a good way off. And when he saw in the distance the flash of the naked sword, he knew the deed was done; and mounting his horse he fled from the place.

159. But this villainous deed only raised up a still more formidable

antagonist, and swift retribution followed. Brian now became King of Thomond: and his first care was to avenge his brother's murder. Proceeding with his fleet to Scattery island where Ivar had taken refuge after the battle of Sulcoit, he slew him and his Danes. Next, in 977, he captured Bruree, Donovan's fortress, and killed Donovan himself, with Harold the son of Ivar and a vast number of their followers.

It was now Molloy's turn: and Brian, marching south in 978, encountered his army in Barnaderg, the very spot where the great crime had been committed two years before. Molloy was defeated with a loss of 1,200 men; and immediately after the battle he himself was found hiding in a hut and was killed without mercy by Murrogh the young son of Brian. After this last battle Brian was acknowledged King of all Munster.

160. Malachi, who we have seen became King of Ireland in 980, now grew jealous of the growing power of Brian; and to humble him he made an inroad into Thomond in 982, and uprooted and destroyed the venerable tree of Magh-Adhair [Moy-Ire] under which the Dalcassian kings had for ages been inaugurated. This led to a war of skirmishes and plundering expeditions, which continued with varying fortunes for several years.

During this period, Malachi never lost an opportunity of attacking the Danes. In 996 he swooped down on Dublin, then and for long after a Danish city, and plundered it. Among the trophies that he brought away were two heirlooms greatly prized by the Norsemen, the ring or collar of the Norwegian Prince Tomar—who had been killed 148 years before—and the sword of Carlus, who fell in battle in 869. This is the incident referred to by Moore in the words:—"When Malachi wore the collar of gold which he won from her proud invader."

At last the two opponents, having crushed all other competitors, found themselves so evenly matched, that they agreed to divide Ireland between them, Malachi to be king of Leth Conn and Brian of Leth Mow.

161. Mailmora King of Leinster was not pleased with the terms of this peace, which placed him permanently under the jurisdiction of Brian. In the very next year—999—he and the Danes of Dublin revolted. Whereupon Brian marched northwards, and being joined by Malachi, encamped at Glenmama near Dunlavin in Wicklow. Here they were attacked by Mailmora and Harold the Dane of Dublin; and in the terrible battle that followed Brian and Malachi defeated them and slow 4,000 of the Danes and Leinstermen.

162. About this time Brian came to the determination to depose Malachi; and the better to strengthen himself he made alliance with those who had lately been his enemies. He married Gormlaith mother of the King of the Dublin Danes (Sitric of the Silken Beard) and sister of Mailmora King of Leinster; he gave his own daughter in marriage to Sitric; and he took Mailmora into favour and friendship.

His next proceeding was to invade Malachi's territory, in 1002, in violation of the treaty of four years before; and he sent to him to demand submission or battle. And Malachi finding he was not strong enough to resist, rode into Brian's encampment with merely a small guard and without any guarantee or protection, and telling him plainly he would fight if he had been strong enough, he made his submission. This was in 1002; and from that year Brian was acknowledged king of Ireland, Malachi going back to his own special kingdom of Meath.

163. And now after forty years of incessant warfare Brian devoted his mind to works of peace. He rebuilt the monasteries that had been destroyed by the Danes, and erected bridges and fortresses all over the country. He founded and restored schools and colleges, and took measures for the repression of crime. The bright picture handed down to us of the peaceful and prosperous state of Ireland from Brian's accession to the battle of Clontarf, is illustrated by the well-known legend, that a beautiful young lady richly dressed, and bearing a ring of priceless value on her wand, traversed the country alone from north to south without being molested—a fiction which Moore has embalmed in the beautiful song "Rich and rare were the gems she wore."

THE BATTLE OF CLONTARF

164. Since the battle of Glenmama the Danes had kept quiet because the king's strong hand held them down. But it was a forced submission; and they only waited for an opportunity to attempt the overthrow of King Brian. The confederacy that led to the battle of Clontarf was originated, however, not by the Danes, but by Mailmora King of Leinster.

165. On one occasion while Mailmora was on a visit at Brian's palace of Kincora,* a bitter altercation arose at a game of chess between him and Murrogh, Brian's eldest son; so that he left the palace in anger and made his way to his own kingdom of Leinster, determined to revolt. And he and his people sent messengers to O'Neill king of Ulster, to O'Ruarc Prince of Brefney (the present Co. Leitrim), and to the chiefs of Carbury in Kildare, all of whom promised their aid.

166. The confederates began by attacking Malachi's kingdom of Meath, as he was now one of Brian's adherents. He defended himself successfully for some time, but he was at last defeated at Drinan near Swords by Mailmora and Sitric with the united armies of Danes and Leinstermen, leaving 200 of his men, including his own son Flann, dead on the Field. After this, Malachi, finding himself unable to defend his kingdom against so many enemies, sent messengers to Brian to demand protection. Moved by the representations of the King of Meath, and alarmed at the menacing movements of the Danes and Leinstermen, Brian and his son Murrogh marched north by two different routes, ravaging the Leinster and Danish territories; and in September, 1013, encamped at Kilmainham, intending to

take Dublin by blockade. But the attempt was unsuccessful, for the Danish garrison kept within walls and the Irish army ran short of provisions; so that the king was forced to raise the siege at Christmas, and return home to Kincora.

167. Mailmora and the Danish leaders now began actively at the work of mustering forces for the final struggle; and Gormlaith, who was among her own people—having been discarded by Brian—was no less active than her relatives. Her son Sitric of the Silken Beard, acting under her directions, engaged Sigurd earl of the Orkneys, as well as Broder and Amlaff of the Isle of Man, the two earls of all the north of England, who promised to be in Dublin on Palm Sunday, the day fixed on for the meeting of all the confederates. Broder had once been a Christian, but now worshipped heathen fiends: "he had a coat of mail on which no steel would bite;" he was both tall and strong, and his black locks were so long that he tucked them under his belt. These two vikings, Broder and Amlaff, who had a great fleet with 2,000 "Danmarkians" are described as "the chiefs of ships and outlaws and Danars of all the west of Europe, having no reverence for God or for man, for church or for sanctuary."

There came also 1,000 men covered with coats of mail from head to foot: a very formidable phalanx, seeing that the Irish fought as usual in tunics. Envoys were despatched in other directions also: and Norse auxiliaries sailed towards Dublin from Scotland, from the Isles of Shetland, from the Hebrides, from France and Germany, and from the shores of Scandinavia.

168. While Sitric and the other envoys were thus successfully prosecuting their mission abroad, Mailmora was equally active at home; and by the time all the foreign auxiliaries had joined muster, and Dublin Bay was crowded with their black ships, he had collected the forces of Leinster and arranged them in three great battalions within and around the walls of Dublin.

169. The Irish monarch had now no time to lose. He collected his forces about the 17th of March; and having encamped at Kilmainham, he set fire to the Danish districts near Dublin, so that the fierce Norsemen within the city could see Fingall the whole way from Dublin to Howth smoking and blazing. And brooding vengeance, they raised their standards and sallied forth to prepare for battle.

On the evening of Thursday the 22nd of April the king got word that the Danes were making preparations to fight next day—Good Friday. The good King Brian was very unwilling to fight on that solemn day; but he was not able to avoid it.

170. On the morning of Friday the 23rd of April 1014 the Irish army began their March from Kilmainham at dawn of day, in three divisions; and the Danes were also in three divisions. Sitric the King of Dublin was not in the battle: he remained behind to guard the city. We are not told the

numbers engaged: but there were probably about 20,000 men each side. The Danes stood with their backs to the sea: the Irish on the land side facing them.

In the march from Kilmainham the venerable monarch rode at the head of the army; but his sons and friends prevailed on him, on account of his age—he was now seventy-three—to leave the chief command to his son Murrogh. When they had come near the place of conflict, the army halted; and the king holding aloft a crucifix in sight of all, rode from rank to rank and addressed them in a few spirited words. He reminded them that on that day their good Lord had died for them; and he exhorted them to fight bravely for their religion and their country. Then giving the signal for battle he withdrew to his tent in the rear.

Little or no tactics appear to have been employed. It was simply a fight of man against man, a series of hand-to-hand encounters; and the commanders fought side by side with their men.

171. The first divisions to meet were the Dalcassians and the foreign Danes; then the men of Connaught and the Danes of Dublin fell on one another; and the battle soon became general. From early morning until sunset they fought without the least intermission. The thousand Danes in coats of mail were marked out for special attack: and they were all cut to pieces; for their armour was no protection against the terrible battle-axes of the Dalcassians.

The old chronicle describes Murrogh as dealing fearful havoc. Three several times he rushed with his household troops through the thick press of the furious foreigners, mowing down men to the right and left; for he wielded a heavy sword in each hand, and needed no second blow. At last he came on earl Sigurd whom he found slaughtering the Dalcassians. But Murrogh struck off his helmet with a blow of the right hand sword, bursting straps and buckles; and with the other felled him to the earth—dead.

Towards evening the Irish made a general and determined attack; and the main body of the Danes at last gave way. Crowds fled along the level shore towards Dublin, vainly hoping to reach either the ships or the city. But Malachi who had stood by till this moment, rushed down with his Meathmen and cut off their retreat.

The greatest slaughter of the Danes took place during this rout, on the level space now covered with streets, from Ballybough Bridge to the Four Courts.

172. We have related so far the disasters of the Danes. But the Irish had their disasters also; and dearly did they pay for their great victory.

After the rout of the Danish main body, scattered parties of Danes continued to fight for life with despairing fury at various points over the plain. On one of those groups came Murrogh, still fighting, but so fatigued that he could scarce lift his hands. Anrad the leader of the band, dashed at him furiously. But Morrogh who had dropped his sword, closing on him, grasped him in his arms, and by main strength pulled his armour over his head: then getting him under, he seized the Norseman's sword and thrust it three times through his body to the very ground. Anrad, writhing in the death agony, plunged his dagger into the prince's side, inflicting a mortal wound. But the Irish hero lived till next morning when he received the solemn rites of the church.

The heroic boy Turlogh, only fifteen years of age, the son of Murrogh, fought valiantly during the day in his father's division, side by side with his elder relatives. After the battle, late in the evening, he was found drowned at the fishing weir of the river Tolka, with his hands entangled in the long hair of a Dane, whom he had pursued into the tide at the time of the great flight.

173. But the crowning tragedy of the bloody day of Clontarf was yet to come. The aged king remained in his tent engaged in earnest prayer, while he listened anxiously to the din of battle. He had a single attendant, Laiten, who stood at the door to view the field; and close round the tent stood a guard. And now came the great rout; and the guards, thinking all danger past, eagerly joined in the pursuit, so that the king and his attendant were left alone.

It happened that Broder, who had fled from the battlefield, came with some followers at this very time toward the tent. "I see some people approaching," said Laiten. "What manner of people are they?" asked the king. "Blue and naked people," replied the attendant. "They are Danes in armour," exclaimed the king, and instantly rising from his cushion, he drew his sword. Broder at that instant rushed on him with a double-edged battle-axe, but was met by a blow of the heavy sword that cut off both legs, one from the knee and the other from the ankle. But the furious Viking, even while falling, cleft the king's head with the axe.

After a little time the guards, as if struck by a sudden sense of danger, returned in haste: but too late. They found the king dead, and his slayer stretched by his side dying.

174. As to the numbers slain, the records differ greatly. According to the annals of Ulster 7,000 fell on the Danish side and 4,000 on the Irish, which is probably near the truth. Almost all the leaders on both sides were slain, and among them Mailmora, the direct inciter of the battle.

The battle of Clontarf was the last great struggle between Christianity and heathenism.

The body of King Brian and that of his son Murrogh were conveyed with great solemnity to Armagh, where they were interred in the cathedral, the archbishop and the clergy celebrating the obsequies for twelve days.

175. After the battle of Clontarf and the death of Brian, Malachi, by

general consent and without any formality, took possession of the throne. He reigned for eight years after, and gave evidence of his old energy by crushing some risings of the Danes—feeble expiring imitations of their ancient ferocious raids—and by gaining several victories over the Leinstermen. He died in 1022 in the seventy-third year of his age, leaving behind him a noble record of self-denial public spirit, and kingly dignity.

* Kincora was situated on the very spot now occupied by the town of Killaloe.

PREPARING THE WAY FOR THE INVADER

176. During the century and a half from the death of Malachi II. to the Anglo Norman invasion, Ireland had no universally acknowledged over-king. To every one there was opposition from some influential quarter or another; which the annalists indicate by the epithet "king with opposition" commonly applied to the kings who during this time aspired to the sovereignty. There were altogether eight "kings with opposition:"— Donogh, Turlogh O'Brien, Dermot Mac Mailnamo, Murkertagh O'Brien, Donall O'Loughlin, Turlogh O'Conor, Murkertagh O'Loughlin, and Roderick O'Conor. During the whole of this period Ireland was in a state of great confusion. The rival claimants waged incessant war with one another; and as a natural consequence, the country became an easy prey to the invaders when they came.

The annalists tell us that for some years after the death of Malachi there was an interregnum; and that the affairs of the kingdom were administered by two learned men, Cuan O'Lochan, a great antiquary and poet, and "Corcran the cleric," a very holy ecclesiastic who lived chiefly in Lismore.

177. Not long after the death of Malachi, Donogh King of Munster, son of Brian Boru, took steps to claim the sovereignty. He is ranked among the kings of Ireland, but he never made any attempt on Ulster.

After some years his nephew Turlogh O'Brien, with the aid of Dermot MacMailnamo King of Leinster deposed him; on which Turlogh became king of Munster; and Donogh, now in his old age, took a pilgrim's staff and fared to Rome where he died in 1064.

178. At the time of Donogh's deposition Dermot of Leinster was the most powerful of the provincial kings, so that he also is reckoned among the kings of Ireland. His most persistent opponent was Conor O'Melaghlin Prince of Meath, the son of Malachi, who at last defeated and slew him in 1072 at the battle of Navan in Meath.

Turlogh O'Brien now marched north from Kincora and forced the kings and chiefs of all the other provinces and minor states, except Ulster, to acknowledge his authority. But when he attempted to reduce the Ulstermen they defeated him in 1075 near Ardee so that he had to retreat south. Some say that he ultimately forced Ulster to submit and pay him tribute. In 1086 this king died peacefully in Kincora.

179. Turlogh's son Murkertagh O'Brien succeeded as King of Munster. In the assertion of his claim to the throne of Ireland he had a formidable competitor, Donall O'Loghlin (or Mac Loghlin) King of Ulster, who belonged to the Northern Hy Neill and who now revived the claims of that princely family. These two men for more than a quarter of a century contended with varying fortunes for the throne of Ireland. Donall marched south in 1088 and destroyed O'Brien's palace of Kincora; on which Murkertagh retaliated by an expedition up the Shannon.

180. At last O'Brien had to acknowledge the supremacy of O'Loghlin. But he soon renewed the war; and in 1101 he marched north with an overwhelming army, destroyed Ailech or Greenan-Elly near Derry, the royal palace of the Northern Hy Neill, in revenge for the destruction of Kincora thirteen years before; and to make the demolition more humiliating, he ordered his soldiers to bring away the very stones of the building all the way back to Kincora. He made the whole circuit of Ireland without meeting any opposition, and brought hostages from every territory to his home in Kincora.

The struggle still went on; and five different times—from 1097 to 1113—when the hostile armies were about to engage, the archbishop of Armagh interposed and persuaded the kings to separate without bloodshed.

181. In 1101 Murkertagh granted the old city of Cashel to the church, and changed his own chief residence to Limerick, which after that time continued to be the seat of the kings of Thomond. The Rock of Cashel now contains on its summit the most interesting group of ruins in Ireland. In the year 1098 Murkertagh gave William Rufus a number of great oak trees from the wood of Oxmanstown near Dublin, wherewith was constructed the roof of Westminster Hall.

182. The long contest between these two powerful rivals—O'Brien and O'Loghlin—remained undecided to the last. They are both spoken of as kings of Ireland, reigning with equal authority, though O'Brien was the more distinguished king. Murkertagh, struck down with a wasting sickness, retired to the monastery of Lismore, where having entered the ecclesiastical state, he died in 1119. With him passed away for ever the predominance of the O'Brien family. Donall retired to the monastery of Derry where he died in 1121.

183. For the past century the struggle for supremacy had been chiefly between the O'Briens of Munster and the O'Loghlins or Mac Loghlins of Ulster—a branch of the northern Hy Neill. For the next half century it was between the O'Neills and the O'Conors of Connaught, ending in the triumph of the O'Conors, till the native monarchy was overthrown for ever by the Anglo Normans. Turlogh O'Conor, who at this time ruled over Connaught—the king who caused the Cross of Cong to be made in 1123—now put forth his claims to the supreme monarchy. He first reduced

Munster and weakened it by dividing it, making one of the O'Briens king of Thomond, and one of the Mac Carthys king of Desmond. But the O'Briens proved formidable adversaries, and still retained at least nominal sway over the whole province. They not only disputed O'Conor's supremacy, but led successful expeditions into the heart of Connaught. And thus the wretched country continued to be torn by feuds and broils; so that, as the Four Masters express it, Ireland was "a trembling sod."

184. The most powerful member of the great Dalcassian family at this time was Turlogh O'Brien who had an army of 9,000 men. O'Conor, determined on crushing him, marched south and caught him at a disadvantage, in 1151, at a place called Moanmore either in Limerick or Tipperary. In the terrible battle fought here O'Brien was defeated and his army almost annihilated: 7,000 of them fell, the greatest slaughter since the day of Clontarf. O'Brien fled to Ulster; but he never recovered this downfall.

185. Murkertagh O'Loglin or Mac Loghlin, Prince of Ailech was now O'Conor's only opponent. In the same year of the battle of Moanmore— 1151—he forced O'Conor to give him hostages. In 1154 O'Conor plundered the coasts of Ulster with a great Connaught fleet; but O'Loghlin met him with a Scoto-Danish fleet quite as large; and a naval battle was fought during a long summer day in which the Danish fleet was defeated and captured; but the Irish commander was killed.

186. King Turlogh O'Conor never relinquished the struggle for supremacy till the day of his death, which occurred in 1156. He was succeeded as king of Connaught by his son Rory, or as he is more commonly called, Roderick O'Connor. Not long after his election, this new king marched towards Ulster to assert his claim to be King of Ireland against O'Loghlin; who however met him in 1159 at Ardee and defeated him. After this O'Conor acknowledged O'Loghlin's supremacy and sent him hostages. But O'Loghlin was soon after (in 1166) killed in battle; and Roderick O'Conor having now no rival of any consequence was formally and solemnly inaugurated king of Ireland.

187. Though most of the great educational establishments had been broken up during the Danish ravages, many rose from their ruins or held their ground. Even to the beginning of the twelfth century Ireland still retained some portion of her ancient fame for learning, and we find the schools of Armagh, Lismore, Clomnacnoise, Monasterboice, and others still attracting great numbers of students, many of them foreigners. At this time flourished the two great scholars and annalists, Flann of Monasterboice and Tighernach of Clonmacnoise.

188. Many grave abuses had crept into the church during the Danish troubles—nearly all caused by the encroachments of the lay chiefs: but they were all disciplinal irregularities: none in doctrine. The ecclesiastical

authorities exerted themselves to correct these abuses; and their solicitude and activity are shown by a number of synods occurring about this time: in the one half century from 1111 to 1169, eleven synods were held at various places through the country.

In 1111 Murkertagh O'Brien caused a synod to be held at a place called Fid-Aengusa near Ushnagh in Westmeath, which was attended by the archbishops of Cashel and Armagh, and by 50 bishops, 300 priests, and 3,000 clergy of inferior orders, as well as by King Murkertagh himself and the chiefs of Leth-Mow.

Another synod was held about the same time at a place called Rathbrassil, at which the several dioceses all over Ireland were clearly defined; and it was ordained that the lands and revenues allotted to the bishops for their support should be exempted from public tax or tribute. The subdivision into parishes gradually followed. Some say that Fid-Aengusa and Rathbrassil were the same.

The most memorable synod of this period was that held at Kells in 1152, presided over by Cardinal Paparo the Pope's legate. Until this time there had been only two archbishops in Ireland, those of Armagh and Cashel; but at this council Dublin and Tuam were constituted archiepiscopal sees; and the Cardinal conferred the four palliums on the four archbishops, declaring that the archbishop of Armagh was primate over the others.

PART III. THE PERIOD OF INVASION

1172-1547.

IN this Third Part is told the story of the Anglo-Norman Invasion, beginning with the expedition of Fitzstephen and Prendergast, and ending with the reign of Henry VIII, the first English monarch who assumed the title of King of Ireland.

The conquest of Ireland, whose history we are now about to enter upon, might have been accomplished in a few years, if only proper measures had been adopted. Why it took so long was pointed out nearly three hundred years ago by Sir John Davies, an Englishman, who was attorney general of Ireland.

The force employed in the first instance was wholly insufficient for conquest.

The king did not reside in Dublin; and there was no adequate representative of royalty with state and power to overawe the whole people both native and colonial.

The great Anglo-Norman lords had too much power in their hands, and for their own selfish ends kept the country in a state of perpetual warfare.

Great tracts of land belonged to absentees living in England, who merely drew their rents and did nothing for the country.

But the most fatal and disastrous mistake of all was this. The native Irish, sick of anarchy, would have welcomed any strong government able and willing to maintain peace and protect them from violence. But the government, instead of treating them as subjects to be cared for, and placing them under the law that ruled the colonists, looked upon them as enemies, and refused them the protection of English law.

Henry II. did not conquer Ireland: it would have been better for both nations if he had. It took more than four centuries to do that—probably the longest conquest-agony recorded in history.

DERMOT MAC MURROGH

189. During the time that the two O'Conors were struggling with Murkertagh O'Loghlin, Dermot Mac Murrogh was King of Leinster. This Dermot, who was in after times often called Dermot-na-Gall (of the English), was a man of great size and strength, stern in manner, brave and fierce in war; and his voice was loud and hoarse from constant shouting in battle. He was cruel, tyrannical, and treacherous, and was hated in his own day as much as his memory has been hated ever since. His whole life was a record of violence and villainy.

190. In 1152, a few months after the battle of Moanmore, where he had fought on the side of O'Conor, he carried off Dervorgilla the wife of Ternan O'Ruarc Prince of Brefney, while O'Ruarc himself was absent from home; and she took away with her all she had brought to her husband as dowry. O'Ruarc appealed for redress to Turlogh O'Conor King of Ireland, who in 1153 marched with an army into Leinster and forced Dermot to restore Dervorgilla and all her rich dowry. She retired after a little time to the abbey of Mellifont, where she spent the rest of her days doing works of penitence and charity, and where she died in 1193 at the age of 85.

191. So long as King Murkertagh O'Loghlin lived he befriended Dermot and secured him in possession of Leinster. But when that king was slain in 1166, Ternan O'Ruarc led an army against Dermot, composed of the men of Brefney and Meath, joined by the Dano-Irish of Dublin under their King Hasculf Mac Turkill, and by the incensed people of Leinster. Seeing that resistance was hopeless, Dermot, breathing vengeance, fled across the sea, resolved to seek the aid of the great King Henry II. of England.

192. Many years before this time Nicholas Breakspear, an Englishman who had been elected Pope with the title of Adrian IV., influenced by an unfair and exaggerated account of the evil state of religion in Ireland, given to him by an envoy of King Henry, issued a bull authorizing the king to take possession of Ireland. Some writers have questioned the issue of this bull. But the evidence is overwhelming on the other side; and there is no sufficient reason to doubt that the Pope, moved by misrepresentations, did really issue the bull, with the firm conviction that it would be for the advancement of religion and for the good of Ireland.

193. Dermot presented himself before the king at Aquitaine, in 1168, and prayed him for help against his enemies, offering to hold his kingdom of

Leinster under him, and to acknowledge him as lord and master. The king eagerly accepted the offer; but being then too busy with the affairs of his own kingdom to go himself, he gave Dermot letters, permitting any of his British or French subjects that pleased to join the expedition.

194. With these letters Dermot proceeded to Bristol, where he engaged the services of Richard de Clare earl of Pembroke, better known by the name of Strongbow; on condition that the earl should get Dermot's daughter Eva in marriage, and should succeed him as King of Leinster.

At St. David's in Wales he engaged a number of the Geraldines, among them Maurice Fitzgerald and Robert Fitzstephen, to whom he promised the town of Wexford and the adjoining district. After this he returned to Ferns where he remained concealed during the winter.

THE FIRST ANGLO-NORMAN ADVENTURERS (1169-1171)

195. In the month of May 1169 a force of 100 knights and men-at-arms in coats of mail and about 600 archers, under Robert Fitzstephen and Maurice Prendergast landed at Bannow in Wexford with Hervey Mountmaurice, Strongbow's uncle. As knights and archers had attendants, the total force was about 2,000. Having been joined by Dermot and his son, Donall Kavanagh, with 500 horsemen, he advanced on the town of Wexford, which after a valiant defence was surrendered to them.

Then Dermot granted Wexford and the adjoining district to Robert Fitzstephen and Maurice Fitzgerald—the latter of whom had not yet arrived. He granted also to Mountmaurice the district lying between the towns of Wexford and Waterford. Dermot and his allies next attacked Ossory and forced its chief Mac Gilla Patrick to submit.

196. King Roderick O'Conor now at last became alarmed, and marched with a large army towards Ferns, where he found the King of Leinster and his foreign auxiliaries strongly entrenched. But the feeble-minded monarch, instead of promptly attacking the rebel king and his few foreign auxiliaries, made peace with Dermot and restored him to his kingdom, on condition—which was kept secret from his new friends—that he should send home the foreigners and bring hither no more of them; and Dermot gave his favourite son Conor and two other relatives as hostages.

But Maurice Fitzgerald landing soon afterwards, Dermot broke his promises, and with all the Anglo-Normans marched on Dublin, which the Danish King Hasculf Mac Turkill was forced to surrender to them.

197. At last Dermot resolved to make himself King of Ireland, and sent to Strongbow urging him to come over. On the 1st of May, 1170, Strongbow, not being yet ready to come himself, despatched a force of about 800 men under Raymond Fitzgerald, commonly known as Raymond le Gros, who fortified himself at a place called Dundonnell on the Wexford coast not far from Waterford.

Here they were soon attacked by a great army from Waterford; but

Raymond defeated them, slaying 500 of them. And after the battle 70 of the principal citizens who had been taken prisoners were cruelly executed.

198. At last, on the 23rd of August 1170, Strongbow landed near Waterford with an army of 3,000 men; and being joined by the others, they captured the city of Waterford, slaughtering great numbers of the inhabitants. Then Dermot carried out his promise: and the marriage of Strongbow and Eva was solemnized.

199. Scarcely had the ceremony ended when tidings came that Hasculf of Dublin had revolted against Dermot. Whereupon Dermot and Strongbow, in this same year 1170, marched over the mountains with an army of 5,000 men; and when the Dublin citizens beheld this formidable army approaching, they were so terrified that they sent their illustrious and saintly archbishop Laurence O'Toole with conditions of surrender. A truce was agreed on till terms of peace should be settled. But even after the conclusion of the truce, Raymond le Gros and Miles de Cogan, with a band of followers, forced their way into the city, and falling on the unresisting citizens butchered them without mercy. Hasculf and a large number of his people made their escape on board ship and sailed for the Scottish isles; and Dermot and Strongbow remained in possession of the city. After this King Roderick caused Dermot's three hostages to be put to death.

200. The progress of the invaders began now to excite general alarm, and a synod of all the clergy of Ireland was convoked at Armagh, who came to the conclusion that the invasion was a judgment from heaven for the crime of Slavery. And the synod decreed that all English slaves should be forthwith restored to freedom.

201. In the Spring of the next year, 1171, the arch traitor Dermot died at Ferns in the 61st year of his age: and immediately after his death earl Richard had himself proclaimed King of Leinster.

202. The fame of the great conquests made by Strongbow got noised abroad, so that it came to the ears of King Henry. Fearing that Strongbow might make himself king, he issued an edict forbidding further intercourse with Ireland: and at the same time he began to prepare for his own expedition.

And now Strongbow, being in want of provisions and reinforcements, was reduced to dire distress; and the little band of Anglo-Normans were preserved from destruction only by their own indomitable bravery.

203. Hasculf Mac Turkill returned to Ireland in 1171 with a great army of Danes, and besieged Dublin. But the governor Miles de Cogan, sallied forth from the gate, and after a terrible struggle he defeated the Danish army, and slew the commander, a fierce Dane named John the Mad. Hasculf himself was captured and put to death.

204. But no sooner was this danger averted than there arose another much more formidable. The patriotic archbishop Laurence O'Toole

persuaded the kings and chiefs to join in an attempt to crush the enemy. And numerous contingents began to march from every side towards Dublin; so that a great army was soon encamped round about the city, under King Roderick's command.

For two whole months (of 1171) the king let his army lie inactive in their tents; but they reduced the garrison to great straits by stopping all supplies. To add to the distress news came that Fitzstephen was surrounded by the Irish in his castle of Carrick near Wexford.

Driven to desperation they came to the resolution to attempt to cut their way in a body through the enemy. About 3 o'clock in the afternoon, the desperate little band, 600 Anglo-Normans with some Irish under Donall Kavanagh, suddenly sallied out and took the Irish completely by surprise; and the king himself, who happened to be in his bath at the time, escaped with much difficulty half naked from the field. The panic spread rapidly, and the various contingents broke up and fled. And the garrison returned triumphant to the city, laden with booty, and with provisions enough for a whole year.

205. Strongbow now marched south to relieve Fitzstephen; but he was too late, for Fitzstephen had been taken prisoner. Immediately afterwards he received a message from King Henry, summoning him to his presence. So hastily crossing the sea he presented himself before the monarch, whom he found with a large army preparing to invade Ireland.

KING HENRY IN IRELAND (1171-1173)

206. On the 18th October 1171, King Henry landed at Crook a little below Waterford, with many of his nobles, and an army of 4,400 knights and men at arms. Counting attendants he probably had 10,000 altogether.

At Waterford he was met by Dermot Mac Carthy King of Desmond, who was the first Irish prince to submit and pay tribute; and the Wexford men delivered up to him in fetters Fitzstephen, whom in a few days he released.

207. Henry next marched by Lismore to Cashel where he received the submission of Donall O'Brien of Limerick and of many others of the southern princes. After this he returned to Waterford; and having taken possession of Wexford, he proceeded to Dublin, where he was received in great state. Here he was visited by most of the other Irish princes, all of whom submitted to him. Roderick O'Conor did not come, but he sent his submission: O'Neill of Ulster neither came nor sent submission. The Irish princes and nobles were invited to spend the Christmas with the king in Dublin; and they were astonished at the magnificence of the display, and much pleased with the attention shown to themselves.

208. Early in the ensuing year, 1172, the king caused a synod of the archbishops and bishops of Ireland and several Anglo-Norman ecclesiastics to be held at Cashel; in which certain decrees were drawn up for the regulation of church discipline. These decrees do not indicate any

very serious state of religious corruption in Ireland, such as had been falsely represented to the Pope.

209. Henry now rewarded his followers by grants of large tracts of country, giving away the lands belonging to the natives without the least scruple. Leinster was granted to Strongbow, with the exception of Dublin and some other maritime towns; Meath—then much larger than now—to Hugh de Lacy; and Ulster to John de Courcy. In all the chief towns he left governors. He granted Dublin to the people of Bristol with De Lacy as governor, who is generally regarded as the first viceroy of Ireland.* Having completed these arrangements, he embarked at Wexford in April 1172, and returned to England.

210. After his departure his arrangements were all disregarded; and his followers did just as they pleased, plundering and harassing the unfortunate natives without mercy and without restraint.

The turmoil began the moment he had left. Ternan O'Ruarc, Dermot's old adversary, was killed by De Lacy in a fray during a conference. Strongbow, returning from a plundering raid through Offaly, was intercepted by its chief, O'Dempsey, and defeated, a great number of his men, with his son-in-law De Quenci, being slain. In the following year— 1173—he was appointed viceroy by the king.

* The governors of Ireland at this time and for centuries after, were designated by various titles, such as viceroy, lieutenant, lord lieutenant, lord justice or justiciary, governor, etc. A person appointed to govern temporarily in place of an absent lord lieutenant or viceroy was designated deputy or lord deputy.

RAYMOND LE GROS (1173-1176)

211. No sooner had Strongbow entered on his new duties as viceroy than troubles began to thicken round him. He found most of the Irish princes in revolt, and the money he had brought was soon spent, so that he had no pay for his soldiers. Mountmaurice was general of the army: but the soldiers hated him and demanded to have Raymond put over them, which was done: on which the new general led the men south and ravaged Offaly and the country round Lismore, carrying off immense spoils in spite of all opposition.

212. Raymond growing more ambitious with continued success, solicited in marriage Strongbow's sister Basilea: and he asked also to be made constable or commander of Leinster. But the earl refused both requests; whereupon Raymond threw up his post in 1174, and returned to Wales; and Mountmaurice was restored to the chief command.

213. And now (1174) Strongbow marched towards Limerick against Donall O'Brien King of Thomond who had revolted. But O'Brien and King Roderick intercepted him at Thurles, defeated him, and killed 1,700 of his men—the best part of his army. Strongbow fled to Waterford and shut

himself up there, but was besieged and in great danger, till Raymond returned and rescued him. Then he gave his sister in marriage to his rescuer and made him constable of Leinster.

214. Raymond next made preparation to avenge on Donall O'Brien the defeat of Thurles. He led his troops, in 1175, to Limerick; and in the face of enormous difficulties he forded the deep and rapid river, stormed the city, and gave it up to slaughter and plunder. Then leaving a sufficient garrison under the command of Miles de Cogan he returned to Dublin.

215. Meanwhile Roderick, finding that he could not prevent the daily incursions of English raiders, determined to claim the protection of King Henry. Accordingly he sent three ambassadors to England, one of whom was archbishop Laurence O'Toole, and a treaty was arranged between the two kings. Under this treaty, which was signed at Windsor in 1175, it was agreed that Roderick was to remain King of Connaught, which he was to hold directly as vassal to Henry; that he was to rule the rest of Ireland also as vassal, except the portions held by the English colony; and that through him the other kings and chiefs of the country were to pay tribute to King Henry.

216. But now Mountmaurice secretly reported to the king that Raymond aimed at making himself king of Ireland; whereupon King Henry ordered that he should be sent to England. But even while Raymond was preparing to obey the command, news came that Donall O'Brien had laid siege to Limerick; and when Strongbow ordered out the army for its relief, the men refused point blank to march under Mountmaurice. So Raymond had to be replaced in command, and marching south he defeated O'Brien and recovered Limerick.

217. One day while he was in the south a courier arrived post haste from Dublin with an odd message from his wife Basilea:—-"Be it known to you that the great jaw-tooth which used to trouble me so much has fallen out. Wherefore return with all speed." She took this enigmatical way of telling him that her brother the earl was dead (A.D. 1176). Knowing well the dangerous position of the colony in Dublin, and fearing the Irish might rise if they knew of his death, she determined to keep the matter secret till Raymond should be present. Raymond understood the meaning and returned; and the earl was interred with great pomp in Christ Church Cathedral.

218. As soon as the king heard of Strongbow's death, being still jealous of the brilliant soldier Raymond, he appointed William Fitz Adelm de Burgo viceroy in 1176, with John de Courcy, Robert Fitzstephen, and Miles de Cogan to assist him. Raymond met them near Wexford, and having given them a most respectful reception, he delivered up all his authority to the new viceroy without a murmur.

After this we hear little more of Raymond le Gros in public life. He retired to his estates in Wexford where he resided quietly till his death, which took place in 1182.

218a. Among the families descended from the Anglo-Norman lords, the most distinguished were the Fitzgeralds or Geraldines, the Butlers, and the De Burgos or Burkes. The Geraldines were chiefly descended from Maurice Fitzgerald. There were two main branches: one in Leinster, whose chiefs became, first, barons of Offaley, then earls of Kildare, and lastly dukes of Leinster: the other in Munster, whose heads were earls of Desmond. The Butlers settled in Leinster, and their chiefs became earls of Ormond. The family of De Burgo was founded by William Fitz Adelm de Burgo: they settled chiefly in Connaught, and were of two main branches as told in Paragraph 262.

JOHN DE COURCY (1177-1204)

219. The new governor was from the first disliked by the colonists: for he wished for peace and discouraged outrage on the natives; whereas war was what the colonists most desired, as it brought them plunder and sure increase of territory.

220. Among all De Burgo's followers not one was so discontented as Sir John de Courcy. He was a man of gigantic size and strength—brave and daring; and he now resolved to attempt the conquest of Ulster, which King Henry II. had granted to him five years before. So gathering round him a small band of about 320 knights and archers, who with their attendants made an army of about 1,000, he set out from Dublin for Ulster.

Passing northwards with all speed, he arrived on the morning of the fourth day—the 2nd of February 1177—at Downpatrick, then the capital of Ulidia. The adventurers were half starved as they entered the town; and now they fell upon everything they could lay hands on: they ate and drank, plundered, killed, and destroyed, till half the town was in ruins.

221. At the end of a week Mac Dunlevy Prince of Ulidia came with a large undisciplined army to attack him. De Courcy nothing daunted, went out to meet them, and chose a favorable position to meet the assault. The Irish rushed on with tumultuous bravery, but they were not able to break the disciplined ranks of the enemy; and after a furious fight they were repulsed with great loss.

222. But the Ulidians continued to offer the most determined resistance. The valiant De Courcy battled bravely through all his difficulties, and three several times in the same year, 1177, he defeated in battle the people of the surrounding districts, But as time went on he met with many reverses, and he had quite enough to do to hold his ground. In the following year he was defeated near Newry with a loss of 450 men; and again he was intercepted in one of his terrible raids, and defeated by the Dalaradian chief Cumee O'Flynn. He escaped from this battlefield with only eleven companions; and having lost their horses they fled on foot for two days and two nights

closely pursued, without food or sleep, till they reached a place of safety. But in several other battles he was victorious, so that as years went by he strengthened his position in Ulster: and as opportunities offered he built many castles.

223. In 1177, the second year of De Burgo's viceroyalty, Miles de Cogan invaded Connaught in violation of the treaty of Windsor; but he was defeated with great loss and driven back across the Shannon by King Roderick.

224. William De Burgo became at last so unpopular with the colonists, that King Henry removed him from the viceroyalty (in 1178), and appointed Hugh de Lacy in his place.

After De Lacy's appointment he married (in 1180) a daughter of King Roderick O'Conor. This marriage greatly increased his power and influence among the Irish, insomuch that it excited the jealousy and suspicion of the king, who in consequence dismissed him from his office. But in a few months he was reinstated: and he built castles all over Leinster.

225. The country still continued to be very much disturbed; and the king determined to send over his son Prince John, hoping that his presence would restore tranquillity. The prince, then 19 years of age, landed at Waterford in 1185 with a splendid retinue and a large body of cavalry. He had the title of Lord of Ireland. His secretary and tutor was a Welsh priest named Gerald Barry, now better known as Giraldus Cambrensis, or Gerald of Wales, who afterwards wrote a description of Ireland and of the Anglo Norman invasion.

226. But Prince John soon raised the whole country in revolt by his silly and vicious conduct; and he even turned the old colonists against him. The Irish chiefs crowded to him in Waterford, both to pay him respect and to acknowledge him as their lord; but his insolent young associates — close shaven dandies — ridiculed their dress and manners, and insulted them by plucking their beards, which they wore long according to the custom of the country.

Incensed by this treatment the proud Irish nobles withdrew to their homes, brooding mischief. The settlements were attacked at all points; and the most active of the assailants was the valiant Donall O'Brien of Thomond. A great number of the strongholds were taken, and many of the bravest of the Anglo-Norman chiefs were slain. The colonists were driven to take refuge in the towns; and almost the whole of John's splendid army perished in the various conflicts.

227. When the country had been for some time in this state of turmoil, King Henry heard how matters stood, and at once recalled the prince, after a stay of about eight mouths, appointing De Courcy viceroy. The prince, both before and after his return, threw the whole blame of the disturbances

on De Lacy; but De Lacy never lived to clear himself. One day in 1186, while with a few attendants he was inspecting his new castle at Durrow, a young Irishman suddenly drew forth a battle-axe from under his cloak, and with one blow struck off the great baron's head: after which he made his escape. This was done to avenge De Lacy's seizure of lands, and his desecration of St. Columkille's venerated monastery of Durrow, which he had pulled down.

228. During De Courcy's viceroyalty he invaded Connaught, burning and slaying after his usual fashion. But before he had advanced far into the province he was confronted by the two kings of Connaught and Thomond — Conor Mainmoy and Donall O'Brien — with their united armies. Not venturing to give battle to this formidable force, he retreated northwards, his only anxiety now being to save himself and his army from destruction. But when he had arrived at Ballysadare, on the coast of Sligo, the Prince of Tirconnell came marching down on him in front, while his pursuers were pressing on close behind. Setting fire to Ballysadare, he fled south-east; but as he was crossing the Curlieu Hills he was overtaken by Conor Mainmoy and O'Brien, who fell upon him and killed a great number of his men; and it was with much difficulty he escaped with the remnant of his army into Leinster.

229. Two years later, A.D. 1200, he was tempted to try his fortune a second time in Connaught; but with no better result than before. He and Hugh de Lacy the younger were both induced by Cahal Crovderg to come to his assistance in the struggle for the throne. But the rival king, Cahal Carrach, caught the allies in an ambuscade in a wood near Kilmacduagh in Galway, and inflicted on them a crushing defeat, slaying more than half of the English army. De Courcy had a narrow escape here, being felled from his horse by a stone. Recovering, however, he fled from the battlefield northwards till he reached Rindown castle on the western shore of Lough Ree, where he proceeded to convey his army in boats across the lake. He had been a week engaged at this, when, on the very last day, Cahal Carrach pounced down on those that still remained at Rindown and killed and drowned great numbers of them; while De Courcy and the rest, being safe at the far side, made good their escape.

230. The chequered career of this extraordinary man ended in ruin and disgrace. Hugh de Lacy (the younger: son of the great De Lacy) took every means to poison King John's mind against him. He was proclaimed a rebel and a traitor; and De Lacy, now lord justice, was commissioned to arrest him. After several unsuccessful attempts De Courcy was at length betrayed by some of his own servants, who led De Lacy's men to his retreat at Downpatrick, where he was taken in 1204. Some records relate that his enemies came down on him on Good Friday, when he was barefoot and unarmed, doing penance in the cathedral of Downpatrick, and that he

snatched the nearest weapon — a great wooden cross standing on a grave — with which he dashed out the brains of thirteen of his assailants before he was overpowered.

KING JOHN IN IRELAND (1189-1210)

231. King Henry died in the year 1189 and was succeeded by his son Richard the Lion Hearted. Richard took no interest in Ireland, and left the whole management of its affairs to his brother John, who, in 1189, appointed Hugh de Lacy lord justice, in place of John de Courcy.

At this time and for long after, Connaught was in a miserable state of turmoil, partly from the contests of the members of the O'Conor family for the provincial throne, and partly on account of the interference of the barons, who always took advantage of the native dissensions to advance their own interests.

232. The disturbances began with the contention of Cahal Crovderg (of the Red-hand) and Cahal Carrach, the former the youngest brother and the latter the grandson of the old King Roderick. After a short struggle Cahal Crovderg triumphed, and in 1190 became King of Connaught. The old King Roderick himself, wearied with care, both public and domestic, retired for a time (in 1183) to the monastery of Cong; and though he subsequently came forth to resume his kingdom, he never afterwards played any important part in the government, and finally retired for life. In 1198 he ended his troubled career in peace and penitence in the same monastery.

233. In 1192 the English of Leinster invaded Munster; but Donall O'Brien King of Thomond defeated them with great loss at Thurles. To avenge this they crossed the Shannon to ravage Thomond; but O'Brien fell on them, and having slain great numbers, drove them back. This brave King Donall O'Brien died two years later (in 1194).

234. Cahal Crovderg, having ruled over Connaught for eight or nine years, was driven from his throne by Cahal Carrach aided by William de Burgo. After several vain attempts to regain his kingdom, aided by De Lacy and John de Courcy Cahal Crovderg finally succeeded, in 1201, in slaying his rival, and reigned from that time forth without opposition. He was one of the most valiant chiefs of those times, and is much celebrated in the annals for his bravery, power, and justice. In the end of his life he retired to the abbey of Knockmoy where he died in 1224.

235. King Richard died in 1199 and was succeeded by his brother John.

The years immediately following the death of Donall O'Brien (in 1194) present a weary record of strife and turmoil. There were wars and broils everywhere, among both the Irish chiefs and the English nobles, causing wide devastation and misery among the people.

236. Even Dublin, the centre of government, felt the effects of the general state of disturbance. On Easter Monday, 1209, the dispossessed

O'Byrnes and O'Tooles fell upon the citizens at Cullenswood near the city and killed 300 of them; from which Easter Monday was for many ages afterwards called Black Monday.

237. King John was kept well informed of the disturbed state of the country. What seems to have troubled him most, so far as Ireland was concerned, was that some of the great nobles, and notoriously the De Lacys and William de Braose, had thrown off all authority and made themselves, to all intents and purposes, independent princes, like John de Courcy. With the object of reducing these turbulent barons to submission and of restoring quiet, the king resolved to visit Ireland. He landed at Crook near Waterford, in the month of June 1210, with a formidable army. In the presence of this great force the country at once became quiet, and the two De Lacys, Hugh and his brother Walter, fled to France. De Braose also escaped, but his wife and son fell into the tyrant's hands, who had them starved to death in prison.

It is stated that the De Lacys had to work in France as gardeners for subsistence, but that the king after some time pardoned and restored them.

The king proceeded to Dublin, and from thence to Meath, where Cahal Crovderg visited him and made submission.

238. As John had no fighting to do, he employed himself more usefully in making arrangements for the better government of the country. Those parts of Ireland which were under English jurisdiction he parcelled out into twelve shires or counties: namely, Dublin, Kildare, Meath, Uriel (or Louth), Carlow, Kilkenny, Wexford, Waterford, Cork, Kerry, Limerick and Tipperary. He directed that in all these counties the English laws should be administered. But it must be always borne in mind that these arrangements, including the administration of the law, were for the settlers only, not for the natives, who were then and long afterwards outside the pale of the law.

The king returned to England in August 1210, leaving John de Grey lord justice, to whom he committed the task of carrying out his arrangements. During the remainder of his reign, Ireland was comparatively quiet.

A CENTURY OF TURMOIL (1210-1314)

239. King John was succeeded, in 1216, by his son Henry III., who was then a boy of nine years old.

The century that elapsed from the death of John to the invasion of Edward Bruce was a period of strife and bloodshed, a period of woe and misery for the common people. There was as usual no strong central government, and the whole nation was abandoned to anarchy.

240. William Marshal earl of Pembroke married Isabel the only child of Strongbow and Eva, through whom he came in for possession of almost the whole of Leinster. Marshal died in 1219, leaving his titles and estates to his son William Marshal the younger. Between him and Hugh de Lacy a war arose in 1224, which continued till the whole of Meath was wasted.

This is sometimes called the War of Meath.

241. While this warfare was going on, Connaught was in a state of strife which lasted for many years; and the struggles among the several claimants of the O'Conor family went on unceasingly: battles, skirmishes, and raids without number. The English, under Marshal, De Burgo, or others, were mixed up in most of these contests, now siding with one of the parties, now with another; but always keeping an eye to their own interests. And thus the havoc and ruin went on unchecked. Meanwhile the wretched hunted people had no leisure to attend to their tillage; famine and pestilence followed; and the inhabitants of whole towns and districts were swept away.

242. There was also a War of Kildare as well as of Meath. After William Marshal's death, his brother Richard, a handsome, valiant, noble-minded knight, inherited his titles and estates. He incurred the anger of King Henry III. and fled to Ireland. But Geoffrey Marisco, Maurice Fitzgerald, and Hugh de Lacy conspired to destroy him, hoping to share his vast estates. Marisco pretended friendship, and in 1234 arranged a conference on the Curragh of Kildare. Here young Marshal was suddenly attacked by De Lacy and the others, and being abandoned by Marisco, he was at length overpowered, wounded, and taken prisoner. He soon after died of his wounds; but his assassins gained nothing by their villainy.

243. Maurice Fitzgerald, who had been twice lord justice, marched with his army northwards through Connaught in 1257, resolved to bring Ulster completely under English rule. But he was intercepted by Godfrey O'Donnell, chief of Tirconnell, at Credran-Kill near Sligo town, where a furious battle was fought. The two leaders, Fitzgerald and O'Donnell, met in single combat and wounded each other severely; the English were routed; and Fitzgerald retired to the Franciscan monastery of Youghal, where he died the same year, probably of his wounds.

244. As for O'Donnell, he had himself conveyed to an island in Lough Veagh in Donegal, where he lay in bed for a whole year sinking daily under his wounds; and all this time the Tirconnellians had no chief to lead them.

There had been, for some time before, much dissension between this O'Donnell and Brian O'Neill, Prince of Tyrone; and now O'Neill ignobly invaded Tirconnell. O'Donnell, still lying helpless, ordered a muster of his army, and had himself borne on a bier at their head to meet the enemy. And while the bier was held aloft in view of the Kinel Connell, the armies attacked each other near the river Swilly, and the Tyrone men were routed. Immediately afterwards the heroic chief died: and the same bier from which he had witnessed his last victory, was made use of to bear him to his grave.

245. Some of the Irish chiefs now attempted to unite against the common

enemy, choosing Brien O'Neill for leader: but in 1260 they were defeated by the English in a bloody battle at Downpatrick; and O'Neill and a large number of chiefs were slain.

246. In the south the Mac Carthys of Desmond, seeing their ancient principality continually encroached upon by the Geraldines, became exasperated and attacked and defeated them in 1261 at Callan near Kenmare; after which they demolished numbers of the English castles. But they soon quarrelled among themselves, and the Geraldines gradually recovered all they had lost.

While this universal strife was raging in Ireland, Henry III. died, and was succeeded by Edward I. in 1272.

247. After the English settlement in 1172 there were two distinct codes of law in force in Ireland—the English and the Brehon. The English law was for the colonists; it did not apply to the Irish: so that an Irishman that was in any way injured by an Englishman had no redress. He could not seek the protection of English law; and if he had recourse to the Brehon law, the Englishman need not submit to it. About this time therefore the Irish several times petitioned to be placed under English law; but though both Edward I. and Edward III. were willing to grant it, the selfish Anglo-Irish barons always prevented it; for it was their interest that the Irish should be regarded as enemies, and that the country should be in a perpetual state of disturbance.

EDWARD BRUCE (1315-1318)

248. The preceding hundred years I have designated a century of turmoil; but it was peace itself compared with the three and a half years of Bruce's expedition to Ireland.

The Irish people, especially those of the north, viewed with great interest and sympathy the struggles of their kindred in Scotland for independence; and Robert Bruce's glorious victory at Bannockburn filled them with joy and hope. Soon after the battle they requested him to send his brother Edward to be king over them. He eagerly accepted the invitation; and on the 25th of May 1315, Edward Bruce, accompanied by many of the Scottish nobles, landed at Larne with an army of 6,000 of the best soldiers of Scotland. He was immediately joined by Donall O'Neill, and by numbers of the northern Irish; and the combined forces overran a great part of Ulster, destroying everything belonging to the English that came in their way, and defeating them in several battles. Moving southwards, they stormed and burned Dundalk and Ardee; and at this latter place they set fire to the church in which a number of people had taken refuge and burned them all to death.

From first to last the campaign was carried on with great cruelty, and with reckless waste of life and property. All food except what was needed for the use of the army was destroyed, though there was a famine, and the people were starving all over the country.

249. The two leading Anglo-Irish noblemen at this time were Richard de Burgo the Red earl of Ulster, and Sir Edmund Butler the lord justice. The Red earl, who was by far the most powerful nobleman in Ireland, raised a large army, chiefly in Connaught, and set out in quest of the invaders. His march north through the Irish districts was perhaps more savagely destructive than that of Bruce.

Felim O'Conor the young King of Connaught had joined De Burgo and accompanied the English army. But he was recalled to Connaught to suppress a rebellion of some of his subjects. This weakened De Burgo, who was now attacked by Bruce at Connor near Ballymena and wholly defeated; and he returned to Connaught with the broken remnants of his forces.

250. A body of the defeated English fled eastwards to Carrickfergus and took possession of the castle, which they gallantly defended for months against the Scots. Soon after the battle Bruce had himself proclaimed King of Ireland and formally crowned.

Marching next into Meath he routed an army of 15,000 men under Roger Mortimer at Kells; and at the opening of the new year—1316—he defeated the lord justice Sir Edmund Butler at Ardscull near Athy.

The harvest of this year was a bad one, and scarcity and want prevailed all over the country. Nevertheless the Scottish army, wherever they went, continued to ravage and destroy all they could not consume or bring away, multiplying tenfold the miseries of the people, both English and Irish.

251. Felim O'Conor, having crushed in blood the revolt in Connaught, now declared for the Scots. Intending to expel all the English from the province, he marched to Athenry with a great army; but was there defeated and slain in 1316 in a great battle by William de Burgo and Richard Birmingham. Eleven thousand of the Irish fell, and among them nearly all the native nobility of Connaught.

252. The band of English who had taken possession of Carrickfergus castle held out most heroically, and now Bruce himself came to conduct the siege in person. Reduced to starvation, the brave garrison at last surrendered on condition that their lives should be spared.

253. King Robert had come over to aid his brother; and early in the spring of 1317 they set out for Dublin with an army of 20,000, destroying everything in their march.

They encamped at Castleknock; but the citizens of Dublin took most determined measures for defence, burning the suburbs in their desperation, both houses and churches, to deprive the Scots of shelter; so that the Bruces did not think it prudent to enter on a siege; and they resumed their destructive march till they reached Limerick. But as they found this city also well prepared for defence, and as there was still great scarcity of provisions, they returned northwards after a short stay. They had to traverse the very districts they had wasted a short time before; and in this most miserable march vast numbers of them perished of cold, hunger, and disease—scourged by the famine they had themselves created.

254. Robert Bruce returned to Scotland; and in the autumn of next year, 1318, Edward again marched southwards, but was met at Faughart two miles north of Dundalk with an army much more numerous than his own, under Sir John Bermingham.

The battle fought here on Sunday, the 14th of October, 1318, terminated the war. The issue was decided chiefly through the bravery of Sir John Maupas, an Anglo-Irish knight, who made a dash at Bruce and slew him in the midst of the Scots. Maupas was instantly cut down; and after the battle his body was found pierced all over, lying on that of Bruce. The Scottish army was defeated with great slaughter. Bermingharn, with barbarous vindictiveness, had the body of Bruce cut in pieces to be hung up in the chief towns in the colony, and brought the head salted in a box to King Edward II., who immediately created him earl of Louth and gave him the manor of Ardee.

255. And so ended the celebrated expedition of Edward Bruce. Though it resulted in failure, it shook the Irish government to its foundation and weakened it for centuries. Ulster was almost cleared of colonists; the native chiefs and clans resumed possession; and there were similar movements in other parts of Ireland, though not to the same extent.

There had been such general, needless, and almost insane destruction of property, that vast numbers of the people lost everything and sank into hopeless poverty. The whole country was thrown into a state of utter disorder from which it did not recover till many generations had passed away. And to add to the misery there were visitations of famine and pestilence—plagues of various strange kinds—which continued at intervals during the whole of this century.

THE STATUTE OF KILKENNY (1318-1377)

256. Edward III. succeeded to the throne of England in 1327, in succession to his father Edward II.

The Irish government emerged from the Bruce struggle weak: it now grew weaker year by year—engaged in defence rather than invasion; and the causes were not far to seek. The Irish, taking advantage of the dissensions and helplessness of the English, recovered a great part of their lands. The English all over the country were fast becoming absorbed into the native population.

257. There were two reasons for this. First: the colonists, seeing the Irish prevailing everywhere, joined them for their own protection, intermarrying with them and adopting their language, dress, and customs. Second: the government had all along made a most mischievous distinction between

New English and Old English—English by birth and English by blood. They favored Englishmen and gave them most of the situations of trust, putting them over the heads of the Old English. This so incensed the old colonists that a large proportion of them turned against the government and joined the Irish all over the country.

These "degenerate English," as they were called, were regarded by the loyal English with as much aversion as the Irish, and returned hate for hate quite as cordially. So completely did they become fused with the native population, that an English writer complained that they had become Hiberniores Hibernicis ipsis, more Irish than the Irish themselves.

258. The whole country was now feeling the consequences of the Bruce invasion. There were murderous broils everywhere among the English themselves. At Bragganstown, near Ardee, Sir John Bermingham, the victor of Faughart, was led into a trap, in 1329, and treacherously slain, together with his brothers, nephews, and retainers, to the number of 160, by the Gernons and Savages. About the same time a similar outrage was perpetrated in Munster; when Lord Philip Hodnet and 140 of the Anglo-Irish were massacred by their brethren, the Barrys, the Roches, and others.

259. The uprising of the Irish became so general and alarming that, in 1330, the viceroy called in the aid of the powerful nobleman in the country, Maurice Fitzgerald, who was at the same time created first earl of Desmond. This only made matters worse; for Fitzgerald, after some successful expeditions, quartered his army, to the number of 10,000, on the colonists, to pay themselves by exacting coyne and livery. This was the first time the English adopted the odious impost, which afterwards became so frequent among them.

260. The Anglo Irish lords had now become so dangerously powerful that King Edward III. determined to pull them down and reduce them to obedience. He made three attempts by three different governors and failed in all.

The first was Sir Anthony Lucy, a stern Northumbrian baron, who was sent over in 1331 as lord lieutenant. He arrested, among others, the earl of Desmond and Sir William Bermingham. Bermingham, who was suspected of being implicated in a rebellious outbreak that had lately taken place in Leinster, was executed in the following year; and Desmond was released after 18 months' imprisonment. But Lucy was not successful in his main object.

261. In 1333 De Burgo the Brown earl of Ulster, then only 21 years of age, was murdered on his way to Carrickfergus church on a Sunday morning by Richard de Mandeville, his own uncle by marriage. The Anglo-Irish people of the place, by whom the young lord was much liked, rose up in a passionate burst of vengeance, and seizing on all whom they suspected of having a hand in the deed, killed 300 of them.

262. The murder of this young earl lost a great part of Ireland to the government, and helped to hasten the incorporation of the English with the Irish. He left one child, a daughter, who according to English law was heir to her father's vast possessions in Ulster and Connaught, about one-fourth of the whole Anglo-Irish territory.

The two most powerful of the Connaught De Burgos seized the estates, declared themselves independent of England, and adopted the Irish dress and language.

They took also Irish names, one of them calling himself Mac William Oughter (Upper) as being lord of upper, or south, Connaught; he was ancestor of the earls of Clanrickard: the other, Mac William Eighter i.e. of Lower or North Connaught, from whom descended the earls of Mayo. And their example was followed by many other Anglo-Irish families, especially in the west and south.

263. The English of the Pale were now so weak that they had to pay some of the Irish septs of their borders to protect them from the attacks of the natives. Payments of this kind subsequently became very common, and were called "Black rents."

264. After a considerable interval, Sir John Morris came in 1341 as deputy, to attempt what Lucy had failed in. He took back all the lands and all the privileges which either the king himself or his father had granted; and he re-claimed all debts that had been cancelled. But there came a much worse measure than this. The king issued an ordinance in 1342 that all natives, whether of Irish or English descent, who were married and held public offices in Ireland, should be dismissed, and their places filled up by English-born subjects who had property in England.

265. These measures caused intense surprise and indignation among the Anglo-Irish of every class. The earls of Desmond and Kildare refused to attend Morris's parliament, and in 1342 convened a parliament of their own in Kilkenny. They spoke openly of armed resistance and drew up a spirited remonstrance to the king. In this document they complained bitterly of the intolerable conduct of the English officials, exposed their selfishness and fraud, and represented that to their corruption and incompetency were due the recent losses of territories and castles. The appeal was successful: the king granted almost everything they asked for; and at the same time requested assistance from them for his French wars.

266. But after all this, still another attempt was to be made. Sir Ralph Ufford was now—in 1344—appointed lord justice, whose wife was Maud, widow of the Brown earl of Ulster. He turned out a most intolerable tyrant, and quite overshot the mark; and his wife was blamed for instigating him to some of his worst deeds. He seized the earl of Desmond's estates, hanged several of his knights, and threw the earl of Kildare into prison. But he died in the midst of his tyranny, "to the great joy of everyone;" and so

fierce was the rage of the people against him, that his wife, who had lived with the grandeur and state of a queen, had now to steal away from Dublin Castle through a back gate, with the coffin containing her husband's body.

267. After his death Kildare was released, and joined the king at the siege of Calais in 1347, where he was knighted for his bravery. Desmond's wrongs were also redressed and he was made lord justice for life.

With these proceedings of Ufford's the attempts of the king to break down the power of the Irish nobles may be regarded as having terminated.

268. During all this time the people of the country, English and Irish alike, were sunk in a state of misery that no pen can describe. At this period the "black death" was in full swing, and was as bad in Ireland as elsewhere. Once it entered a house, all the family generally fell victims; and it swept away the inhabitants of whole towns, villages, and castles. The plague was not all: the people's cup of misery was filled to overflowing by perpetual war and all its attendant horrors. The inhabitants of the Pale were perhaps in a worse condition than those of the rest of Ireland; for they were tyrannised over and robbed by the soldiers.

The colonists, exposed to all sorts of exactions and hardships, and scourged by pestilence, quitted the doomed country in crowds—every one fled who had the means—and the settlement seemed threatened with speedy extinction.

269. In this critical state of affairs King Edward resolved to send over his third son Lionel, afterwards duke of Clarence, as lord lieutenant. This young prince had married Elizabeth the only child of the Brown earl of Ulster, and in her right had become earl of Ulster and lord of Connaught. With a force of 1,500 experienced soldiers he came to Ireland in 1361; and twice afterwards he came as lord lieutenant, in 1364 and 1367. Believing, after this much experience, that it was impossible to subdue the Irish, he caused the government, during his last visit—in 1367—to frame and pass an act of parliament—the celebrated Statute of Kilkenny—in order to save the miserable remnant of the settlement.

270. This act contains thirty-five chapters, of which the following are the most important provisions: Intermarriage, fosterage, gossipred, traffic, and intimate relations of any kind with the Irish, were forbidden as high treason:—punishment, death.

If any man took a name after the Irish fashion, used the Irish language, or dress, or mode of riding (without saddle), or adopted any other Irish customs, all his lands and houses were forfeited, and he himself was put into jail till he could find security that he would comply with the law. The Irish living among the English were permitted to remain, but were forbidden to use the Irish language under the same penalty. To use or submit to the Brehon law or to exact coyne and livery was treason.

No Englishman was to make war on the Irish without the special warrant of the government, who would conduct, supply, and finish all such wars, "so that the Irish enemies shall not be admitted to peace until they be finally destroyed or shall make restitution fully of the costs and charges of that war."

The Irish were forbidden to booley or pasture on those of the march lands belonging to the English; if they did so the English owner of the lands might impound the cattle as a distress for damage; but in doing so he was to keep the cattle together, so that they might be delivered up whole and uninjured to the Irish owner if he came to pay the damages.

According to Brehon law, the whole sept were liable for the offences and debts of each member. In order to avoid quarrels, the act ordains that an English creditor must sue an Irish debtor personally, not any other member of the sept. This at least was a wise provision.

No native Irish clergyman was to be appointed to any position in the church within the English district, and no Irishman was to be received into any English religious house in Ireland.

It was forbidden to receive or entertain Irish bards, pipers, story-tellers, or mowers, because these and such like often came as spies on the English.

271. The Statute of Kilkenny, though not exhibiting quite so hostile a spirit against the Irish as we find sometimes represented, yet carried out consistently the vicious and fatal policy of separation adopted by the government from the beginning. It was intended to apply only to the English, and was framed entirely in their interests. Its chief aim was to withdraw them from all contact with the "Irish enemies"—so the natives are designated all through the act—to separate the two races for evermore.

272. But this new law designed to effect so much, was found to be impracticable, and turned out after a little while a dead letter. Coyne and livery continued to be exacted from the colonists by the three great earls, Kildare, Desmond, and Ormond; and the Irish and English went on intermarrying, gossiping, fostering, and quarrelling on their own account, just the same as before.

273. The reign of Edward III. was a glorious one for England abroad, but was disastrous to the English dominion in Ireland. At the very time of the battle of Cressy, the settlement had been almost wiped out of existence— not more than four counties now remained to the English. If one-half of the energy and solicitude expended uselessly in France had been directed to Ireland, which was more important than all the French possessions, the country could have been easily pacified and compacted into one great empire with England.

274. Almost as soon as the English had made permanent settlements in Ireland the evil of absenteeism began to make itself felt. A number of speculators got possession of large tracts of lands; and while they lived out of the country and discharged none of the duties expected from holders of

property, they drew their rents from their Irish estates and drained the country of its capital. Many attempts to remedy this evil were made about this time; and acts were passed to enforce residence: those who did not reside had to pay two-thirds of their income as fine. But these acts were evaded and produced no lasting results; and absenteeism has descended through seven centuries to our own times.

ART MAC MURROGH KAVANAGH (1377-1417)

275. The man that gave most trouble during the reign of Richard II (from 1377 to 1399) was Art Mac Murrogh Kavanagh, King of Leinster, born in 1357. In early youth, even in his sixteenth year, he began his active career as defender of the province; and at eighteen (in 1375) he was elected King of Leinster.

Some time after his election, he married the daughter of Maurice Fitzgerald fourth earl of Kildare; whereupon the English authorities seized the lady's vast estates, inasmuch as she had violated the statute of Kilkenny by marrying a mere Irishman. In addition to this, his black rent—eighty marks a year—was for some reason stopped, soon after the accession of Richard II. Exasperated by these proceedings, he devastated and burned many districts in the counties of Wexford, Kilkenny, Carlow, and Kildare; till the Dublin council were at last forced to pay him his black rent.

276. Meantime Ireland had been going from bad to worse; and at last the king resolved to come hither himself with an overwhelming force, hoping thereby to overawe the whole country into submission and quietness. He made great preparations for this expedition; and on the 2nd of October 1394, attended by many of the English nobles, he landed at Waterford with an army of 34,000 men, the largest force ever yet brought to the shores of Ireland.

277. As soon as Mac Murrogh heard of this, far from showing any signs of fear, he swept down on New Ross, then a flourishing English settlement strongly walled, burned the town, and brought away a vast quantity of booty. And when the king and his army marched north from Waterford to Dublin, he harassed them on the way after his usual fashion, attacking them from the woods and bogs and catting off great numbers.

278. The Irish chiefs however saw that submission was inevitable. At a place called Ballygorry near Carlow, Mowbray earl of Nottingham received the submission of a number of the southern chiefs in 1395, and amongst them Mac Murrogh, the most dreaded of all. The king himself received the northern chiefs at Drogheda. Altogether about 75 chiefs submitted to the king and to Mowbray.

They were afterwards invited to Dublin, where they were feasted sumptuously for several days by the king, who knighted the four provincial kings, O'Neill of Ulster, O'Connor of Connaught, Mac Murrogh of Leinster, and O'Brien of Thomond.

279. In a letter to the duke of York, the English Regent King Richard describes the Irish people as of three classes:—Irish savages or enemies; Irish rebels (colonists in rebellion); and English subjects; and he says the rebels were driven to revolt by ill usage.

280. But this magnificent and expensive expedition produced no useful result whatever. As for the submission and reconciliation of the Irish chiefs, it was all pure sham. They did not look upon King Richard as their lawful sovereign; and as the promises they had made had been extorted by force, they did not consider themselves bound to keep them.

281. After a stay of nine months the king was obliged to return to England in 1395, leaving as his deputy his cousin young Roger Mortimer earl of March, who, as Richard had no children, was heir to the throne of England. Scarcely had he left sight of land when the chiefs one and all renounced their allegiance, and the fighting went on again; till at last, in a battle fought at Kells in Kilkenny in 1397, against the Leinster clans, amongst them a large contingent of Mac Murrogh's kern, the English suffered a great overthrow, and Mortimer was slain.

282. And now the king, greatly enraged, resolved on a second expedition to Ireland, in order as he said, to avenge the death of his cousin, and especially to chastise Mac Murrogh. Another army was got together quite as numerous as the former. In the middle of May 1399 the king landed with his army at Waterford, and after a short time he marched to Kilkenny on his way to Dublin. But instead of continuing on the open level country, he turned to the right towards the Wicklow highlands to attack Mac Murrogh: and here his troubles began.

Making their way slowly and toilsomely through the hills, they at length descried the Leinster army under Mac Murrogh, about 3,000 in number, high up on a mountain side, coolly looking down on them, with dense woods between. The king having forced 2,500 of the peasantry, whose houses he had burned, to cut a way for his army through the woods, pushed on, determined to overwhelm the little body of mountaineers. But he was soon beset with difficulties of all kinds, bogs, fallen trees, hidden gullies, and quagmires in which the soldiers sank up to their middle. At the same time the Irish continually attacked him and killed great numbers of his men. They could get little or no provisions, and hundreds perished of hunger and fatigue.

283. In this dire strait the army made their way across hill, moor, and valley, men and horses starving, and perishing with rain and storm; till at the end of eleven days of toil and suffering, they came in sight of the sea, somewhere on the south part of the Wicklow coast. Here they found three ships laden with provisions, which saved the army from destruction. Next day they resumed march, moving now along the coast towards Dublin; while Mac Murrogh's flying parties hung on their rear and harassed their

retreat, never giving them an hour's rest.

284. But now Mac Murrogh sent word that he wished to come to terms; and the young earl of Gloucester was despatched by the king to confer with him.

When they had come to the place of conference, Mac Murrogh was seen descending a mountain-side between two woods, accompanied by a multitude of followers. He rode, without saddle, a noble horse that had cost him four hundred cows, and he galloped down the face of the hill as swiftly as a stag. He brandished a long spear, which, when he had arrived near the meeting place, he flung from him with great dexterity. Then his followers fell back, and he met the earl alone near a small brook; and those that saw him remarked that he was tall of stature, well knit, strong and active, with a fierce and stern countenance.

285. But the parley ended in nothing, for Gloucester could not agree to Mac Murrogh's demands. On the king's arrival in Dublin he made arrangements to have Mac Murrogh hunted down. But before they could be carried out he was recalled to England by alarming news; and when he had arrived he was made prisoner in 1399, and a new king, Henry IV., was placed on the throne.

286. After the king's departure, Mac Murrogh's raids became so intolerable that the government agreed to compensate him for his wife's lands. Two years later—in 1401—he made a terrible raid into Wexford, in which numbers of the settlers were slain. But this was avenged soon after by the English of Dublin, who in 1402 marched south along the coast, led by the mayor, John Drake, and defeated the O'Byrnes near Bray, killing 500 of them. For this and other services, the king granted to the city of Dublin the privilege of having a gilt sword carried before the mayor.

287. After a short period of quietness Mac Murrogh renewed the war in 1405, plundered and burned Carlow and Castledermot, two English settlements, and again overran the county Wexford. But now came a turn of ill fortune. The deputy Sir Stephen Scroope utterly defeated him in 1407 near Callan in Kilkenny, and immediately afterwards surprised O'Carroll lord of Ely, and killed O'Carroll himself and 800 of his followers. Altogether 3,000 of the Irish fell in these two conflicts—the greatest reverse ever sustained by Mac Murrogh.

288. This defeat kept him quiet for a time. But in 1413 he inflicted a severe defeat on the men of Wexford. Three years after this—in 1416—the English of Wexford combined, with the determination to avenge all the injuries he had inflicted on them. But he met them on their own plains, defeated them with a loss of 320 in killed and prisoners, and so thoroughly frightened them that they were glad to escape further consequences by making peace and giving hostages for future good behaviour.

289. This was the old hero's last exploit. He died in New Ross a week

after the Christmas of 1417, in the sixtieth year of his age, after a reign of forty-two years over Leinster. O'Doran his chief brehon, who had been spending the Christmas with him, died on the same day, and there are good grounds for suspecting that both were poisoned by a woman who had been instigated by some of Mac Murrogh's enemies.

He was the most heroic, persevering, and indomitable defender of his country, from Brian Boru to Hugh O'Neill; and he maintained his independence for nearly half a century just beside the Pale, in spite of every effort to reduce him to submission.

DURING THE WARS OF THE ROSES (1413-1485)

290. Henry V, who ascended the throne in 1418, was so engrossed with France that he gave hardly any attention to Ireland; so that there was little or no change in Irish affairs during his reign; and there was strife everywhere.

Matters at last looked so serious that in 1414 the king sent over an able and active military rnan as lord lieutenant, Sir John Talbot Lord Furnival, subsequently earl of Shrewsbury, who became greatly distinguished in the French wars. He made a vigorous circuit round the Pale, and reduced O'Moore, Mac Mahon, O'Hanlon, and O'Neill. But this brought the Palesmen more evil than good; for the relief was only temporary; and when the brilliant exploits were all over he subjected them, in violation of the Statute of Kilkenny, to coyne and livery, having no other way of paying his soldiers. No sooner had he left than the Irish resumed their attacks, and for years incessantly harried and worried the miserable Pales-men, except indeed when kept quiet in some small degree by the payment of black rent.

291. The accession of Henry VI, in 1422, made no improvement in the country, which continued to be everywhere torn by strife. Ireland was now indeed, and for generations before and after, in a far worse condition than at any time under native management, even during the anarchical period after the battle of Clontarf.

The people of the Pale probably fared neither better nor worse than those of the rest of the country. But to add to their misfortunes, there arose, about the time of the king's accession, a deadly quarrel between the Butlers, headed by the carl of Ormond, and the Talbots, headed by Richard Talbot archbishop of Dublin and his brother Lord Furnival, who came twice again to Ireland as lord lieutenant. This feud was so violent that it put a stop to almost all government business for many years.

292. Meantime in 1423 the Irish of Ulster made a terrible raid on Louth and Meath, defeated the army sent against them, and carried off great booty; till at last the inhabitants had to buy peace by agreeing to pay black rent.

In 1449 Richard Plantagenet duke of York, a prince of the royal blood and heir to the throne of England, was appointed lord lieutenant for ten years. He won the affections of the Irish both of native and English descent, treating them with fairness and consideration.

293. In an act of parliament of this time we have a frightful picture of the condition of the colonists of the Pale. In time of harvest companies of the soldiers were in the habit of going with their wives, children, servants, and friends, sometimes to the number of a hundred, to the farmers' houses, eating and drinking, and paying for nothing. They robbed and sometimes killed the tenants and husbandmen; and their horses were turned out to graze in the meadows and in the ripe corn, ruining all the harvest.

294. The parliament held by the duke in 1449, asserted for the first time the independence of the Irish legislature: that they had a right to a separate coinage, and that they were absolutely free from all laws except those passed by the lords and commons of Ireland.

295. The duke had not been in Ireland for more than a year when Jack Cade's rebellion broke out; on which he went to England in 1451 to look after his own interests.

296. For the past century and a half the English kings had been so taken up with wars in France, Scotland, and Wales, that they had little leisure to attend to Ireland. Accordingly we have seen the Irish encroaching, the Pale growing smaller, and the people of the settlement more oppressed and more miserable year by year.

But now about this time—1454—began in England the tremendous struggle between the houses of York and Lancaster, commonly known as the Wars of the Roses, which lasted for about thirty years, and during which the colony fared worse than ever. The Geraldines sided with the house of York, and the Butlers with the house of Lancaster; and they went to England with many others of the Anglo-Irish to take part in the battles. Then the Irish rose up everywhere, overran the lands of the settlers, and took back whole districts. The Pale became smaller than ever, till it included only the county Louth and about half those of Dublin Meath and Kildare. At one time not more than 200 men could be got together to defend it.

The duke of York was at last defeated at the battle of Wakefield in 1460, where fell a great part of the Anglo-Irish nobility and gentry; and he himself was taken and beheaded on the battlefield. The very next year, however—1461—witnessed the triumph of the Yorkists; and the duke's eldest son was proclaimed King of England as Edward IV., the first king of the house of York.

297. The Geraldines, both of Desmond and Kildare, were now in high favour, while the Butlers were in disgrace. These two factions enacted a sort of miniature of the Wars of the Roses in Ireland. In 1462 they fought a battle at Pilltown in Kilkenny, where the Butlers were defeated and 400 or 500 of their men killed. As a curious illustration of how completely these

Anglo-Irish families had adopted the Irish language and customs, it is worthy of mention that the ransom of Mac Richard Butler, who had been taken prisoner in the battle, was two Irish manuscripts, the Psalter of Cashel and the Book of Carrick. A fragment of the Psalter of Cashel is still preserved in the Bodleian Library in Oxford, and in one of its pages is written a record of this transaction.

298. Thomas the eighth earl of Desmond—the Great Earl as he was called—was appointed lord deputy, in 1463, under his godson the young duke of Clarence, the king's brother, who though appointed lord lieutenant, never came to Ireland. Desmond was well received by the Irish of both races. His love for learning is shown by the fact that he founded the college of Youghal, which was richly endowed by him and his successors; also a university in Drogheda; but this latter project fell to the ground for want of funds.

299. The Irish parliament passed an act in 1465 that every Irishman dwelling in the Pale was to dress and shave like the English, and take an English surname:—from some town as Trim, Sutton, Cork; or of a color as Black, Brown; or of some calling, as Smith, Carpenter, etc., on pain of forfeiture of his goods. Another and more mischievous measure forbade ships from fishing in the seas of Irish countries, because the dues went to make the Irish people prosperous and strong. But the worst enactment of all was one providing that it was lawful to decapitate thieves found robbing "or going or coming anywhere" unless they had an Englishman in their company. And whoever did so, on bringing the head to the mayor of the nearest town, was licensed to levy a good sum off the barony.

This put it in the power of any evil-minded person to kill the first Irishman he met, pretending he was a thief, and to raise money on his head. This indeed was not the intention of the legislators; the act was merely a desperate attempt to keep down marauders who swarmed at this time all through the Pale.

300. With all the earl of Desmond's popularity he was unable to restore tranquillity to the distracted country. He was defeated in open fight in 1466 by his own brother-in-law O'Conor of Offaly, who took him prisoner and confined him in Carbury castle in Kildare; from which however he was rescued in a few days by the people of Dublin. Neither was he able to prevent the septs from ravaging the Pale.

301. The Great Earl was struck down in the midst of his career by an act of base treachery under the guise of law. He was first replaced in 1467 by John Tiptoft earl of Worcester—"the Butcher" as he was called from his cruelty—who came determined to ruin him. Acting on the secret instructions of the queen, he caused the earls of Desmond and Kildare to be arrested; and had them attainted for exacting coyne and livery, and for making alliance with the Irish, contrary to the Statute of Kilkenny.

Desmond was at once executed; Kildare was pardoned; and "the Butcher" returned to England, where he was himself executed soon after.

POYNINGS' LAW (1485-1494)

302. The accession in 1485, of Henry VII., who belonged to the Lancastrians, was the final triumph of that great party.

At this time all the chief state offices in Ireland were held by the Geraldines; but as the new king felt that he could not govern the country without their aid, he made no changes, though he knew well they were all devoted Yorkists. Accordingly the great Earl of Kildare, who had been lord deputy for several years, with a short break, was still retained.

303. But the Irish retained their affection for the house of York; and accordingly when the young impostor Lambert Simnel came to Ireland and gave out that he was the Yorkist Prince Edward earl of Warwick, he was received with open arms, not only by the deputy, but by almost all the Anglo-Irish: nobles, clergy, and people. But the city of Waterford rejected him and remained steadfast in its loyalty; whence it got the name of Urbs Intacta, the "untarnished city."

304. After a little time an army of 2,000 Germans came to Ireland to support the impostor; and in 1487 he was actually crowned as Edward VI., by the bishop of Meath, in Christchurch Cathedral, Dublin, in presence of the deputy Kildare, the archbishop of Dublin, and a great concourse of Anglo-Irish nobles, ecclesiastics, and officers. But this foolish business came to a sudden termination when Simnel was defeated and taken prisoner in England. Then Kildare and the others humbly sent to ask pardon of the king; who dreading their power if they were driven to rebellion, took no severer steps than to send over Sir Richard Edgecomb to exact new oaths of allegiance. In the following year the king invited them to a banquet at Greenwich; and one of the waiters who attended them at table was their idolized Prince Lambert Simnel.

305. A little later on reports of new plots in Ireland reached the king's ears; whereupon in 1492 he removed Kildare from the office of deputy. These reports were not without foundation, for now a second claimant for the crown, a young Fleming named Perkin Warbeck, landed in Cork in 1492 and announced that he was Richard duke of York, one of the two princes that had been kept in prison by Richard III. And he was at once accepted by the Anglo-Irish citizens of Cork.

It was chiefly the English colonists who were concerned in the episodes of Simnel and Warbeck; the native Irish took little or no interest in either claimant.

306. The king now saw that his Irish subjects were ready to rise in rebellion for the house of York at every opportunity. He came to the resolution, therefore, to lessen their power by destroying the independence of their parliament; and having given Sir Edward Poynings instructions to

this effect, he sent him over as deputy.

307. Poynings' first act was to lead an expedition to the north against O'Hanlon and Magennis, who had given shelter to some of the supporters of Warbeck. But he heard a rumour that the earl of Kildare was conspiring with O'Hanlon and Magennis to intercept and destroy himself and his army; and news came also that Kildare's brother had risen in open rebellion and had seized the castle of Carlow. On this Poynings returned south and recovered the castle.

308. He convened a parliament at Drogheda in November, 1494, the memorable parliament in which the act since known as "Poynings' law" was passed. The following are the most important provisions of this law:

1. No parliament was in future to be held in Ireland until the Irish chief governor and privy council had sent the king information of all the acts intended to be passed in it, with a full statement of the reasons why they were required, and until these acts had been approved and permission granted by the king and privy council of England. This single provision is what is popularly known as "Poynings' law."

2. All the laws lately made in England affecting the public weal should hold good in Ireland. This referred only to English laws then existing; it gave no power to the English parliament to make laws for Ireland in the future.

3. The Statute of Kilkenny was revived and confirmed, except the part forbidding the use of the Irish tongue, which could not be carried out, as the language was now used everywhere, even through the English settlements.

4. For the purpose of protecting the settlement, it was made felony to permit enemies or rebels to pass through the marches; and the owners of march lands were obliged to reside on them or send proper deputies on pain of losing their estates.

5. The exaction of coyne and livery was forbidden in any shape or form.

6. Many of the Anglo-Irish families had adopted the Irish war-cries; the use of these was now strictly forbidden.*

In this parliament the earl of Kildare was attainted for high treason, mainly on account of his supposed conspiracy with O'Hanlon to destroy the deputy; in consequence of which he was soon afterwards arrested and sent a prisoner to England.

309. Up to this the Irish parliament had been independent; it was convened by the chief governor whenever and wherever he pleased; and it made its laws without any interference from the parliament of England. Now Poynings' law took away all this power and made the parliament a mere shadow, entirely dependent on the English king and council.

This indeed was of small consequence at the time; for the parliament was only for the Pale, and no native Irishman could sit in it. But when at a later period English law was made to extend over the whole country, and the Irish parliament made laws for all the people of Ireland, then Poynings' law which still remained in force was felt by the people of Ireland to be one of their greatest grievances.

310. During the whole time that this parliament was sitting the Warbeck party were actively at work in the south. But Warbeck had at last to fly; and the rest of his career belongs to English rather than to Irish history. In 1499 he was lunged at Tyburn, with John Walter, mayor of Cork, his chief supporter in that city.

311. A double ditch or wall was at this time built all along on the boundary of the Leinster settlement from sea to sea to keep out the Irish. This little territory was called the Pale; and it remained so circumscribed for many years, but afterwards became enlarged from time to time.

* The war-cry of the O'Neills was Lamh-derg abu, i.e., the Red-hand to victory (lamh, pron. lauv, a hand). That of the O'Briens and Mac Carthys, Lamh-laidir abu, the Strong-hand to victory (laidir, pron. lauder, strong). The Kildare Fitzgeralds took as their cry Crom abu, from the great Geraldine castle of Crom or Croom in Limerick; the earl of Desmond Shanit abu, from the castle of Shanid in Limerick. Most of the other chiefs, both native and Anglo-Irish, had their several cries.

GARRETT, THE GREAT EARL OF KILDARE (1477-1513)

312. Garrett or Gerald Fitzgerald, who is known as the Great earl of Kildare, became the eighth earl in 1477. His sister Eleanora was married to Conn O'Neill chief of Tyrone (father of Conn Bacach). He was at this time in custody in London, but only on mere suspicion. The king now resolved to govern Ireland through him: but first brought him up to answer the charges. A whole crowd of enemies came forward to accuse him. He was charged with burning the church of Cashel, to which he replied, that it was true enough, but that he would not have done so only he thought the archbishop was in it. The archbishop himself was present listening; and this reply was so unexpectedly plain and blunt that the king burst out laughing.

The king advised him to have the aid of counsel, saying that he might have anyone he pleased; to which the earl answered that he would have the best counsel in England, namely, the king himself; at which his majesty laughed as heartily as before. At last when one of his accusers exclaimed with great vehemence: "All Ireland cannot rule this man!" the king ended the matter by replying: "Then if all Ireland cannot rule him, he shall rule all Ireland!"

Thus the great earl triumphed; and the king restored him, and made him lord lieutenant of Ireland. (1496.)

313. There was at this time a bitter war between the O'Neills and O'Donnells; and the earl often went north to aid his brother-in-law Conn

O'Neill.

314. The most important event the great earl was ever engaged in was the battle of Knockdoe, which came about in this way. O'Kelly chief of Hy Many, having a quarrel with Mac William Burke of Clanrickard, applied for help to the earl of Kildare. Kildare and O'Kelly enlisted on their side the chiefs of almost all the north of Ireland except O'Neill. On the other side Burke, knowing what was coming, collected a considerable army, being joined by many of the native chiefs of the south, among others O'Brien of Thomond, Macnamara, and O'Carroll; and he awaited the approach of his adversary on a low hill called Knockdoe—the hill of tiie battle-axes—about eight miles from Galway.

The battle that followed, which was fought in 1504, was the most obstinate, bloody, and destructive fought in Ireland since the invasion, with the single exception of the battle of Athenry. The southern men, who were far outnumbered by the earl's forces, held the field for several hours; but in the end they suffered a total overthrow, with a loss of upwards of 2,000. The victors encamped on the battle-field for twenty-four hours; and the next day Galway and Athenry opened their gates to the earl.

315. On the accession of Henry VIII. in 1509 the great earl was made lord deputy. The next year, 1510, he set out on an expedition, which did not end so well for him as the battle of Knockdoe. Having overrun a good part of south Munster, he invaded Thomond, but was utterly routed near Limerick by O'Brien and Burke of Clanrickard, and saved himself and the remnant of his army by flight.

316. This defeat did not check the warlike activity of the earl. Two years later, in 1512, he captured Roscommon; after which he went north, took the castle of Belfast, and plundered the Glens of Antrim, the Scottish Mac Donnells' district. In 1513 he made an unsuccessful attempt to take O'Carroll's castle of Leap in King's County; and soon after died at Athy.

GARRETT, NINTH EARL OF KILDARE (1513-1534)

317. After the death of the Great earl of Kildare his son Garrett Oge (the young) was appointed lord deputy by the king. The new deputy followed in the footsteps of his father. He defeated the O'Moores, of Leix, the O'Reillys, of Brefney, and the O'Tooles, of Wicklow; and he captured after a week's siege O'Carroll's castle of Leap, which had baffled his father.

Turning his arms next against the north, he took the strong castle of Dundrum, and captured and burned the castle of Dungannon.

318. This career of uninterrupted success excited the jealousy of some of the other Anglo-Irish lords, especially the Butlers, the hereditary foes of his house, who employed every means in their power to turn the king against him. But Kildare counteracted all these schemes so skilfully, that for a long time his enemies were unsuccessful; till at last Ormond managed to gain the ear of Cardinal Wolsey, through whose influence Kildare was

summoned to England to answer charges of enriching himself from the crown revenues and of holding traitorous correspondence with the Irish enemies.

319. Soon after his arrival in England, Thomas Howard earl of Surrey was, at Wolsey's instance, sent to Ireland as lord lieutenant (in 1520). He marched north against Conn (Bacach) O'Neill, Prince of the O'Neills of Tyrone, who had suddenly invaded the English settlements of Meath; but O'Neill retreated to his Ulster fastnesses, whither Surrey could not follow him. This chief made his peace soon after; and the king sent Surrey a chain of gold for him as a token of pardon and friendship.

Surrey next made peace between the earls of Ormond and Desmond, who had been actively keeping up the old feuds of their families. He took O'Conor's castle of Monasteroris; but O'Conor obstinately refused to come to terms, saying he would make no peace till the English were driven from the country.

320. In 1521 James earl of Desmond invaded the territories of two powerful chiefs of the Mac Carthys; but they defeated him at Mourne Abbey or Ballinamona between Mallow and Cork, and slew 2,000 of his men. In the end Surrey made peace between them.

321. From the very day of Surrey's arrival he applied himself to collect evidence against the earl of Kildare; taking down vague reports of every kind, aided all through by Pierce Roe of Ormond. Meantime Kildare married Lady Elizabeth Grey, a near relative of the king, which stopped for the time all further proceedings against him.

Surrey at last became heartily tired of his mission. He grew sick in mind and sick in body; and besought the king for leave to retire. This was at last granted; and he returned to England in 1521, after a stay of nearly two years.

322. In 1522 one of the ever-recurring feuds between the O'Neills and the O'Donnells broke out, and attained such magnitude as almost to deserve the name of civil war. The chief of the O'Neills, Conn Bacach, who had been inaugurated three years before, made a great gathering, determined to march into Tirconnell and bring the O'Donnells under thorough subjection. O'Donnell had an army very much smaller; but what he wanted in numbers he made up in generalship. After a good deal of skirmishing be surprised O'Neill's camp at night at Knockavoe near Strabane, and almost before the sentinels were aware of how matters stood, the two armies were fighting furiously in pitch darkness in the midst of the camp. After a long and fearful struggle, in which men found it hard to distinguish friend from foe, the O'Neills were routed with a loss of 900 men; and O'Donnell took possession of the camp, with an immense quantity of booty.

This battle of Knockavoe, which was one of the bloodiest ever fought between the Kinel Connell and Kinel Owen, did not end the quarrel.

Kildare, who was Conn Bacach O'Neill's first cousin, tried hard to make peace; but in spite of his efforts the war continued for many years afterwards.

323. Let us now return to Earl Garrett. When Surrey went back to England in 1521, Pierce Roe, earl of Ormond, Kildare's old enemy, was appointed lord deputy. The chief use he made of his power was to injure Kildare, several of whose castles he took and destroyed. But while he was still deputy, Kildare was at last permitted to return to Ireland; and as might have been expected, the feud now blazed up with tenfold fury; so that the king had to send over commissioners to investigate the dispute. Their decision was for Kildare; whom they appointed deputy in 1524 in place of Ormond.

324. Kildare was now directed by the king to arrest the earl of Desmond, who had been holding correspondence with the King of France about an invasion of Ireland. He led an army southwards on this unpleasant mission; but Desmond eluded pursuit, and the deputy returned without him to Dublin. It was afterwards alleged against him that he had intentionally allowed Desmond to escape arrest, which was probably true.

325. Kildare's enemies especially the two most powerful, Pierce Roe in Ireland, and Wolsey in England, still kept wideawake watching his proceedings and continually sending damaging reports about him. They succeeded at last so far as to have him summoned to England to answer several charges. He was not brought to trial; but at his own urgent request he was examined by the lords of the privy council: and he successfully defended himself against the bitter accusations of Wolsey, who, not being able to have him condemned, sent him back to the Tower.

326. Meantime things began to go on very badly in Ireland; and the Pale was attacked and plundered by O'Conor of Offally and several other chiefs. These disturbances were laid at the door of Kildare, who was openly accused of having, by messages from London, incited O'Conor and the others to attack the Palesmen.

327. But Kildare's extraordinary influence and good fortune again prevailed; he was released and restored to confidence. Sir William Skeffington was appointed lord deputy, and Kildare was sent with him to Ireland to advise and aid him. It was easy to foresee that this arrangement would not last long; for Kildare was too high and proud to act as subordinate to any English knight.

328. In 1531 Skeffington marched north against O'Neill. Kildare accompanied him to save appearances; for it is not to be supposed that he was earnest in taking part in a war on Conn O'Neill, his cousin and friend. There had been before this time jealousies and bickerings between Skeffington and Kildare, and while they were in the north, the old enmity between Kildare and the earl of Ormond, now earl of Ossory, almost broke

out into open war. So this expedition, led as it was by divided commanders who hated each other heartily, was not likely to be very formidable; and on the appearance of O'Neill with his army, they did not wait to be attacked, but retreated southwards.

329. The enmity between Kildare and the deputy at last broke out openly; and the earl proceeded to England and laid his case before the king. The result was that Skeffington was removed, and Kildare became deputy once more.

As Wolsey was now dead, there was no single enemy that Kildare feared; and he used his great power unsparingly. He removed archbishop Allen from the chancellorship, and put George Cromer archbishop of Armagh in his place. He drew around him the most powerful of the Irish chiefs, and gave one of his daughters in marriage to O'Conor of Offaly, and another to O'Carroll tanist of Ely. He ravaged the territory of the Butlers in Kilkenny, and at his instigation his brother James Fitzgerald and his cousin Conn O'Neill entered Louth—a part of the Pale—burned the English villages, and drove away the cattle.

330. All these proceedings were eagerly watched and reported with exaggeration by Kildare's enemies; and at last the Dublin council, one of whom was the deposed chancellor archbishop John Allen, sent the master of the rolls, whose name was also John Allen, with reports to the king and to the English chancellor, Thomas Cromwell.

The result was that for the third time Kildare was summoned to England by the king to give an account of his government. There is some reason to suspect that he contemplated open rebellion and resistance; for now he furnished his castles with great guns, pikes, powder, etc., from the government stores in the castle of Dublin. At any rate he delayed obeying the order as long as he could. But at last there came a peremptory mandate; and the earl, with a heavy heart, set about preparing for his journey.

331. The Geraldines had become thoroughly Irish. They were always engaged in war, exactly like the native chiefs, they spoke and wrote the Irish language, read and loved Irish books and Irish lore of every kind, kept bards, shanachies, and antiquaries, as part of their household; and intermarried, fostered and gossiped with the leading Irish families. They were as much attached to all the native customs as the natives themselves; and when the Reformation came, they were champions of the Catholic religion. When we add to all this that they were known to be of an ancient and noble family, which told for much in Ireland, we have a sufficient explanation of the well-known fact that the native Irish were rather more attached to those Geraldines than to their own chiefs of pure Celtic blood.

THE REBELLION OF SILKEN THOMAS (1534-1537)

332. When the lord deputy, Garrett Oge Fitzgerald, went to England in obedience to the king's mandate, he left his son, the young Lord Thomas,

as deputy in his place. On his arrival in London he was sent to the Tower, on various charges. He might possibly have got through his present difficulties, as he had through many others, but for what befel in Ireland, which will now be related.

333. Lord Thomas Fitzgerald, who was afterwards known as "Silken Thomas," from the gorgeous trappings of himself and his retinue, was then in his twenty-first year, brave, open and generous. But the earl his father could not have made a more unfortunate choice as deputy; for there were in Dublin plotting enemies who hated all his race, and they led the young man to ruin by taking advantage of his inexperience, and of his unsuspicious disposition.

334. They now—1534—spread a report that his father had been beheaded in England. Whereupon with his brilliant retinue of seven score horsemen he rode through the streets to St. Mary's Abbey; and entering the chamber where the council sat, he openly renounced his allegiance, and proceeded to deliver up the sword and robes of state.

His friend Archbishop Cromer, now lord chancellor, besought him with tears in his eyes to forego his purpose; but at that moment the voice of an Irish bard was heard from among the young nobleman's followers, praising the Silken Lord, and calling on him to avenge his father's death. Casting the sword from his hand, he rushed forth with his men to enter on that wild and hopeless struggle which ended in the ruin of himself and his family.

The earl, his father, on hearing of his son's rebellion, took to his bed, and being already sick of palsy, died in a few days.

335. Collecting a large force of the Irish septs in and around the Pale, Lord Thomas led them to the walls of Dublin. The city had been lately weakened by a plague, and the inhabitants on promise of protection admitted him. He then laid siege to the castle, to which several of the leading citizens, including Archbishop Allen, had retired on the first appearance of danger.

336. The archbishop, having good reason to dread the Geraldines, for he had always been bitterly hostile to them, attempted during the siege to make his escape by night in a vessel that lay in the Liffey. But he was taken and brought before Lord Thomas at Artaine. He threw himself on his knees to beg for mercy, and the young lord, pitying him, ordered his attendants to take him away in custody. But they, wilfully misinterpreting him, murdered the archbishop. This fearful crime brought a sentence of excommunication against Lord Thomas and his followers.

337. As time went on, O'Conor Faly, O'Moore, and O'Carroll—three powerful chiefs—joined his standard; and he had on his side also O'Neill of Tyrone, and O'Brien of Thomond. He and O'Conor Faly now invaded Meath, and burned Trim, Dunboyne, and the surrounding territory.

338. The new deputy Sir William Skeffington remained inactive during

the whole winter. But in March, 1535, he laid siege to the castle of Maynooth, the strongest of Fitzgerald's fortresses, which was defended by 100 men. After a siege of nine days, during which the castle was battered by artillery, then for the first time used in Ireland, he took it by storm, except the great keep; and the garrison who defended this, now reduced to thirty-seven men, seeing the case hopeless, surrendered, doubtless expecting mercy. But, they were all executed. The fall of Maynooth damped the spirits of his adherents; and one of his best friends, O'Moore of Leix, was induced by the earl of Ossory to withdraw from the confederacy.

339. The rebellion had already brought the English Pale to a frightful state, three-fourths of Kildare and a great part of Meath burned and depopulated; while to add to the ruin and misery of the people, the plague was raging all over the country. Lord Leonard Grey, marshal of Ireland, was directed to place himself at the head of the army and to take more active measures. He made short work of the rebellion. Lord Thomas's remaining allies rapidly fell off; and he and his faithful friend O'Conor sent offers of submission. O'Conor was received and pardoned; and Lord Thomas delivered himself up to Lord Grey, on condition that his life should be spared.

340. Lord Thomas was conveyed to England in 1535 and imprisoned in the Tower. Here he was left for about eighteen months neglected and in great misery. There is extant a pitiful letter written by him while in the Tower to an old servant in Ireland, asking that his friend O'Brien should send him £20 to buy food and clothes:— "I never had any money since I came into prison, but a noble, nor I have had neither hosen, doublet, nor shoes, nor shirt but one; nor any other garment but a single frieze gown, for a velvet furred with budge [i.e. instead of a velvet furred with lambskin fur], and so I have gone wolward [shirtless] and barefoot and barelegged divers times (when it hath not been very warm); and so I should have done still, but that poor prisoners of their gentleness hath sometimes given me old hosen and shoes and shirts."

341. At the time of his arrest his five uncles were treacherously taken; and though it was well known that three of them had openly discountenanced the rebellion, and notwithstanding the promise made to the young lord, the whole six were executed at Tyburn in 1537.

342. And this was the end of the Rebellion of Silken Thomas, which had been brought about by the villainy of his enemies, and during which, though it lasted little more than a year, the county Kildare was wasted and depopulated, and the whole Pale, as well as the country round it, suffered unspeakable desolation and misery. It was a reckless enterprise, for there never was the remotest chance of success: the only palliation was the extreme youth and inexperience of Lord Thomas Fitzgerald.

343. Notwithstanding the efforts of King Henry VIII. to extirpate the

house of Kildare, there remained two direct representatives, sons of the ninth earl by Lady Elizabeth Grey. Gerald (or Garrett) the elder, then about twelve years of age, succeeded to the earldom on the death of Lord Thomas. At the time of the apprehension of his uncles (in 1535) he was at Donore in Kildare, sick of small-pox. His faithful tutor Thomas Leverous, afterwards bishop of Kildare, fearing for his safety, wrapped him up warm in flannels, and had him secretly conveyed in a cleeve or basket to Thomond, where he remained under the protection of O'Brien. The other son, then an infant, was in England with his mother. The reader should be reminded that Leonard Grey, now lord justice, was uncle to these two children, for their mother Lady Elizabeth was his sister.

344. Great efforts were now made to discover the place of young Gerald's retreat; and certain death awaited him if he should be captured. But he had friends in every part of Ireland, for the Irish, both native and of English descent, had an extraordinary love for the house of Kildare. By sending him from place to place disguised, his guardians managed to baffle the spies that were everywhere on the watch for him. Sometimes the Irish chiefs that were suspected of protecting him were threatened, or their territories were wasted by the lord justice; and large bribes were offered to give him up; but all to no purpose.

345. When Thomond became an unsafe asylum, he was sent by night to Kilbrittain in Cork, to his aunt Lady Eleanor Mac Carthy, who watched over him with unshaken fidelity. While he was under her charge, Manus O'Donnell chief of Tirconnell made her an offer of marriage, and she consented, mainly, it is believed, for the sake of securing a powerful friend for her outlawed nephew. In the middle of June, 1537, the lady travelled with young Gerald all the way from Cork to Donegal, through Thomond and Connaught, escorted and protected everywhere by the chiefs through whose territories they passed. The illustrious wayfarers must have been well known as they travelled slowly along, yet none of the people attempted to betray them. The journey was performed without the least accident; and she and O'Donnell were immediately married.

346. At the end of two years Lady Eleanor, having reason to believe that her husband was about to betray Gerald, had him placed, disguised as a peasant, on board a vessel which conveyed him to St. Malo. On the Continent he was received with great distinction. He was however dogged everywhere by spies greedy to earn the golden reward for his capture; but he succeeded in eluding them all. And he was pursued from kingdom to kingdom by the English ambassador, who in vain demanded from the several sovereigns that he should be given up. He found his way at lost to Rome to his kinsman Cardinal Pole, who gave him safe asylum, and educated him as became a prince.

347. After many extraordinary vicissitudes and narrow escapes, he was

reinstated in all his possessions by Edward VI., in 1552; and in 1554 Queen Mary restored his title, and he became the eleventh earl of Kildare.

GENERAL SUBMISSION (1535-1547)

348. A few years before the time we have now arrived at, King Henry VIII. had begun his quarrel with Rome, the upshot of which was that he threw off all allegiance to the Pope, and made himself supreme head of the church in his own kingdom of England. He made little or no change in religion; on the contrary he did his best to maintain the chief doctrines of the Catholic church, and to resist the progress of the Reformation. All he wanted was that he, and not the Pope, should be head.

349. Henry was now determined to be head of the church in Ireland also; and to carry out his measures he employed the deputy Skeffington, the earl of Ormond, and George Brown, formerly a London friar, whom the king appointed archbishop of Dublin in place of archbishop Allen.

Brown now—1535—went to work with great energy; but he was vehemently opposed by Cromer archbishop of Armagh; and he made no impression on the Anglo-Irish of the Pale, who showed not the least disposition to go with him.

350. A parliament was convened in Dublin in 1536, which passed an act making the king supreme spiritual head of the church. The members representing the church, called proctors, two from each diocese, opposed it; but they were deprived of the right of voting; and the act was passed by laymen. An oath of supremacy was to be taken by all government officers, i. e. an oath that the king was spiritual head of the church; and any one who was bound to take it and refused was adjudged guilty of treason. All monasteries, except a few in some remote districts, were suppressed: and their property was either kept for the king or given to laymen.

351. About this time the Irish chiefs showed a general disposition for peace, and the king was equally anxious to receive them. At this important juncture, in 1540, a sensible man—Sir Anthony Sentleger—was by good chance appointed lord deputy. He was all for a conciliatory policy, and he told the king in a letter "I perceive them [the chiefs] to be men of such nature that they will much sooner be brought to honest conformity by small gifts, honest persuasions, and nothing taking of them, than by great rigour." Accordingly he took full advantage of their present pacific mood; and by skilful management he induced them to submit. They all acknowledged the king's temporal and spiritual authority. As to the spiritual supremacy, it had not been much brought into notice before that time, and they hardly knew what they were doing. Besides it was only the chiefs; the body of the people knew nothing of it, and the doctrine of the king's spiritual supremacy made no headway in the country.

352. Hitherto the English kings from the time of John, had borne the title of lord of Ireland; it was now resolved to confer on Henry the title of King

of Ireland. With this object a parliament was assembled in Dublin on the 12th June, 1541; and in order to lend greater importance to its decisions, a number of the leading Irish chiefs were induced to attend it.

The act conferring the title of King of Ireland on Henry and his successors was passed through both houses rapidly, and with perfect unanimity.

353. Titles were conferred on many of the chiefs. Conn Bacach O'Neill was made earl of Tyrone, and his (reputed) son Ferdoragh or Matthew was made baron of Dungannon with the right to succeed as earl of Tyrone. O'Brien was made earl of Thomond; and Mac William Burke, who is commonly known as Ulick-na-gann, was made earl of Clanrickard. O'Donnell was promised to be made earl of Tirconnell; but the title was not actually conferred till a considerable time after.

354. With the career of Henry VIII. in England we have no concern here: I am writing Irish, not English history. Putting out of sight the question of supremacy and the suppression of the Irish monasteries, Henry's treatment of Ireland was on the whole considerate and conciliatory, though with an occasional outburst of cruelty. He persistently refused to expel or exterminate the Irish to make room for new colonies, though often urged to do so by his mischievous Irish officials. The result was that the end of his reign found the chiefs submissive and contented, the country at peace and the English power in Ireland stronger than ever it had been before. Well would it have been, both for England and Ireland, if a similar policy had been followed in the succeeding reigns.

PART IV. THE PERIOD OF INSURRECTION, CONFISCATION, AND PLANTATION

1172-1547.

THERE were four great rebellions during this period:—the rebellion of Shane O'Neill; the Geraldine rebellion; the rebellion of Hugh O'Neill; and the rebellion of 1641; besides many smaller risings. And after all these came the War of the Revolution.

The causes of rebellion were mainly two:—First, the attempt to extend the Reformation to Ireland: Second, the Plantations, which though the consequence of some rebellions were the cause of others. These and other influences of less importance will be described in a general way in the next chapter, and in more detail in those that follow.

Whenever a rebellion took place, the invariable course of events may be briefly summed up as:—Rebellion, Defeat, Confiscation, Plantation.

The Plantations began immediately after the confiscation of Leix and Offaly and continued almost without a break during the whole of this period, that is for a century and a half.

NEW CAUSES OF STRIFE

355. If there had been no additional disturbing influences after the reign of Henry VIII., it is probable that Ireland would have begun to settle down, and that there would have been no serious or prolonged resistance. But now two new elements of discord were introduced; for the government entered on the task of forcing the Irish people to become Protestant; and at the same time they began to plant various parts of the country with colonies of settlers from England and Scotland, for whom the native inhabitants were to be expelled. The Irish on their part resisted, and fought long and resolutely for their religion and their homes; and the old struggle was intensified and embittered by religious feelings. The Plantations succeeded, though not to the extent expected; the attempt to Protestantise the Irish, though continued for three centuries, was a failure. These two projects were either directly or indirectly the causes of nearly all the dreadful wars that desolated this unhappy country during the period comprised in the present part of our history.

356. There were other evil influences also. When a chief who had got a title from the king died, his son or next heir succeeded to title and land, according to English law; but according to the Irish law of Tanistry, he whom the tribe elected succeeded to the chiefship and to the mensal land. Thus when this titled chief died, English and Irish law came, in a double sense, into direct antagonism; and there was generally a contest, in which the government supported the heir, and the tribe the tanist. This was the origin of many disturbances.

357. The disturbing influence next to be mentioned was in some respects the most general and far-reaching of all. Ireland was then, as it has always

been, the weak point of the empire in case of invasion from abroad. For some time before the accession of Elizabeth, and all through her reign, there were continual reports, both in England and Ireland, of hostile expeditions from Spain or France to Ireland. These reports, some of which, as we shall see, were well founded, generally caused great terror, sometimes panic, on the part of the government.

358. The best plan to provide against this danger would have been to govern the people so as to attach them to the empire and make them ready to rise in its defence. But the government took the other course: they governed the people by force and kept them down to prevent them giving aid to an invader; and they made themselves intensely unpopular by needless harshness. The consequence of this was that any invader, no matter from what quarter, would have been welcomed and aided, by both native Irish and Anglo Irish.

359. All this again had a further result. If a chief encouraged by the prospect of help from abroad, rose in rebellion, it was not enough, as it would be under ordinary circumstances, to reduce him to submission, inflict reasonable punishment, and take guarantees for future good behaviour. He was executed or banished, or brought prisoner to London; and the people, who were mostly blameless, were expelled or exterminated, and the whole district turned into a desert, in order that an invader should have neither help nor foothold.

360. A disquieting agency less serious than any of the preceding, but still a decided element of disturbance, was the settled policy of the Tudors to anglicise the Irish people. To accomplish this the government employed all the agencies at their disposal, and employed them in vain. Acts of parliament were passed commanding the natives to drop their Irish language and learn English, and to ride, dress, and live after the English fashion. The legislators undertook to regulate how the hair was to be worn and how the beard was to be clipped; and for women, the colour of their dresses, the number of yards of material they were to use, the sort of hats they were to wear, with many other such like silly provisions. These laws were, as might he expected, almost wholly inoperative; for the people went on speaking Irish, shaving, riding, and dressing just the same as before. But like all such laws, they were very exasperating; and they were among the causes that rendered the government of that time so universally odious in Ireland.

THE STATE RELIGION

361. King Henry died in 1547 and was succeeded by his son Edward VI., then a boy of nine years old. His death removed all check to the Reformation, which was now pushed forward vigorously in England. In 1551, the fifth year of Edward's reign, the chief Protestant doctrines and forms of worship were promulgated in Ireland by Sir Anthony Sentleger.

George Brown archbishop of Dublin exerted himself to forward the Reformation; but he was resolutely opposed by the archbishop of Armagh, George Dowdall, a man of the highest character; whereupon, in 1552, the lord deputy Croft deprived him of the primacy of all Ireland, which had hitherto been held by the archbishops of Armagh, and conferred it on Brown and his successors in the see of Dublin.

362. In this same year the venerable monastery of Clonmacnoise was plundered by the English of Athlone, who carried away everything they could lay hands on. But there was on the whole little disturbance in Ireland on the score of religion during Edward's short reign. No serious attempt was made to impose the reformed doctrines on the general body of Catholics, either of Dublin or elsewhere, and the Reformation took no hold on the country.

363. Queen Mary who succeeded Edward VI in 1553, restored the Catholic religion in England and Ireland.

During Mary's reign Ireland was quite free from religious persecution. The Catholics were now the masters; but they showed no disposition whatever to molest the few Protestants that lived among them. Ireland indeed was regarded as such a haven of safety, that many Protestant families fled hither during the troubles of Mary's reign.

364. On the death of Mary in 1558, Elizabeth became queen. Henry VIII. had transferred the headship of the church from the Pope to himself; Edward VI. had changed the state religion from Catholic to Protestant; Mary from Protestant to Catholic; and now there was to be a fourth change, followed by results far more serious and lasting than any previously experienced.

365. A parliament was assembled in Dublin in 1560, to restore the Protestant religion; and in a few weeks the whole ecclesiastical system of Mary was reversed. The act of supremacy was revived, and all officials and clergymen were to take the oath or be dismissed. The act of uniformity was also re-introduced; i.e. an act commanding all people to use the Book of Common Prayer (the Protestant Prayer Book), and to attend the new service on Sunday under pain of censure and a fine of twelve pence for each absence—about twelve shillings of our money.

366. Wherever these new regulations were enforced, the Catholic clergy had of course to abandon their churches, for they could not hold them without taking the oath. But they went among the people, administered the rites of the church, and took good care of religion just the same as before.

367. In many places the new statute of uniformity was now brought sharply into play. In Dublin fines were inflicted on those who absented themselves from church; and to avoid the penalty many went to Mass in the morning and to church in the evening. But the church wardens tried to prevent even this by calling a roll of the parishioners at the morning

service.

This compulsion prevailed however only in the Pale and in some few other places. In far the greatest part of Ireland the government had no influence, and the Catholics were not interfered with. Even within the Pale the great body of the people took no notice of proclamations, the law could not be enforced, the act of uniformity was a dead letter, and the greater number of the parishes remained in the hands of the priests.

From the time of Elizabeth Protestantism remained the religion of the state in Ireland, till the disestablishment of the church in 1869.

SHANE O'NEILL (1547-1567)

368. On the accession of Edward VI. in 1547, Sentleger was continued as deputy. As there were some serious disturbances in Leinster, Edward Bellingham, an able and active officer, was sent over in May this year as military commander, bringing a small force of 600 horse and 400 foot. He reduced O'Moore of Leix and O'Conor of Offaly, and sent them to London, in 1548, where they were treated kindly and got pensions. Meanwhile the two territories were annexed to the Pale, and Bellingham built a number of castles to keep down the people for the future. How land and people were dealt with is told in Chapter V.

369. We have seen that when Conn Bacach O'Neill was created Earl of Tyrone, his (reputed) son Matthew was made baron of Dungannon with the right to succeed to the earldom. Conn had adopted this Matthew, believing him to be his son, though there was then, as there has been to this day, a doubt about it.

370. The earl's eldest legitimate son Shane, afterwards well known by the name of Shane-an-diomais or John the Proud, was a mere boy when Matthew was made baron. But now that he was come of age and understood his position, he claimed the right to be his father's heir and to succeed to the earldom, alleging that Matthew was not an O'Neill at all. The father, who took Shane's part, was brought prisoner to Dublin: whereupon Shane rose in open war against Matthew and the government. The deputy Croft attempted to reduce him; marching three times to Ulster in 1551 and 1552, but without success.

371. From the earliest time the two leading families of Ulster were the O'Neills of Tyrone and the O'Donnells of Tirconnell, who were rivals and very often at war. In 1557 Shane, meaning to make himself king of all Ulster, invaded Tirconnell with a large army. But Calvagh O'Donnell chief of Tirconnell surprised his camp at night and utterly defeated him.

372. Shane soon recovered this disaster; and in the next year, 1558, the year of Queen Elizabeth's accession, some of his people killed his rival, Matthew the baron of Dungannon, in a night attack, so unfairly that it almost deserved the name of assassination. But Shane himself was not present. In the following year the earl his father died, and Shane was

elected "The O'Neill" in open defiance of English law.

373. These movements of the great chief gave the government much uneasiness; and in 1560 they raised up rivals all round him: but he quickly defeated them all. In 1561 the lord deputy—the earl of Sussex—marched north against him; but Shane defeated him, and soon after made himself master of all Ulster.

374. At last the queen invited him to London. He went there in December 1561, much against the wishes of Sussex, who suggested that he should be treated coldly. But the queen received him very graciously. The redoubtable chief and his retainers, all in their strange native attire, were viewed with curiosity and wonder. He strode through the court to the royal presence, between two lines of wondering courtiers; and behind him marched his galloglasses, their heads bare, their long hair curling down on their shoulders and clipped short in front just above the eyes. They wore a loose wide-sleeved saffron-dyed tunic, and over this a short shaggy mantle flung across the shoulders. On the 6th of January 1562 he made formal submission to the queen in presence of the court and the foreign ambassadors.

The London authorities took an unfair advantage of his presence to make him sign certain severe conditions; but though he signed them, it was against his will, and it would seem he had no intention to carry them out. He returned to Ulster in May 1562 with the queen's pardon, all his expenses having been paid by the government.

375. But he was very indignant at being forced to sign conditions: and he now quite disregarded them and renewed the war. At last the queen heartily sick of the quarrel, instructed Sussex to end it by reasonable concessions; and peace was signed in November 1563 in O'Neill's house at Benburb, on terms much to his advantage. After this there was quietness for some time.

376. There were at this time in Antrim great numbers of Scottish settlers from the western coasts and islands of Scotland, of whom the most distinguished were the Mac Donnells—the "Lords of the Isles." They were greatly feared and disliked by the government who made many ineffectual attempts to expel them.

377. One of the conditions that Shane had to sign in London bound him to make war on these Scots and reduce them to obedience. Whether it was that he wished to carry out this condition, or what is more likely, that he himself dreaded the Scots as neighbours, he attacked and defeated them in 1565 at Glenshesk in Antrim, where 700 of them were killed.

378. The news of this victory at first gave great joy to the English; but seeing how much it increased his power, their joy soon turned to jealousy and fear. And they sent two commissioners to have an interview with him; to whom he said among many other things:—"For the queen, I confess she is my sovereign: but I never made peace with her but at her own seeking.

My ancestors were kings of Ulster, and Ulster is mine, and shall be mine. O'Donnell shall never come into his country, nor Bagenall into Newry, nor Kildare into Dundrum or Lecale. They are now mine. With the sword I won them: with this sword I will keep them."

379. The defeat that finally crushed the great chief was inflicted, not by the government, but by the O'Donnells. Hugh O'Donnell chief of Tirconnel made a plundering excursion into Tyrone, Shane's territory, in 1567. Shane retaliated by crossing the Swilly into Tirconnell; but he was met by O'Donnell at the other side and utterly routed; and Shane himself, crossing a ford two miles higher up, barely escaped with his life.

380. This action, in which 1,300 of his men perished, utterly ruined him. He lost all heart, and now formed the insane resolution of placing himself at the mercy of the Scots, whose undying enmity he had earned by the defeat at Glenshesk two years before. He came to their camp at Cushendun (in 1567) with only fifty followers, trusting in their generosity. They received him with a show of welcome and cordiality; but in the midst of the festivities they raised a dispute, which obviously had been prearranged, and suddenly seizing their arms, they massacred the chief and all his followers.

381. O'Neill's rebellion cost the government £147,407, about a million and three-quarters of our present money, besides the cesses laid on the country and the damages sustained by the subjects. At the time of his death he was only about forty years of age.

THE GERALDINE REBELLION (1565-1583)

382. The Fitzgeralds and the Butlers were at perpetual war. The earl of Desmond, the head of the southern Geraldines, was a Catholic, and took the Irish side; the earl of Ormond, the leader of the Butlers, had conformed to the Protestant faith, and had taken the side of the English all along. By the tyranny and oppression of these two earls, as well as by their never-ending disputes, large districts in the south were devastated, and almost depopulated.

383. On one occasion Desmond, who claimed jurisdiction over Decies in Waterford, crossed the Blackwater with his army to levy tribute, in the old form of coyne and livery. The chief of the district, Sir Maurice Fitzgerald, a relative of the Butlers, called in the aid of the earl of Ormond. Desmond, taken unawares, was defeated in a battle fought in 1565 at Affane in the county Waterford, beside the Blackwater, and he himself was wounded and taken prisoner. It is related that while he was borne from the field on a litter, one of his captors tauntingly asked him:—"Where is now the great earl of Desmond?" To which he instantly replied, "Where he ought to be: on the necks of the Butlers."

384. At the same time Connaught was in a state almost as bad, by the broils of the earl of Clanrickard and his sons with each other, and with the

chiefs all round.

385. The deputy, Sir Henry Sydney, a very able man, endeavoured to make peace. He undertook a journey south and west in 1567; and having witnessed the miseries of the country, he treated the delinquents with merciless severity as he went along, hanging and imprisoning great numbers. He brought Desmond a prisoner to Dublin, leaving his brother John Fitzgerald, or John of Desmond as he is called, to govern South Munster in the earl's absence.

386. He convened a parliament in Dublin in which during 1569, 1570, and 1571 were passed acts to spread the Reformation and to attaint Shane O'Neill and confiscate his lands.

387. In 1567, at Ormond's instigation, John of Desmond was treacherously seized without any cause, and he and his brother the earl were sent to London and consigned to the Tower, where they were detained for six years. All this was done without the knowledge of Sydney, who afterwards quite disapproved of it. It made a rebel of John Fitzgerald, who had been up to that time well affected towards the government.

388. There had been reports that large districts in Ireland were to be taken from the owners and planted with colonies; and this, coupled with the proceedings in Dublin to force the Reformation produced great alarm and discontent. Matters were brought to a crisis by the arrest of Desmond and John Fitzgerald. James Fitzmaurice Fitzgerald, the earl's first cousin, now went among the southern chiefs and induced them all, both native Irish and Anglo-Irish, to unite in defence of their religion and their lands: and thus was formed what was called the Geraldine League. Thus also arose the Geraldine rebellion.

389. When Sydney heard of these alarming proceedings he proclaimed the chiefs traitors, and in 1569 made a journey south with his army, during which he and his officers acted with great severity. This circuit of Sydney's went a good way to break up the confederacy, and many of the leaders were terrified into submission.

390. But Fitzmaurice never thought of yielding. On the approach of winter he took refuge in the great wooded Glen of Aherlow in the Galty mountains; and next spring, in 1570, he suddenly attacked Kilmallock, then held by an English garrison. Scaling the walls before sunrise, he plundered the town; after which he set it on fire and retired to Aherlow, leaving the stately old capital a mere collection of blackened walls.

391. About this time Sydney appointed "Presidents" to govern Munster and Connaught. The object was to produce peace; but it did the very reverse; for the presidents used their great power so mercilessly that they drove both chiefs and people to rebellion everywhere. Sir Edward Fitton and Sir Richard Bingham, two presidents of Connaught, were perhaps the worst, and Sir John Perrott, a brave old soldier, who was made President of

Munster in 1571, though very severe, was about the best and most reasonable of all.

392. Perrott took Fitzmaurice's castles one after another, and at last, in 1573, forced him to submit. After this, as the rebellion was considered at an end, the earl of Desmond and his brother were released.

393. Sydney had been lord justice in 1558; and after that he was three times lord deputy, 1565, 1568. 1575. In 1577 during his last deputyship, he raised a great disturbance at home by attempting to impose an illegal tax on the people of Dublin and the Pale, without obtaining the consent of the Irish parliament. His harshness on this occasion caused great excitement and discontent among the loyal people of the Pale, and helped to drive some into rebellion. In the end the matter was compromised.

394. Fitzmaurice fled to France after his submission; and the Geraldine rebellion slumbered for about six years. In 1579 the Pope, on the recommendation of Philip II. of Spain, fitted out for him a small squadron of three ships with 700 Italian soldiers, intended for Ireland, which was placed under the command of Thomas Stukely, a clever unprincipled English adventurer. This man had managed to hoodwink his employers into the belief of his sincere attachment to the cause of Ireland. But touching at Lisbon on his way, he joined another expedition led by the King of Portugal; and the Irish never heard any more of him or his squadron.

395. Meantime Fitzmaurice embarked for Ireland in 1579 in three small ships which he had procured in Spain, with about eighty Spaniards, accompanied by Dr. Allen, a Jesuit, and by Dr. Sanders, a celebrated English ecclesiastic, the Pope's legate. He landed at the little harbour of Smerwick in Kerry, and took possession of a fort called Dunanore, perched on top of a rock jutting into the sea. Here he was joined by Desmond's two brothers, John and James Fitzgerald.

396. But Fitzmaurice was soon forced to abandon his fort, and flying northwards towards the Shannon, he was killed, in the same year, in a skirmish with the Burkes of Castleconnell.

397. John Fitzgerald now took command of the Munster insurgents; and soon collected a considerable force. The earl of Desmond came to lord justice Drury, who was then at Kilmallock, to assure him he had nothing to do with the rebellion; and Drury forced him to give up his only son James, then a child, as a hostage for his loyalty.

398. Lord Justice Drury and Sir Nicholas Malbie pursued the insurgents; and two battles were fought in 1579; one at Gort-na-tubbrid or Springfield in the county Limerick, where Fitzgerald defeated the government forces; the other near Croom where he was defeated by Malbie.

399. Malbie was joined by Sir William Pelham the newly appointed lord justice, and by the earl of Ormond general of the army: and they goaded

Desmond to join the rebellion.

400. The frightful civil war broke out now more virulently than before; and brought the country to such a state as had never yet been witnessed. Several hostile bands belonging to both sides traversed the country for months, destroying everything and wreaking vengeance on the weak and defenceless.

Desmond utterly ruined the rich and prosperous town of Youghal, leaving not one house fit to live in; but in his marches through those parts of the country belonging to the English he did not massacre the inhabitants. Not so with Pelham and Ormond, who carried fire and sword through the country, sparing no living thing that fell in their way.

401. For the rebels it was a losing game all through. Pelham and Ormond took Desmond's strongholds one by one. James Fitzgerald, the earl's youngest brother, was captured while making a raid on the territories of Sir Cormac Mac Carthy, the sheriff of Cork; and he was sent to Cork and executed. A little later on his brother, John of Desmond, was intercepted and killed.

402. Meantime the insurrection blazed up in Leinster under James Eustace viscount Baltinglass, who exasperated by Sidney's proceedings, flew to arms.

The newly appointed justice, Lord Grey of Wilton, who succeeded Pelham, at once mustered his men, and in August 1580 marched into the heart of Wicklow in pursuit of the insurgent army, who had retired into Glenmalure. Here he was suddenly attacked by viscount Baltinglass and by the great chief Fiach Mac Hugh O'Byrne; and his army was almost annihilated.

403. The insurgents had long expected aid from the Continent, which at length arrived: 700 Spaniards and Italians landed about the 1st October 1580 from four vessels at Smerwick. They took possession of the ill-omened old fort of Dunanore, and proceeded to fortify it. They expected to see the people join them in crowds: but Ormond and Pelham had done their work so thoroughly that the peasantry held aloof, trembling with fear.

404. After about six weeks Lord Grey laid siege to the fort; at the same time Admiral Winter arrived early in November with the English fleet, so that it was invested both by sea and land. After the cannon had battered the fort for some days the garrison surrendered. The Irish authorities assert they had promise of their lives; the English say they surrended at discretion. Anyhow, Grey had the whole garrison massacred. This deed of horror caused great indignation all over England and on the Continent.

405. During the next year, 1581, Grey and his officers carried on the war with relentless barbarity; till at length it began to be felt that instead of quieting Ireland he was rather fanning rebellion; and in 1582 the queen recalled him.

406. And now the great earl of Desmond, the master of almost an entire province, the inheritor of vast estates, and the owner of numerous castles, was become a homeless outlaw with a price on his head, dogged by spies everywhere, and hunted from one hiding place to another. Through all his weary wanderings he was accompanied by his faithful wife, who never left him, except a few times when she went to intercede for him. On one of these occasions she sought an interview with Lord Justice Pelham himself, and on her knees implored mercy for her husband; but her tears and intreaties were all in vain. After many narrow escapes he was at length taken and killed in 1583 by some soldiers and peasants in Kerry. This ended the great Geraldine rebellion.

407. The war had made Munster a desert. In the words of the Four Masters:—"The lowing of a cow or the voice of a ploughman could scarcely be heard from Dunqueen in the west of Kerry to Cashel."

To what a frightful pass the wretched people had been brought by the constant destruction and spoiling of their crops and cattle, may be gathered from Edmund Spenser's description of what he witnessed with his own eyes:—"Notwithstanding that the same [province of Munster] was a most rich and plentiful countrey, full of corne and cattle, yet ere one yeare and a halfe they [the people] were brought to such wretchedness as that any stony hart would have rued the same. Out of every corner of the woods and glynnes they carne creeping forth upon their hands, for their legges could not beare them, and if they found a plot of watercresses or shamrocks there they flocked as to a feast for the time: that in short space of time there were none [i.e. no people] almost left, and a most populous and plentifull country suddainely left voide of man and beast."

THE PLANTATIONS

408. In the time of Queen Mary, who succeeded Edward VI. in 1553, an entire change was made in the mode of dealing with Irish territories whose chiefs had been subdued. Hitherto whenever the government deposed or banished a troublesome chief, they contented themselves with putting in his place another, commonly English or Anglo-Irish, more likely to be submissive, while the general body of occupiers remained undisturbed. But now when a rebellious chief was reduced, the lands, not merely those in his own possession, but also those occupied by the whole of the people over whom he ruled, were confiscated—seized by the crown—and given to English adventurers, undertakers as they were commonly called. These men got the lands on condition that they should bring in or plant on them a number of English or Scotch settlers; for whom it was of course necessary to clear off the native population.

409. After the banishment of O'Moore and O'Conor in 1548 their districts of Leix and Offaly were given to an Englishman named Francis Bryan and to some others, who proceeded straightway to expel the native people and

parcel out the lands to new tenants, chiefly English. But the natives resisted; and the fighting went on during the whole of the reign of Edward VI., with great loss of life to both sides.

410. As this settlement did not succeed, the whole district was made crown property in 1555 and 1556, during the reign of Queen Mary, and replanted. But the natives still struggled for their homes; and a pitiless war of mutual extermination went on for many years, till the original owners were almost completely banished or exterminated.

411. After the attainder of Shane O'Neill more than half of Ulster was confiscated; and the attempt to clear off the old natives and plant new settlers was commenced without delay. In 1570 the peninsula of Ardes in Down was granted to the queen's secretary Sir Thomas Smith, who sent his illegitimate son with a colony to take possession. But this plantation was a failure; for the owners, the O'Neills of Clandeboy, not feeling inclined to part with their rights without a struggle, attacked and killed the young undertaker in 1573.

412. The next undertaker was a more important man, Walter Devereux earl of Essex. In 1573 he undertook to plant the district now occupied by the county Antrim, together with the Island of Rathlin.

He waged savage war on the natives, stopping short at no amount of slaughter and devastation—burning their corn and depopulating the country to the best of his ability by sword and starvation. He treacherously seized young O'Donnell of Tirconnell and Brian O'Neill chief of Clandeboy and sent them prisoners to Dublin. And he massacred hundreds of the Scots of Clandeboy and of Rathlin Island to gain possession of their lands. Yet after all this fearful work he failed, and he had to return to Dublin where he died.

413. After the death of the earl of Desmond his vast estates, and those of 140 of his adherents, nearly a million acres, all in Munster, were confiscated by a parliament held in Dublin in 1585.

414. In 1586 proclamation was made all through England, inviting gentlemen to "undertake" the plantation of this great and rich territory. Estates were offered at two pence or three pence an acre, and no rent at all was to be paid for the first five years. Every undertaker who took 12,000 acres was to settle eighty-six English families as tenants on his property, but no Irish; and so in proportion for smaller estates down to 4,000 acres.

Sir Walter Raleigh got 42,000 acres in Cork and Waterford, and resided at Youghal, where his house is still to be seen. Edmund Spenser the poet received 12,000 acres in Cork, and took up his residence in one of Desmond's strongholds, Kilcolman Castle, the ruin of which, near Buttevant, is still an object of interest to visitors.

In the most important particulars, however, this great scheme turned out a failure. The English farmers and artisans did not come over in sufficient numbers; and the undertakers received the native Irish everywhere as tenants, in violation of the conditions. Some English came over indeed; but they were so harassed and frightened by the continual attacks of the dispossessed owners that many of them returned to England. And lastly, more than half the confiscated lands remained in possession of the owners, as no others could be found to take them. So the only result of this plantation was to root out a large proportion of the old gentry and to enrich a few undertakers.

415. There were many other plantations during these times and subsequently, all resembling in their main features those sketched here.

HUGH ROE O'DONNELL (1584-1592)

416. Sir John Perrott was lord deputy from 1584 to 1588. He treated the Irish with some consideration, much against the wishes of his Dublin council, many of whom were his bitter enemies. Yet his action was not always straight, as the following narrative will shew.

417. In anticipation of hostilities with Spain, where the Armada was at this time in preparation, he had already secured hostages from many of the Irish chiefs, but none from the O'Donnells, whom he feared more than all. In this strait he bethought him of a treacherous plan to seize either Sir Hugh O'Donnell or his son and heir.

418. Sir Hugh O'Donnell chief of Tirconnell had a son Hugh, commonly known as Hugh Roe (the Red), who was born in 1572, and who was now— 1587—in his fifteenth year. Even already at that early age, he was remarked for his great abilities and for his aspiring and ambitious disposition. "The fame and renown of the above-named youth, Hugh Roe,"—say the Four Masters—"had spread throughout the five provinces of Ireland even before he had come to the age of manhood, for his wisdom, sagacity, goodly growth, and noble deeds; and the English feared that if he should be permitted to arrive at the age of maturity, he and the earl of Tyrone [Hugh O'Neill his brother-in-law] might combine and conquer the whole island."

419. Perrott's plan for entrapping young Red Hugh was skilfully concocted and well carried out. In the autumn of 1587 he sent a merchant vessel laden with Spanish wines to the coast of Donegal on pretence of traffic. The captain entered Lough Swilly and anchored opposite the castle of Rathmullen, where the boy lived with his foster father Mac Sweeny. When Mac Sweeny heard of the arrival of the ship, he sent to purchase some wine. The messengers were told that no more was left to sell; but that if any gentlemen wished to come on board they were quite welcome to drink as much as they pleased. The bait took. A party of the Mac Sweenys, accompanied by Hugh, unsuspectingly went on board. The captain had previously called in all his men; and while the company were enjoying themselves, their arms were quietly removed, the hatchway door was

closed down, and the ship weighed anchor. When the people on shore observed this they were filled with consternation, and flocked to the beach; but they were quite helpless, for they had no boats ready. Neither was it of any avail when Mac Sweeny rushed to the point of shore nearest the ship, and cried out in the anguish of his heart, offering any amount of ransom and hostages. Young Hugh O'Donnell was brought to Dublin and safely lodged in Bermingham Tower in the Castle.

420. This transaction, however, so far from tending to peace, as Perrott no doubt intended, did the very reverse; for, as Leland justly observes, it was "equally impolitic and dishonourable." It made bitter enemies of the O'Donnells, who had been hitherto for generations on the side of the government. In young O'Donnell himself more especially, it engendered feelings of exasperation and irreconcilable hatred; and it was one of the causes of the O'Neill war which brought unmeasured woe and disaster to both English and Irish.

421. Three years and three months passed away: Perrott had been recalled, and Sir William Fitzwilliam was now, 1590, lord deputy; when O'Donnell, in concert with some of his fellow prisoners, made an attempt to escape. Round the castle there was a deep ditch filled with water, across which was a wooden bridge opposite the door of the fortress. Early one dark winter's evening, before the guard had been set, they let themselves down on the bridge by a long rope, and immediately fastened the door on the outside. They were met on the bridge by a youth of Hugh's people with two swords, one of which Hugh took, the other was given to Art Kavanagh, a brave young Leinster chief. They made their way noiselessly through the people along the dimly lighted streets, guided by the young man, while Kavanagh brought up the rear with sword grasped ready in case of interruption. Passing out through one of the city gates which had not yet been closed for the night, they crossed the country towards the hills, avoiding the public road, and made their way over that slope of the Three Rock Mountain overlooking Still-organ. They pushed on till far in the night; when being at last quite worn out, they took shelter in a thick wood, somewhere near the present village of Roundwood, where they remained hidden during the remainder of the night. Next morning O'Donnell was so fatigued that he was not able to keep up with his companions; for the thin shoes he wore had fallen in pieces with wet, and his feet were torn and bleeding from sharp stones and thorns. So, very unwillingly, his companions left him in a wood and pursued their journey, all but one servant who went for aid to Castlekevin, a little way off, near the mouth of Glendalough, where lived Felim O'Toole, one of Hugh's friends, who at once took steps for his relief.

422. After the fugitives had left the castle, the guards going to lock them up in their cells for the night missed them, and instantly raising an alarm,

rushed to the door; but finding themselves shut in, they shouted to the people in the houses at the other side of the street, who removed the fastening of the door and released them. They were not able to overtake the fugitives, who had too much of a start, but they traced them all the way to the hiding-place. O'Toole now saw that his friend could no longer be concealed, for the soldiers had surrounded the wood; and making a virtue of necessity, he and his people arrested him and brought him back to Dublin. The council were delighted at his capture; and for the better security they shackled him and his companions in the prison with heavy iron fetters.

423. Another weary year passed away. On Christmas night, 1591, before supper time, Hugh and his two companions Henry and Art O'Neill, the sons of Shane O'Neill, who were also in the prison, cut through their iron fetters with a file which had somehow been conveyed to them, and let themselves down on the bridge by a long silken rope. They crept through the common sewer of the castle, and, making their way across the ditch, were met at the other side by a guide sent by the great chief Fiach Mac Hugh O'Byrne of Glenmalure.

424. They glided through the dim streets as in their former attempt at escape, the people taking no notice of them; and passing out at one of the city gates which had not been closed, they made their way across the country; but in this part of their course they lost Henry O'Neill in the darkness. Greatly distressed at this, they still pressed on; but they found it hard to travel and suffered keenly from cold; for the snow fell thick, and they had thrown aside their soiled outer mantles after leaving the castle. They crossed the hills, shaping their way this time more to the west, up by Killakee and along the course of the present military road.

But Art O'Neill, who had grown corpulent in his prison for want of exercise, was unable to keep pace with the others: and Hugh and the attendant had to help him on at intervals by walking one on each side, while he rested his arms on their shoulders. In this manner they toiled on wearily across the snowy waste through the whole of that Christmas night and the whole of next day without food, hoping to be able to reach Glenmalure without a halt. But they became at last so worn out with fatigue and hunger, that they had to give up and take shelter under a high rock, while the servant ran on for help. Fiach despatched a small party with a supply of food, who found the two young men lying under the rock to all appearance dead:—"Unhappy and miserable" —write the Four Masters— "was the condition [of the young chiefs] on their arrival. Their bodies were covered over with white-bordered shrouds of hailstones freezing around them, and their light clothes and fine-threaded shirts adhered to their skin, and their large shoes and leather thongs to their legs and feet: so that covered as they were with snow, it did not appear to the men who had arrived that they were human beings at all, for they found no life in their members, but just as if they were dead."

They raised the unhappy sufferers and tried to make them take food and drink, but neither food nor drink could they swallow, and while the men were tenderly nursing them Art O'Neill died in their arms. And there they buried him under the shadow of the rock. Hugh, being hardier, however, fared better: after some time he was able to swallow a little ale, and his strength began to return. But his feet still remained frozen and dead so that he could not stand: and when he had sufficiently recovered, the men carried him on their shoulders to Glenmalure. Here he was placed in a secluded cottage, where he remained for a time under cure, till a young chief named Turlogh O'Hagan, a trusty messenger from Hugh O'Neill earl of Tyrone, came for him.

425. Meantime, the council hearing that O'Donnell was in Glenmalure with O'Byrne, placed guards on the fords of the Liffey to prevent him from passing northwards to Ulster. Nevertheless, as O'Neill's message was urgent, Fiach sent O'Donnell away with O'Hagan, and a troop of horse for a guard; but the young chief's feet were still so helpless that he had to be lifted on and off his horse. They crossed the Liffey at a deep and dangerous ford just beside Dublin, which had been left unguarded. Here O'Byrne's escort left them; and from Dublin they made their way northwards, attended by Felim O'Toole and his brother. Having escorted them to a safe distance beyond Dublin, the O'Tooles "bade Hugh farewell, and having given him their blessing, departed from him."

There were now only two, O'Donnell himself and O'Hagan, and they rode on till they reached the Boyne a little above Drogheda: here O'Donnell crossed in a boat while O'Hagan brought the horses round by the town. They next reached Mellifont, where resided a friend, Sir Garrett Moore, a young Englishman, with whom they remained for the night; and in the evening of the following day set off with a fresh pair of horses.

They arrived at Dundalk by morning, and rode through the town in open day without attracting any notice: and at last they reached the residence of Hugh O'Neill's half brother, chief of the Fews in Armagh. Next day they came to the city of Armagh, where they remained in concealment for one night. The following day they reached the house of earl Hugh O'Neill at Dungannon, where O'Donnell rested for four days; but secretly, for O'Neill was still in the queen's service.

The earl sent him with a troop of horse as an escort to Enniskillen Castle, the residence of O'Donnell's cousin Maguire of Fermanagh, who rowed him down Lough Erne, at the far shore of which he was met by a party of his own people. With these he arrived at his father's castle at Ballyshannon, where he was welcomed with unbounded joy.

426. There is good reason to believe that the deputy Fitzwilliam, who

was very avaricious and unprincipled, was bribed by Hugh O'Neill earl of Tyrone to connive at the escape of O'Donnell and the two O'Neills.

427. At Ballyshannon Hugh remained under cure for two months. The physicians had at last to amputate his two great toes; and a whole year passed away before he had fully recovered from the effects of that one terrible winter night in the mountains.

In May this year, 1592, a general meeting of the Kinel-Connell was convened; and Sir Hugh O'Donnell, who was old and feeble, having resigned the chieftainship, young Hugh Roe—now in his twentieth year—was elected The O'Donnell, chief of his race.

HUGH O'NEILL, EARL OF TYRONE (1585-1594)

428. Hugh O'Neill, the subject of our present sketch, was the son of Matthew baron of Dungannon. He was born about 1545, and succeeded as baron of Dungannon on the death of his elder brother. He was educated among the English, and began his military life in the queen's service as commander of a troop of horse.

429. In the parliament of 1585, which he attended as baron of Dungannon, he was made earl of Tyrone in succession to his (reputed) grandfather Conn Bacach; and in 1587 the queen granted him the inheritance; but he was to give up 240 acres on the Blackwater as a site for a fort. This fort was built soon after and called Portmore; it commanded a ford which was the pass from Armagh into Tyrone, O'Neill's territory; and its site is now marked by the village of Blackwatertown.

430. Not long after this the earl and Mabel Bagenal, sister of Sir Henry Bagenal marshal of Ireland, fell in love with each other and wished to be married. But Bagenal opposed it and sent the lady to Dublin, whither O'Neill followed her; and they were married in the house of a friend at Drumcondra. The marshal from that day forth was O'Neill's deadly enemy; and he kept the lady's fortune, £1,000, which her father had left her.

431. In 1593 the government made him master of all Tyrone. But his movements were now considered suspicious; he was continually drilling men; and he brought home vast quantities of lead to roof his new house at Dungannon, which it was reported was not intended for roofs but for bullets.

432. Still he was in the queen's service, and in the same year, 1593, fought with deputy Fitzwilliam against O'Ruarc, who had been goaded into rebellion by the sheriff of Fermanagh. In 1594 Fitzwilliam took Maguire's castle at Enniskillen. But Maguire and O'Donnell besieged it immediately after; and when the deputy sent forces to relieve the garrison, they were intercepted at a ford near Enniskillen by Maguire and O'Neill's brother Cormac, and defeated. And in their flight they abandoned all the provisions intended for the garrison; so that the place got the name of Bellanabriska, the ford of the biscuits. But no one could tell whether or not it was with

O'Neill's consent his brother joined Maguire.

THE REBELLION OF HUGH O'NEILL (1595-1597)

433. The friendly relations between the earl and the government may be said to have ended with the close of the year 1594. He had adopted the course of action related in last Chapter without any intention of rebelling, and while maintaining his rights he endeavoured to conciliate the authorities. But he was continually harassed by the untiring machinations of Marshal Bagenal, who intercepted many of his letters of explanation; and this and his determination to regain all the ancestral power of his family in Ulster gradually drew him into rebellion.

434. There were now many alarming signs and rumours of coming disturbance; and at the request of the deputy a force of 3,000 troops was sent over early in 1595, under the command of Sir John Norris president of Munster, an officer of great ability and experience, on whom was conferred the title of "lord general."

435. O'Neill evidently regarded this movement as the first step towards the subjugation of the whole country, including his own province of Ulster; and he decided on immediate action. His young brother Art seized Portmore; and he himself plundered the English settlements of Cavan.

436. He next, in the same year—1595—laid siege to Monaghan and reduced its English garrison to great distress. Norris and his brother Sir Thomas managed to relieve the town. But on their return march to Newry they found O'Neill with his army drawn up on the far bank of a small stream at Clontibret, six miles from Monaghan. After a brave contest the English were defeated; the two Norrises were severely wounded: and O'Neill himself slew in single combat a gigantic officer named Segrave, who had attacked him.

437. In Midsummer of this year—1595—lord general Norris marched north; but he was opposed and harassed by O'Neill and O'Donnell, and returned without much result.

438. There were next many negotiations and conferences, in which O'Neill always insisted, among other conditions, that the Catholics should have full liberty to practise their religion; but this was persistently refused, and the war still went on.

439. The queen was anxious for peace, and she was greatly exasperated when she heard of the cruelties of Sir Richard Bingham president of Connaught, who had driven nearly all the chiefs of that province into rebellion. She removed him in January 1597, and sent in his place Sir Conyers Clifford, a just and humane man.

440. Thomas Lord Borough was appointed lord deputy in 1597, and made preparation for a combined attack on Ulster from three different points;—he himself to march from Dublin towards Portmore against O'Neill; Sir Conyers Clifford to move from Galway, to Ballyshannon

against O'Donnell; and young Barnewell, son of Lord Trimblestone, to proceed from Mullingar: all three to form a junction near Ballyshannon. O'Neill and O'Donnell made preparations to intercept them.

441. In July 1597 the deputy marched with his Leinster forces towards Portmore, and after much destructive skirmishing O'Neill attacked him in force and defeated him at Drumflugh on the Blackwater. Borough himself and the earl of Kildare were wounded, and both died soon after. But the deputy accomplished one important object:—he regained Portmore, and left in it a garrison of 300 men in charge of a brave and capable officer, Captain Williams.

442. Sir Conyers Clifford forced his way across the Erne and laid siege to O'Donnell's castle of Ballyshannon. But the garrison, commanded by a Scotchman named Crawford, after desperate fighting forced the attacking party to retire with considerable loss. Clifford was attacked daily by O'Donnell and reduced to great distress: till at last he was forced to recross the river and retreat back to Connaught, abandoning all his cannons, carriages, and stores to O'Donnell.

443. Young Barnewell marched with 1,000 men from Mullingar; but he was intercepted by Captain Tyrrell at Tyrrell's Pass, where his army was exterminated, and he himself was taken and sent prisoner to the earl of Tyrone.

THE BATTLE OF THE YELLOW FORD (1597-1598)

444. Portmore was now—1597—occupied by captain Williams and his garrison of three hundred. No sooner had lord deputy Borough turned southward after his defeat at Drumflugh than O'Neill laid siege to it; and watching it night and day, tried every stratagem; but the vigilance and determination of Williams completely baffled him. At last he attempted a storm by means of scaling ladders; but the ladders turned out too short, and the storming party were met by such a fierce onslaught that they had to retire discomfited, leaving thirty-four of their men dead in the fosse. After this O'Neill tried no more active operations, but sat down, determined to starve the garrison into surrender.

445. When this had continued for some time, Williams and his men began to suffer sorely; and they would have been driven to surrender by mere starvation but for the good fortune of having seized and brought into the fort a number of O'Neill's horses, on which they now chiefly subsisted. Even with this supply they were so pressed by hunger that they ate every weed and every blade of grass they could pick up in the enclosure: but still the brave captain resolutely held out.

446. When tidings of these events reached Dublin, the council sat in long and anxious deliberations; but at last Marshal Bagenal persuaded them to entrust him with the perilous task of relieving the fort.

447. The marshal arrived at Armagh with an army of 4,000 foot and 350

horse. The five miles highway between the city and Portmore was a narrow strip of uneven ground, with bogs and woods at both sides; and right in the way, at Bellanaboy or the Yellow Ford, on the little river Callan, two miles north of Armagh, O'Neill had marshalled his forces, and determined to dispute the passage. His army was perhaps a little more numerous than that of his adversary, well trained and disciplined, armed and equipped after the English fashion, though not so well as Bagenal's army—they had no armour for instance, while many of the English had; and he had the advantage of an excellent position selected by himself. He had with him Hugh Roe O'Donnell, Maguire, and Mac Donnell of the Glens, all leaders of ability and experience. At intervals along the way he had dug deep holes and trenches, and had otherwise encumbered the line of march with felled trees and brushwood; and right in front of his main body extended a trench a mile long, five feet deep, and four feet across, with a thick hedge of thorns on top. Over these tremendous obstacles, in face of the whole strength of the Irish army, Bagenal must force his way if he is ever to reach the starving little band cooped up in Portmore.

448. But Bagenal was not a man easily daunted; and on the morning of the 14th August 1598 he began his march with music and drum. The army advanced in six regiments forming three divisions. The first division—two regiments—was commanded by colonel Percy, the marshal himself, as commander-in-chief, riding in the second regiment. The second division, consisting of the third and fourth regiments, was commanded by colonel Cosby and Sir Thomas Wingfield, and the third division by captains Coneys and Billings. The horse formed two divisions, one on each wing, under Sir Calisthenes Brooke, with captains Montague and Fleming. The regiments marched one behind another at intervals of 600 or 700 paces.

449. On the night before, O'Neill had sent forward 500 light-armed kern, who concealed themselves till morning in the woods and thickets along the way, and the English had not advanced far when these opened fire from both sides which they kept up during the whole march past. Through all obstacles—fire, bog, and pitfalls—the army struggled and fought resolutely, till the first regiment reached the great trench. A determined rush across, a brief and fierce hand to hand struggle, and in spite of all opposition they got to the other side. Instantly reforming, they pushed on, but had got only a little way when they were charged by a solid body of Irish and utterly overwhelmed.

450. It now appeared that a fatal mistake in tactics had been made by Bagenal. The several regiments were too far asunder, and the men of the vanguard were almost all killed before the second regiment could come up. When at last this second line appeared, O'Neill with a body of horse, knowing that Bagenal was at their head, spurred forward to seek him out and settle wrong and quarrel hand to hand. But they were not fated to meet.

The brave marshal, fatigued with fighting, lifted his visor for a moment to look about him and take breath; but hardly had he done so when a musket ball pierced his brain and he fell lifeless.

451. Even after this catastrophe the second regiment passed the trench, and were augmented by those of the first who survived. These soon found themselves hard pressed; which Cosby becoming aware of, pushed on with his third regiment to their relief; but they were cut to pieces before he had come up. A cannon had got bogged in Cosby's rear, straight in the line of march, and the oxen that drew it having been killed, the men of the fourth regiment made frantic efforts to free it, fighting for their lives all the time, for the Irish were swarming all round them. Meantime during this delay Cosby's regiment was attacked and destroyed, and he himself was taken prisoner.

452. While all this was taking place in the English front, there was hard fighting in the rear. For O'Neill, who with a small party of horse had kept his place near the trench, fighting and issuing orders, had, at the beginning of the battle, sent towards the enemy's rear O'Donnell, Maguire, and Mac Donnell of the Glens, who passing by the flank of the second division, hotly engaged as they were, fell on the last two regiments, which after a prolonged struggle to get forward, "being hard sett to, retyred foully [in disorder] to Armagh."

453. The fourth regiment, at last leaving their cannon, made a dash for the trench; but scarcely had they started when a waggon of gunpowder exploded in their midst, by which they were "disrancked and rowted" and great numbers were killed, "wherewith the traitors were encouraged and our men dismayed." O'Neill, observing the confusion, seized the moment for a furious charge. The main body of the English had been already wavering after the explosion, and now there was a general rout of both middle and rear. Fighting on the side of the English was an Irish chief, Mailmora or Myles O'Reilly, who was known as Mailmora the Handsome, and who called himself the queen's O'Reilly. He made two or three desperate attempts to rally the flying squadrons, but all in vain; and at last he himself fell slain among the others.

454. The multitude fled back towards Armagh, protected by the cavalry under captain Montague, an able and intrepid officer, for Sir Calisthenes Brooke had been wounded; and the Irish pursued them—as the old Irish chronicler expresses it—"by pairs, threes, scores, and thirties." Two thousand of the English were killed, together with their general and nearly all the officers; and the victors became masters of the artillery, ammunition, and stores of the royal army. On the Irish side the loss is variously estimated from 200 to 700. This was the greatest overthrow the English ever suffered since they had set foot in Ireland.

455. The fugitives to the number of 1,500 shut themselves up in Armagh,

where they were closely invested by the Irish. But Montague, with a body of horse, most courageously forced his way out and brought the evil tidings to Dublin. In a few days the garrisons of Armagh and Portmore capitulated—the valiant captain Williams yielding only after a most pressing message from Armagh—and were permitted to retire to Dundalk, leaving colours, drums, and ammunition behind.

456. When the southern chiefs heard of O'Neill's great victory, the Munster rebellion broke out like lightning. The confederates attacked the settlements to regain the lands that had been taken from them a dozen years before; they expelled the settlers; and before long they had recovered all Desmond's castles. The lord lieutenant and Sir Thomas Norris president of Munster were quite unable to cope with the rebellion, and left Munster to the rebels.

457. O'Neill, who now exercised almost as much authority as if he were King of Ireland, conferred the title of earl of Desmond on James Fitzgerald, who is known in history as the Sugan earl: he was nephew of the late (or rebel) earl.

THE EARL OF ESSEX (1599-1600)

458. Matters had now become very serious in Ireland; and at this grave juncture the queen, in March, 1599, appointed as lord lieutenant Robert Devereux second earl of Essex, son of Essex of the Plantations. He brought an army of 20,000 men, and got distinct instructions to direct all his strength against the earl of Tyrone and the other rebels of Ulster, and to plant garrisons at Lough Foyle and Ballyshannon. This latter direction he quite neglected, and the other he delayed.

459. Having scattered a large part of his army by sending them to various stations, he set out for the south on the 21st of May with 7,000 men, chiefly with the object of chastising the Geraldines. Through the whole of this disastrous journey, which occupied about six weeks, the insurgents constantly hung round the army and never gave him an hour's rest, so that he had to fight every inch of his way.

460. The O'Moores killed 500 of his men at the "Pass of the Plumes" near Maryborough. He pushed on for Caher in Tipperary, where he took the castle, the only successful exploit of the whole expedition. Passing round by Limerick, Fermoy, Lismore, and Waterford, he returned to Dublin in June, the soldiers being weary, sick and incredibly diminished in numbers.

461. Sir Conyers Clifford marched from Galway this year—1599—to relieve the castle of Collooney in Sligo, which was besieged by O'Donnell. Having arrived at Boyle, he started to cross the Curlieu Hills into Sligo; but he was intercepted by O'Donnell in a difficult part of the mountain road, called Ballaghboy or the Yellow Pass. After a very sharp fight the English were defeated and fled; and Sir Conyers, endeavouring to rally his men,

was killed in the pass. He was greatly regretted by the Irish, who buried him with much respect.

462. Essex's fine army of 20,000 had melted away in a few months; and at his own request he now got 2,000 more from the queen. In August, 1599, he set out at last for the north, with only 2,500 men: but he found O'Neill so strongly entrenched in his camp that he did not dare to attack him.

O'Neill now requested a conference, which was granted; and a truce was agreed on. But nothing came of it; for immediately afterwards Essex suddenly sailed for England. The remainder of his short career, ending in the block, belongs to the history of England.

463. O'Neill visited Munster in January, 1600, and encamped with his army at Inniscarra on the Lee near Cork. Here most of the southern chiefs visited him and acknowledged him as their leader.

For the last two years victory and success had attended the Irish almost without interruption; and Hugh O'Neill earl of Tyrone had now attained the very summit of his power. But after this the tide began to turn; and soon came the day of defeat and disaster.

LORD MOUNTJOY AND SIR GEORGE CAREW (1600-1601)

464. The person chosen by the queen to succeed Essex as deputy was Charles Blount, better known as Lord Mountjoy, a man of great ability and foresight, and a more formidable adversary than any yet encountered by O'Neill.

He came to Ireland in February, 1600. As soon as O'Neill heard of his arrival he broke up his camp at Inniscarra, where he had tarried for six weeks, and returned to Ulster.

465. Along with Mountjoy came Sir George Carew as president of Munster, a man quite as able and courageous as Mountjoy, but crafty and avaricious. He had an intense hatred of the Irish, mainly because his brother had been killed by them in the battle of Glenmalure.

466. Carew directed all his energies against the Munster rebels. He captured their castles one after another, and caused his soldiers to destroy the crops wherever he went in order to produce a famine. The famine ultimately came and the people—men, women, and children —perished by thousands of starvation.

467. He put forth all his efforts to capture the Sugan earl, who was an able leader of the insurgents, offering large rewards to any one who would betray him: but for a long time he was unsuccessful. The earl was at last taken in the great Mitchelstown cave by his old adherent the white knight, who delivered him up to Carew for a reward of £1,000. He was tried and found guilty of high treason; but he was not executed, lest his brother might be set up in his place and give more trouble.

468. While these events were taking place in the south, O'Neill and

O'Donnell were kept busy in the north. It had long been the intention of the government to plant garrisons on the shores of Lough Foyle. For this purpose a powerful armament of 4,000 foot and 200 horse, under the command of Sir Henry Docwra, with abundance of stores and building materials, sailed for Lough Foyle in May, 1600. At the same time, in order to divert O'Neill's attention and draw off opposition, Mountjoy marched north from Dublin as if to invade Tyrone. While O'Neill and O'Donnell were opposing Mountjoy, Docwra succeeded in building forts at Culmore at the mouth of the river Foyle, at Derry, then almost uninhabited, and at Dunnalong five miles from Derry up the river.

469. Leinster had shared in the O'Neill rebellion: and Owney O'Moore, the chief of Leix, had succeeded in winning back most of his principality. The country had quite recovered from the wars of the Plantations: the land was well cultivated, and the people were prosperous and contented.

470. But now to punish them for their part in the rebellion, Mountjoy proceeded in August, 1600, from Dublin, with a large force and a supply of sickles, scythes, and harrows to tear up the corn; and he soon destroyed the crops of the whole district; after which he returned to Dublin, leaving the people to despair and hunger, their smiling district turned to a black ruin.

471. Soon after this he marched north and employed himself in the same manner, till he had destroyed the people's means of subsistence over a large part of Ulster.

472. Niall Garve O'Donnell was married to Red Hugh O'Donnell's sister, and was one of the ablest and most trusted of the Ulster confederates. But on a sudden he betrayed his trust and went over to the English. This greatly crippled O'Neill and O'Donnell in their efforts to oppose Docwra; who still bravely held his ground in spite of all they could do.

473. By the middle of 1601 the rebellion may be said to have been crushed in the three southern provinces. In Ulster, though O'Neill and O'Donnell were still actively engaged in defensive warfare, they had become greatly circumscribed. But the rebellion was now fated to be renewed in another quarter of the island.

THE SIEGE AND BATTLE OF KINSALE (1601-1602)

474. On the 23d of September, 1601, a Spanish fleet entered the harbour of Kinsale with 3,400 troops under the command of Don Juan del Aguila. They immediately took possession of the town: and Del Aguila despatched a message to Ulster to O'Neill and O'Donnell to come south without delay. Mountjoy and Carew mustered their forces, and at the end of three weeks encamped on the north side of Kinsale with an army of 12,000 men.

475. On the receipt of Del Aguila's message the northern chiefs made a hasty preparation to march south. O'Donnell was first: and crossing the Shannon into Tipperary he encamped near Holy-cross. But here his further progress was barred; for Carew, whom Mountjoy had sent to intercept him,

lay right in his path near Cashel; the Slieve Felim mountains on his right—to the west—were impassable for an army with baggage on account of recent heavy rains; and he dared not go through Kilkenny, as he might encounter the army of the Pale. At the same time, wishing to reserve his strength, he was determined to reach Kinsale without fighting.

Luckily there came a sudden and intense frost on the night of the 22d of November, which hardened up bog and morass and made them passable. The Irish general, instantly taking advantage of this, set out that night westwards, crossed the Slieve Felim mountains, reached Croom the next night after a march of forty English miles —"the greatest march with [incumbrance of] carriage," says Carew, "that hath been heard of."

476. During the month of November the English had carried on the siege vigorously. The ordnance made a breach in the walls, and a storming party of 2,000 attempted to force their way in, but after a desperate struggle were repulsed. On the other hand, one stormy night, 2,000 of the Spaniards made a determined sally to destroy some siege works, but were driven off after sharp fighting.

477. After O'Donnell's arrival things began to go against the English, who were hemmed in by the town on one side, and by the Irish army on the other, so that they were now themselves besieged. They were threatened with famine, and the weather was so inclement that they lost numbers of their men every day by cold and sickness.

478. O'Neill arrived on the 21st December with an army of about 4,000, and encamped at Belgooly north of the town, about three miles from the English lines. His advice was, not to attack the English, but to let their army melt away; for already 6,000 of them had perished. But he was overruled in a council of war, and a combined attack of Irish and Spaniards was arranged for the night of the 3d of January, 1602. Meantime an Irish traitor sent secret information to the English.

479. The night was unusually dark, wet, and stormy; the guides lost their way, and the army wandered aimlessly and wearily, till at length at the dawn of day, O'Neill unexpectedly found himself near the English lines, which he saw were quite prepared to receive him.

His own men were wearied and his lines in some disorder, so he ordered the army to retire a little, either to place them in better order of battle or to postpone the attack. But Mountjoy's quick eye caught the situation, and he hurled his cavalry on the retreating ranks. For a whole hour O'Neill defended himself, still retiring, till his retreat became little better than a rout. All efforts to rally his ranks were vain; by some mistake Del Aguila's attack did not come off; and the Irish lost the battle of Kinsale.

480. Soon after the battle Del Aguila surrendered the town; and having agreed also to give up the castles of Baltimore, Castlehaven, and Dunboy, which were garrisoned by Spaniards, he returned to Spain.

481. On the night following that fatal day, the Irish chiefs retired with their broken army to Innishannon. Here they held a sad council, in which it was resolved to send O'Donnell to Spain for further help; leaving his Tirconnellian forces in command of his brother Rory. Philip King of Spain received him most cordially, and assured him that he would send with him to Ireland an armament much more powerful than that of Del Aguila.

482. But Red Hugh O'Donnell never saw his native Ulster more. He took suddenly ill at Simancas, and his bodily ailment was intensified by sickness of heart, for he had heard of the surrender of Kinsale and of the fall of Dunboy; and he died on the 10th of September 1602 in the twenty-ninth year of his age.

THE SIEGE OF DUNBOY (1602)

483. THE Irish chiefs were very indignant with Del Aguila for surrendering Kinsale; and they were incensed beyond measure when they heard that he had agreed to hand over to the deputy the castles of Baltimore, Castle-haven, and Dunboy. The castles had not yet been given up however, and Donall O'Sullivan Beare, the owner of Dunboy, resolved to regain possession of it and defend it.

484. In February 1602, he threw in a body of native troops under the command of Richard Mac Geoghegan and Thomas Taylor an Englishman. The Spaniards were overpowered and sent away; and now Mac Geoghegan's whole garrison amounted to 143 men, who straightway began to make preparations for a siege.

It might seem an act of madness for such a small garrison to attempt a defence against the overwhelming force at the disposal of Carew: but O'Sullivan hoped that O'Donnell would return with help from King Philip, and that the fortress could hold out till the arrival of the Spaniards.

485. Carew set out from Cork with 3,000 men, sending round his ships with ordnance and stores. At Bantry Sir Charles Wilmot joined him with 1,000 more. The whole army was conveyed to Great Beare Island by sea in the first few days of June; and encamped near the ill-starred castle. The devoted little garrison never flinched at sight of the powerful armament of 4,000 men, and only exerted themselves all the more resolutely to strengthen their position.

486. And now the siege was begun in good earnest, and day after day the ordnance thundered against the walls. On the 17th of June the castle was so shattered that Mac Geoghegan sent to Carew offering to surrender, on condition of being allowed to march out with arms: but Carew's only answer was to hang the messenger and to give orders for a final assault. The storming party were resisted with desperation and many were killed on both sides; but the defenders were driven from turret to turret by sheer force of numbers: till at last they had to take refuge in the eastern wing which had not yet been injured.

487. The only way to reach this was by a narrow passage where firearms could not be used; and a furious hand to hand combat was kept up for an hour and a half, while from various standpoints the defenders poured down bullets, stones, and every available missile on the assailants, killing and wounding great numbers.

While this was going on some of the besiegers, by clearing away a heap of rubbish, made their way in by a back passage, so that the garrison found themselves assailed on all sides; whereupon forty of them sallying out, made a desperate rush for the sea, intending to swim to the island. But before they had reached the water they were intercepted and cut down, all but eight who plunged into the sea; and for these the president had provided by stationing a party with boats outside, "who," in Carew's words, "had the killing of them all."

488. This furious struggle had lasted during the whole long summer day, and it was now sunset; the castle was a mass of ruins, and the number of the garrison was greatly reduced. Late as it was the assault was vigorously renewed; and after another hour's fighting the assailants gained all the upper part of the castle; and the Irish, now only seventy-seven, took refuge in the cellars. Then Carew, leaving a strong guard at the entrance, withdrew his men for the night; while those in the castle enjoyed their brief rest as best they could, knowing what was to come with the light of day.

489. On the next morning—the 18th of June—Taylor was in command; for Mac Geoghegan was mortally wounded; and the men resolved to defend themselves to the last, except twenty-three who laid down their arms and surrendered. Carew now directed his cannons on the cellars till he battered them into ruins on the heads of the devoted band; and at length Taylor's men forced him to surrender. When a party of English entered to take the captives, Mac Geoghegan, who was lying on the floor, his life ebbing away, snatched a lighted candle from Taylor's hand, and exerting all his remaining strength, staggered towards some barrels of powder which stood in a corner of the cellar. But one of Carew's officers caught him and held him in his arms, while the others killed him with their swords.

490. On that same day Carew executed fifty-eight of those who had surrendered. He reserved Taylor and fourteen others to tempt them to give information; but as they firmly refused to purchase their lives on such terms, he had them all hanged.

491. It is from Carew himself that this account of the siege is chiefly taken: and he concludes by saying that of the 143 defenders of Dunboy "no one man escaped, but were either slaine, executed, or buried in the ruins; and so obstinate and resolved a defence had not been seene within this kingdom." The powder that was in the vaults was heaped together and ignited; and all that remained of Dunboy was blown into fragments, except

two parallel side walls which still remain.

THE RETREAT OF O'SULLIVAN BEARE (1603)

492. After the capture of Dunboy, Donall O'Sullivan the lord of Beare and Bantry had no home; and finding that he could no longer maintain himself and his followers where he was, he resolved to bid farewell to the land of his inheritance and seek a refuge in Ulster. On the last day of the year 1602 he set out from Glengarriff on his memorable retreat, with 400 fighting men, and 600 women, children, and servants. The march was one unbroken scene of conflict and hardship. They were everywhere confronted or pursued by enemies, who attacked them when they dared; and they suffered continually from fatigue, cold, and hunger.

493. They fled in such haste that they were able to bring with them only one day's provisions, trusting to be able to obtain food as they fared along; for O'Sullivan had plenty of money, which had been sent to him from Spain. But they found the country people too much terrified by Carew's threats to give them help or shelter or to sell them provisions. As they could not buy, they had either to take by force or starve, which explains much of the hostility they encountered; for no man will permit his substance to be taken without resistance. Scarce a day passed without loss: some fell behind or left the ranks overcome with weariness; some sank and died under accumulated hardships; and others were killed in fight.

494. The first day they made their way to Ballyvourney, after a journey of about twenty-four miles over the mountains. Here they rested for the night. On next through Duhallow, till they reached Liscarroll, where John Barry of Buttevant attacked their rear as they crossed the ford, and after an hour's fighting killed four of their men, but lost more than four himself. Skirting the north base of the Ballyhoura Mountains, they encamped one night beside the old hill of Ardpatrick. Their next resting place was the Glen of Aherlow, where among the vast solitudes of the Galtys they could procure no better food than herbs and water: and the night sentries found it hard to perform their duty, oppressed as they were with fatigue and hunger. For the first part of their journey they made tents each evening to sleep in; but they were not able to continue this, so that they had to lie under the open sky, and they suffered bitterly from the extreme cold of the nights.

495. Next northwards from the Galtys across the Golden Vale, over the great plain of Tipperary, fighting their way through enemies almost every hour. While one detachment of the fighting men collected provisions, the others remained with the main body to protect the women and children; and the whole party were preserved from utter destruction only by the strict discipline maintained by the chief.

496. O'Sullivan's wife, who accompanied the party, carried and nursed so far through all her hardships her little boy, a baby two years old; but now she had to part with him. She intrusted him to the care of one of her

faithful dependents, who preserved and reared him up tenderly, and afterwards sent him to Spain to the parents. We are not told how it fared with this lady and some others; but as they did not arrive with the rest at the end of the journey, they must, like many others, have fallen behind during the terrible march, and been cared for, as they are heard of afterwards.

497. The ninth day of their weary journey found them beside the Shannon near Portland in the north of Tipperary; and here they rested for two nights. But their enemies began to close in on them from the Tipperary side, and no time was to be lost; so they prepared to cross the broad river opposite the castle of Kiltaroe or Redwood. Among them was a man, Dermot O'Hoolahan by name, skilled in making curraghs or hide boats. Under his direction they constructed boat-frames of boughs, interwoven with osier twigs in the usual way. They then killed twelve of their horses, and carefully husbanding the flesh for food, they finished their curraghs by covering the skeleton boats with the skins. In these they crossed the river; though at the last moment their rearguard had a sharp conflict with the sheriff of Tipperary, Donogh Mac Egan the owner of Redwood Castle, who with his party came up, and in spite of O'Sullivan's earnest expostulations, attacked them, and attempted to throw some of the women and children into the river. But O'Sullivan turned on him, and killed himself and many of his men.

498. Nothing better awaited them on the other side of the Shannon. Pushing on northwards through O'Kelly's country, they had to defend themselves in skirmish after skirmish. As most of the horses had by this time quite broken down, O'Sullivan had to abandon the wounded to their certain fate; and their despairing cries rang painfully in the ears of the flying multitude. Sometimes when they came near a village, a party was despatched for provisions, who entered the houses and seized everything in the shape of food they could lay hands on, satisfying their own hunger while they searched, and bringing all they could gather to their starving companions.

499. At Aughrim they were confronted by captain Henry Malbie with a force much more numerous than their own. O'Sullivan, addressing his famished and desperate little band of fighting men in a few encouraging words, placed them so that they were protected on all sides except the front, where the assailants had to advance on foot through a soft boggy pass. Malbie, despising the fugitives, sprang forward at the head of his followers, but fell dead at the first onset. On rushed O'Sullivan and his men: it must be either victory or destruction; and after a determined and bitter fight, they scattered their assailants, and freed themselves from that great and pressing danger.

500. Onwards over Slieve Mary near Castlekelly, and through the

territory of Mac David Burke, where the people, headed by Mac David himself, harassed them all day long to prevent them from obtaining provisions. Near Ballinlough in the west of Roscommon they concealed themselves in a thick wood, intending to pass the night there. But they got no rest: for a friendly messenger came to warn them that Mac David and his people were preparing to surround them in the morning and slay them all. So they resumed their march and toiled on wearily through the night in a tempest of sleet, splashing their way through melting snow, and in the morning found themselves pursued by Mac David, who however was cowed by their determined look, and did not dare to come to close quarters.

501. Arriving at another solitary wood, they found the people friendly; and they lighted fires and refreshed themselves. They next crossed the Curlieu Hills southwards to Knockvicar, beside the river Boyle where it enters Lough Key, and here they took some rest. For days past they had undergone unspeakable sufferings. Avoiding the open roads, they had to cross the country by rugged, rocky, and unfrequented ways, walking all the time, for horses could not be used. The weather was inclement, snow falling heavily, so that they had sometimes to make their way through deep drifts; and many of those who continued able to walk had to carry some of their companions who were overcome by fatigue and sickness.

502. Their hope all through had been to reach the territory of O'Ruarc of Brefney; and next morning when the sun rose over Knockvicar, their guide pointed out to them, a few miles off, the towers of O'Ruarc's residence, Leitrim Castle. At eleven o'clock the same day they entered the hospitable mansion, where a kind welcome awaited them.

They had set out from Glengarriff a fortnight before, one thousand in number; and that morning only thirty-five entered O'Rourke's castle: eighteen armed men, sixteen servants, and one woman, the wife of the chief's uncle, Dermot O'Sullivan. A few others afterwards arrived in twos and threes; all the rest had either perished I or dropped behind from fatigue, sickness, or wounds.

503. How it fared with South Munster after the capture of Dunboy may be told in a few words.

Though the province was now quiet enough, yet several of the rebels were still at large, and there were rumours of other intended risings. Against these dangers Carew took precautions of a very decided character; he had the country turned into a desert:—"Heereupon "—says Carew — "Sir Charles Wilmot with the English regiments overran all Beare and Bantry, destroying all that they could find meet for the reliefe of men, so as that country was wholly wasted. . . . The president therefore [i.e. Carew himself], as well to debarre those straglers from releefe as to prevent all means of succours to Osulevan if hee should returne with new forces, caused all the county of Kerry and Desmond, Beare, Bantry, and Carbery to be left absolutely wasted, constraying all the Inhabitants thereof to withdraw their Cattle into the East and Northern parts of the County of Corke."

THE FLIGHT OF THE EARLS (1602-1608)

504. From the autumn of 1600 to the end of 1602, the work of destroying crops, cattle, and homesteads was busily carried on by Mountjoy and Carew, and by the governors of the garrisons, who wasted everything and made deserts for miles round the towns where they were stationed. We have already seen how thoroughly this was done in Munster and Leinster: it was now the turn of Ulster. In June 1602 Mountjoy himself marched north to prosecute the rebels, and remained in Ulster daring the autumn and winter, traversing the country in all directions, and destroying the poor people's means of subsistence.

505. And now the famine so deliberately planned swept through the whole country, and Ulster was, if possible, in a worse condition than Munster. For the ghastly results of the deputy's cruel policy we have his own testimony, as well as that of his secretary the historian Moryson. Mountjoy writes:—"We have seen no one man in all Tyrone of late but dead carcases merely hunger starved, of which we found divers as we passed. Between Tullaghoge and Toome [seventeen miles] there lay unburied 1,000 dead, and since our first drawing this year to Blackwater there were about 3,000 starved in Tyrone." But this did not satisfy him; for soon after he says:—"To-morrow I am going into the field, as near as I can utterly to waste the county Tyrone."

Next hear Moryson. "Now because I have often made mention formerly of our destroying the rebels' corn, and using all means to famish them, let me by one or two examples show the miserable estate to which the rebels were thereby brought." He then gives some hideous details, which show, if indeed showing were needed, that the women and children were famished as well as the actual rebels. And he goes on to say:—"And no spectacle was more frequent in the ditches of towns than to see multitudes of these poor people dead with their mouths all coloured green by eating nettles, docks, and all things they could rend up above ground."

506. O'Neill was not able to make any headway against Mountjoy and Docwra, both of whom continued to plant garrisons all through the province. With the few followers that remained to him, he retired into impenetrable fastnesses; and far from taking active measures, he had quite enough to do to preserve himself and his party from utter destruction. But he refused to submit, still clinging to the hope of help from abroad.

507. The news of the death of Red Hugh O'Donnell crushed the last hopes of the chiefs; and Rory O'Donnell and O'Conor Sligo submitted in December, and were gladly and favourably received. O'Neill himself, even in his fallen state, was still greatly dreaded; for the government were now,

as they had been for years, haunted by the apprehension of another and more powerful armament from Spain. At length Mountjoy, authorised by the queen, sent Sir Garrett Moore, O'Neill's old friend, to offer him life, liberty, and pardon, with title and territory.

508. While the negotiations were going on, Mountjoy received private intelligence that the queen had died on the 24th March 1603. Keeping the news strictly secret, he hurried on the arrangements. On the 30th of March at Mellifont near Drogheda the chief made his submission to the deputy.

509. James I. of England, who had been James VI. of Scotland, was the first English king who was universally acknowledged by the Irish as their lawful sovereign; and they accepted him partly because he was descended in one line from their own ancient Milesian kings, and partly because they believed that though outwardly a Protestant he was at heart a Catholic.

510. Soon after the submission of O'Neill and O'Donnell they both went to England with Mountjoy. The king received them kindly and graciously; confirmed O'Neill in the title of earl of Tyrone; made Rory O'Donnell earl of Tirconnell; and restored both to most of their possessions and privileges.

511. There was now a very general belief in Ireland that the Catholic religion would be restored, as it was on the accession of Mary: and the citizens of some of the southern cities took back their churches and had Mass openly celebrated. But Mountjoy marched south and promptly stopped the movement, restoring the churches to the ministers of the Established Church.

512. In 1603 and 1604. English law was established in Tyrone and Tirconnell; Tanistry and Gavelkind were abolished; and the inheritance of land all through Ireland was made subject to English law.

513. Notwithstanding that the earl of Tyrone had been received so graciously by the king, and was now settled down quietly as an English subject, yet he was looked upon with suspicion and hatred by the officials and adventurers, who could not endure to see him restored to rank and favour. Those who had looked forward to the forfeiture of his estates and to the confiscation of Ulster were bitterly disappointed when they found themselves baulked of their expected prey, and they determined to bring about his ruin. He was now constantly subjected to annoyance and humiliation, and beset with spies who reported the most trivial incidents of his everyday life. At the same time the earl of Tirconnell was persecuted almost as systematically.

514. At last matters reached a crisis. In 1607 a false report of a conspiracy for another rebellion was concocted and spread by Christopher St. Laurence baron of Howth, a man wholly devoid of principle, who had served against the Irish under lord Mountjoy: but probably he was in collusion with others.

The whole story of the conspiracy was an invention without the least foundation; yet rambling and absurd as St. Laurence's statement was it led to very important consequences; for in a short time the whole country was startled by the news that the two earls of Tyrone and Tirconnell had secretly fled from Ireland.

515. Tyrone had been on a visit at Slane with the deputy Chichester when he heard of the matter; and at the same time both he and Tirconnell were assured that it was intended to arrest them. Keeping his mind to himself he took leave of the deputy and went to Sir Garrett Moore of Mellifont, where he remained for a few days. On a Sunday morning he and his attendants took horse for Dundalk. He knew that he was bidding his old friend farewell for the last time; and Sir Garrett, who suspected nothing, was surprised to observe that he was unusually moved, blessing each member of the household individually, and weeping bitterly at parting. They rode on in haste till they reached Rathmullan on the western shore of Lough Swilly, where a ship that had been purchased by O'Rourke awaited them. Here he was joined by the earl of Tirconnell and his family.

516. The total number of exiles taking ship was about one hundred. At midnight on the 14th of September 1607 they embarked, and bidding farewell for ever to their native country, they made for the open sea. After a long, stormy, and perilous voyage, they landed in France, where they were received with great distinction by all, from the king downwards. From France the earls and their families proceeded by leisurely stages to Rome, where they took up their residence, being allowed ample pensions by the Pope and the King of Spain. O'Donnell died in the following year, 1608; and O'Neill, aged, blind, and worn by misfortune and disappointment, died in 1616. His son Henry was mysteriously murdered in Brussels in 1617; at whose death that branch of the family became extinct.

517. The profound quiet that followed the rebellion was suddenly broken by the hasty and reckless rising of Sir Cahir O'Doherty. This chief, then only twenty-one years of age, had hitherto been altogether on the side of the English; and his rebellion was a mere outburst of private revenge, having nothing noble or patriotic about it.

518. On one occasion, in 1608, he had an altercation with Sir George Paulett governor of Derry, who being a man of ill-temper, struck him in the face. O'Doherty, restraining himself for the time, retired and concerted his measures for vengeance; and he was joined by Niall Garve O'Donnell. He invited his friend Captain Harte the governor of Culmore fort and his wife to dinner. After dinner the governor was treacherously seized by O'Doherty's orders, and threatened with instant death if he did not surrender the fort. Harte firmly refused; but his wife, in her terror and despair, went to the fort and prevailed on the guards to open the gates. O'Doherty and his men rushed in and immediately took possession: and

having supplied himself with artillery and ammunition from the fort, he marched on Derry that same night. He took it by surprise, slew Paulett, slaughtered the garrison, and sacked and burned the town. He was joined by several other chiefs, and held out from May to July 1608, when he was shot dead near Kilmacrenan in a skirmish with marshal Wingfield. The rising then collapsed as suddenly as it had begun. Some of those implicated were executed, and others were sent to the Tower of London, among whom were Niall Garve O'Donnell and his son, who were kept there in confinement for the rest of their days.

THE PLANTATION OF ULSTER (1605-1625)

519. We shall now go back a few years. The Catholics still clung to the hope that their religion would be restored. But they found their mistake when King James, in 1605, caused the two penal Acts of supremacy and uniformity to be revived.

520. By the Act of supremacy no Catholic, without taking the oath of supremacy, could hold any office under government, could practise as a lawyer, act as a magistrate, be appointed judge, or take possession of an estate to be held from the king.

By the Act of uniformity any Catholic might be brought up and fined if he absented himself from Protestant worship on a Sunday; and many of the leading citizens of Dublin were at this time actually fined or imprisoned.

The Roman Catholics who refused to attend Protestant worship were called "Recusants."

521. But except in or near Dublin, it was impossible to carry out these laws, for the people were nearly all Catholics. And even in Dublin the law, for the same reason, could not be enforced to any extent; and numbers of Catholic magistrates, lawyers, and government officers, were permitted to discharge their duties unmolested.

522. Though the two earls of Tyrone and Tirconnell had committed no treasonable or unlawful act, yet nearly all the fertile land of six counties—Donegal, Derry, Tyrone, Armagh, Fermanagh, and Cavan—amounting to 511,465* acres—was confiscated to the crown and given to settlers: Sir Arthur Chichester had the management of this Plantation, which was commenced in 1608.

523. The "lots" were of three sizes:—2,000, 1,500, and 1,000 acres. The planters were of three classes:—First: English and Scotch undertakers, who got the 2,000-acre lots, and who were required to people them with English and Scotch tenants—no Irish—and to build a castle and a bawn (a large walled enclosure near the castle). Second: "servitors," i.e. those who had served the crown in Ireland—all to be Protestants. These got the 1,500-acre lots; they might take English, Scotch, or Irish tenants, all to be Protestants; and they should build a strong house and a bawn. The 1,000-acre lots might be taken by English, Scotch, or Irish planters, who might be either

Protestants or Catholics, and the Catholics were not required to take the oath of supremacy.

524. Vast tracts were given to London companies of merchants or tradesmen, and to certain high officials. Chichester had for his share the whole of Innishowen, Sir Cahir O'Doherty's territory. Large tracts were granted for religious and educational purposes, all Protestant: Trinity College, Dublin, got 9,600 acres.

525. Of the whole body of old Irish proprietors, only 286 were provided for: these got 58,000 acres—about one-ninth of the escheated lands. All the rest of the natives were ordered "to depart with their goods and chattels at or before the first of May next [1609] into what other part of the realm they pleased." But the greater number, instead of migrating to a distance, clung to their native place, and betook them to the hills, glens, and bogs, where they eked out a scanty subsistence, with bitter memories in their hearts.

526. This turned out by far the most successful of all the plantations; and in a short time vast numbers of English Protestants and Scotch Presbyterians were settled on the rich lowland farms all over the confiscated counties.

527. To help to pay the expenses of this plantation, the king, in 1611, created the order of "baronets"; who were to bear on their coat of arms the "bloody hand" of the O'Neills. Each new baronet had to pay for the maintenance of thirty soldiers for three years at 8d. a day each (about £1,095). The title is hereditary.

528. The lord deputy now resolved to summon a parliament, the first for many years: and in order to enable him to pass measures pleasing to the king, he took steps to have a Protestant majority, by creating forty spurious "boroughs," nearly all among the settlers of Ulster; each returning two Members. This parliament, which met in 1613, consisted of 232 members of the house of commons, of whom less than half were Catholic "recusants"; and fifty lords, of whom twenty-five were Protestant bishops, with several others lay Protestants.

529. A violent scene occurred on the election of a speaker the Catholics proposing Sir John Everard, and the Protestants Sir John Davies; and others equally violent followed; so that deputy Chichester, finding it impossible to carry on business, prorogued parliament.

530. On the expostulation of the Catholics some concessions were made; and when parliament next assembled business was carried on quietly. Large sums were voted for the king, who was always in want of money: and some old penal statutes against natives of Irish blood were repealed.

531. English law was extended to the whole of Ireland, a concession the Irish had often previously asked for in vain, and for which King James I. should get full credit. An act was passed for the attainder of the earls of Tyrone and Tirconnell, though they had committed no offence to warrant

such a proceeding. This parliament was disolved in 1615.

532. Chichester was succeeded in 1616 by Oliver St. John, who enforced all the penal statutes against Catholics. He deprived Waterford of its charter, because the corporation refused the oath of supremacy. But his proceedings caused such dangerous commotion that the king removed him, and in 1622 appointed lord Falkland deputy in his place.

533. About this time King James, bent on following up the plantations, appointed a commission of inquiry into titles. The country swarmed with persons called "discoverers" who made their living by finding flaws, of pretended flaws, in titles; these either got the estates themselves, or shared with the king the increase of rent the proprietors had to pay to buy themselves off. They unsettled titles all over Leinster: and a great part of the province was given to English undertakers, the owners being turned off; and those who were allowed to remain had to pay a largely increased rent. These proceedings resulted in several other minor plantations in different parts of the country.

534. The discoverers extended their evil practices into Connaught also; but here matters were delayed till next reign. Iniquitous law proceedings unsettled everything; the whole country was in a state of uncertainty; and no man was sure of his property for a day.

* About three quarters of a million English acres. There was bog and waste land besides: the total area of these six counties is about 3 ¾ millions of English acres; so that the waste land was at that time four times the extent of the arable land.

THE "GRACES" (1625-1641)

535. In the midst of all this inquietude King James I. died in 1625, and was succeeded by his son Charles I. This king was in perpetual straits for money: and the Catholics hoped that by granting him subsidies he would have the penal laws relaxed. The Protestants also had their troubles, for many of them—as well as the Catholics —were threatened with the loss of their estates through the knaveries of the discoverers.

536. Accordingly the Irish gentry, Catholic and Protestant, encouraged by Falkland, offered to pay £120,000 in instalments to the king, who agreed to grant certain concessions or "graces" as they were called.

537. There were altogether fifty-one graces, of which the most important were:—(1) Defects of title were not to be searched for farther back than sixty years; so that those who could prove sixty years title without a flaw were to be secure. Previous to this the discoverers had often gone back to the time of Henry II. This grace affected Protestants as well as Catholics. (2) Recusants were to be required to take an oath of allegiance only (which any subject might take): not an oath of supremacy (which no Catholic could take). (3) The people of Connaught to have their titles confirmed: and (4) the exactions and oppressions of the soldiery on the people, which

had by this time grown intolerable, to be restrained.

538. The graces could not be granted without the confirmation of the Irish parliament. But though the people continued to pay the instalments, the king and Falkland dishonestly evaded the summoning of parliament; and the graces remained unconfirmed. Meantime the Catholics were allowed some toleration for the time; and never suspecting any duplicity, they hoped that the next parliament would make matters right.

539. But the Dublin council were so provoked to see the Catholics openly practising their religion, and building churches and schools, that they pressed lord Falkland to put a stop to it. So Falkland issued a proclamation forbidding such practices, which ended in nothing. For he was a mild tolerant sort of man who did not wish to persecute any one; and though the proclamation was there, he did not attempt to enforce it: so that things went on the same as before. At last the king had to recall him in 1629: and then the government was committed to the hands of viscount Ely, lord chancellor, and Richard Boyle earl of Cork, lord high treasurer, a man who had made himself rich and great by cunning and fraud: these held office for four years.

540. This was an evil change for the Catholics; for the two new justices proceeded to enforce the laws, especially that which compelled attendance at Protestant worship. By their orders & file of soldiers entered a chapel where some Carmelites were celebrating Mass, and carried off the priest in his vestments, who however was immediately rescued by the congregation. This so incensed the authorities, that they seized sixteen Catholic religious houses in Dublin and closed them up; and suppressed the Catholic college. But the king at last bethought him that he could get more money by milder treatment, and ordered the justices to desist.

541. In 1688 the king sent over as deputy, Lord Wentworth, afterwards the earl of Strafford, the most despotic ruler the Irish had yet experienced. He adopted a new course, for he cared nothing about any man's religion. His two main objects were to carry out the behests of the king and to raise money for him; which he pursued through right and wrong, and trampled on all that crossed him, Protestants and Catholics alike. The recusants were induced to give him £20,000 for the king, on promise that the penal statutes against them should not be enforced.

542. The Irish landholders, still feeling insecure, induced the deputy to summon a parliament, with the object of having the graces confirmed; paying at the same time another year's subsidy. Parliament met in 1634 and passed subsidies amounting to £240,000; but Wentworth, partly by bullying, and partly by trickery, succeeded in evading the graces.

543. The motives of all this soon appeared; for in 1635, immediately after the dissolution, he proceeded to break the titles all over Connaught, on the plea that they had not been enrolled in the time of Elizabeth when

the estates had been re-granted; so that he confiscated nearly the whole province.

544. There was a regular trial for each case; and he obtained verdicts in all, for the good reason that he threatened, punished, and imprisoned sheriffs, juries, and lawyers who thwarted him—Catholics and Protestants without distinction. This caused a great outcry; but he persisted in his reckless course, though admonished by his friends, who saw dark clouds ahead. There was no use in appealing against this intolerable tyranny; for his master the king, who was pursuing much the same course in England, supported him in everything.

545. By similar dishonest means he confiscated the whole of Clare and a large part of Tipperary. Over all those vast tracts, in Connaught and Munster, plantation went on for years; and the only thing that prevented a complete clearing out of the inhabitants was want of a sufficient number of settlers. One main object he accomplished all through; for out of every transaction he made money for the king.

546. At this time there was a flourishing Irish trade in wool and woollen cloths; but he adopted measures that almost destroyed it, lest it should interfere with the woollen trade of England. On the other hand he took means—purchasing seed and bringing skilled workmen from France —to create a linen trade, which could do no harm in England; and he thus laid the foundation of what has turned out a great and flourishing industry in Ulster.

547. Meantime the king was getting more deeply into trouble in England, and was in sore need of money. So Wentworth once more summoned parliament in 1639, and heading the subscription list himself with £20,000, he succeeded in having a large sum voted.

548. He was now, 1640, made earl of Strafford; and he raised an army of 9,000 men in Ireland, nearly all Catholics, who were well drilled and well armed, intending them to be employed in the service of the king. But his career was drawing to a close. He was recalled in 1640 to take command against the Scotch covenanters. Soon afterwards he was impeached by the English House of Commons; some of the most damaging charges against him coming from Ireland: and in May 1641 he was beheaded on Tower Hill.

THE REBELLION OF 1641 (1641-1642)

549. This great rebellion was brought about by the measures taken to extirpate the Catholic religion; by the plantations of Chichester and Strafford; and by the non-confirmation of the graces, which made the people despair of redress. There were complaints from every side about religious hardships. As to the plantations, no one could tell where they might stop; and there was a widespread fear that the people of the whole country might be cleared off to make place for new settlers. Besides all

this, those who had been dispossessed longed for the first opportunity to fall on the settlers and regain their homes and farms.

550. Some of the Irish gentry held meetings to force a redress of these hardships by insurrection. The leading spirit was Roger or Rory O'Moore of Leix, a man of unblemished character; and among the others were Sir Phelim O'Neill of the family of Tyrone and his brother Turlogh, lord Maguire of Fermanagh and his brother Rory, Magennis, O'Reilly, and some of the MacMahons.

551. They hoped for help from abroad; for many of their banished kindred had by this time risen to positions of great influence in France, Spain, and the Netherlands. And they sent for Owen Roe O'Neill, a soldier who had greatly distinguished himself in the service of Spain, nephew of the great Hugh O'Neill, Earl of Tyrone, inviting him home to lead the insurgent army. He replied urging an immediate rising and holding out hopes of French help from cardinal Richelieu.

552. The 23rd of October 1641 was the day fixed on for a simultaneous rising. Dublin Castle with its large store of arms, and many of the fortresses and garrisons all over the country were to be seized, and the arms taken. Instructions were given to make the gentry prisoners, but to kill no one except in open conflict; and in general to have as little bloodshed as possible. The Ulster settlers from Scotland, being regarded as kinsmen, were not to be molested.

553. On the evening of the 22nd of October, when the preparations had been completed in Dublin, a man named Owen O'Connolly, to whom MacMahon had confided the secret, went straight to Sir William Parsons one of the lords justices, and told him of the plot. Parsons at first gave no heed to the story, for he perceived that O'Connolly was half drunk. But on consultation with his colleague Sir John Borlase, they arrested Maguire and MacMahon on the morning of the 23rd: these were subsequently tried in London and hanged. Rory O'Moore and some others then in Dublin escaped. Instant measures were taken to put the city in a state of defence.

554. But though Dublin was saved, the rising broke out on the 23rd all through the north. Sir Phelim O'Neill, by a treacherous stratagem, obtained possession of Charlemont fort. The rebels gained possession of Newry, Dungannon, Castleblayney, and many smaller stations. Sir Phelim exhibited a forged commission, giving him authority, which he alleged he had received from King Charles, to which was attached the great seal he had found in one of the castles.

555. At the end of a week nearly all Ulster was in the hands of the rebels, and Sir Phelim had an army of 30,000, armed with knives, pitchforks, scythes, and every weapon they could lay hands on. During the first week of the rising the original intention was carried out, and there was hardly any bloodshed. But most of the people who rose up were persons who had

been deprived of their lands, and after a time they broke loose from all discipline and wreaked their vengeance without restraint and without mercy on the settlers. The country farm houses all over the settlements were attacked by detached parties. Multitudes were stripped and turned out half naked from house and home—old and young, men, women, and children; and hundreds, vainly trying to make their way to Dublin or others of the Government stations, perished by the wayside, of exposure, hardship, and hunger.

But there was even worse: for numbers were murdered, often with great cruelty. Some of these excesses were carried out by the orders of O'Neill himself; but the greatest number were the acts of irresponsible persons wreaking vengeance for their own private wrongs.

556. The numbers of victims have been wildly exaggerated: but Dr. Warner, an English writer, a Protestant clergyman, who made every effort to come at the truth, believes that in the first two years of the rebellion, 4,000 were murdered, and that 8,000 died of ill usage and exposure. But even this is probably in excess.

557. There were wholesale murders also on the other side. Some of the refugees who had fled to Carrickfergus, burning with their own wrongs, sallied out in November with the Scottish garrison, and slaughtered a number of harmless people in Island Magee, who had taken no part in any disturbance.

The two lords justices sent parties of military from Dublin through the country all round, who slaughtered all the people they met, whether engaged in rebellion or not. Their general, Sir Charles Coote, committed horrible cruelties, especially in Wicklow.

558. Many Protestants were protected by individual Catholics. The priests exerted themselves, often at the risk of their own lives, sometimes hiding the poor fugitives under the very altar cloths. The Protestant bishop, Dr. Bedell, who was very popular, was not molested; and numbers of fugitive settlers had a safe asylum in his house. The people at last confined him in Cloghoughter Castle merely to protect him; and on his death in February 1642, they attended his funeral in crowds with great expressions of regret.

559. The sanguinary episode of this memorable year in Ulster reminds us of what took place on a much larger scale forty years before in the same province. One was an unpremeditated outburst of merciless popular rage: the other the slower and surer destruction of much larger numbers by the carefully planned arrangements of Mountjoy.

560. Towards the end of 1641, the old Anglo-Irish nobility of the Pale, who were all Catholics and all loyal, hearing of some threats uttered by Sir Charles Coote to extirpate the whole Catholic population, and finding themselves slighted and insulted by the lords justices on account of their

religion, and their houses burned by Coote, combined for their own protection; and soon all the Pale was in revolt. In a short time the rebellion extended through all Ireland.

At this time King Charles and his parliament were in open hostility in England: and the Puritans and the Scotch Presbyterians were amongst the most successful of his opponents.

561. At the opening of 1642 we find in the distracted country four distinct parties, each with an army:—The old Irish, who aimed at complete separation from England; the old Anglo-Irish Catholics, who wanted religious and civil liberty, but not separation; the Puritans under general Munro, the most determined of the king's enemies, including the Scots of Ulster; and lastly the Protestant loyalist party in the Pale, who held Dublin.

The native Irish party, led by Rory O'Moore, were the special opponents of the Puritans.

562. The war went on during the early part of this year, 1642, with varying fortunes sometimes the rebels victorious, sometimes the Government forces. In Ulster the rebels were losing ground, and losing heart, chiefly through the incompetency of Sir Phelim O'Neill. The Scottish army there soon amounted to 20,000 men under Munro, who acted and fought as it were for themselves, for they were equally opposed to both the king and the Catholics of both sections.

563. Owen Roe O'Neill arrived in Ireland in July 1642, with a single ship and a hundred officers, and taking command in place of Sir Phelim, immediately set about organising the scattered Irish forces. He soon changed the whole aspect of affairs. He strongly denounced the past cruelties, and severely punished some of the worst offenders. Soon afterwards another important leader landed to join the confederates, colonel Preston, brother of lord Gormanstown, with 500 officers and some stores.

THE CONFEDERATION OF KILKENNY (1642-1649)

564. Hitherto the old Irish and the old Anglo-Irish Catholics had acted without concert. But the Catholic clergy exerted themselves to bring about union; and on the 24th of October 1642 a general assembly or parliament—delegates of the most distinguished persons from both sides—met in Kilkenny: this is known as the "Confederation of Kilkenny." They earnestly repudiated the appellation of rebels, maintaining that they were loyal subjects, standing up for the king, who they said would do them justice if he were not restrained by the Puritans.

565. There were eleven bishops, fourteen lords, and 226 commoners. The assembly took upon themselves for the time the government of the country—or of that part of it outside the influence of Ormond—and appointed generals over the army: O'Neill for Ulster and Preston for Leinster. To manage affairs with greater facility they elected from their

number a "Supreme council." And they issued a decree for raising money and for levying men, who were to be drilled by the officers that had come with Preston and O'Neill.

566. In 1643 the king endeavoured to come to terms with the Confederates, hoping to use them against his own refractory parliament: but the justices Borlase and Parsons, who though nominally in the king's service, really sympathised with the parliament, threw obstacles in the way of union; and the forces of the confederates and those of the king continued in open hostility.

567. Preston was at first successful in Leinster, but was badly defeated in March 1643 at Ross in Wexford, by the marquis of Ormond. In Ulster O'Neill, held his ground with difficulty, and was once defeated by one of Monro's generals. But in several other actions he was victorious.

568. Meantime in spite of the opposition of the lords justices, negotiations went on between the king and the confederates: in September 1643, a cessation of arms for one year was arranged; and the confederates agreed to send the king a gift of £30,000. But the English parliament directed the Puritan party in Ulster to pay no attention to the truce.

569. The king had removed Borlase from his post, and in 1644 appointed the marquess of Ormond lord lieutenant. But this did not mend matters; for Ormond played a double part. Pretending to act for the king, he really worked in the interest of the parliament, and he prevented any final peace between the king and the confederates.

570. The king, finding he could do nothing through Ormond, sent over the earl of Glamorgan in 1645, who made a secret treaty with the confederates. They were to give the king men and money; he was to grant full toleration for religion. But when, a little afterwards, the parliament accidentally discovered this, King Charles, with his usual duplicity, disavowed it.

571. In this same year, 1645, the Pope sent to the confederates as Nuncio, Baptist Rinuccini archbishop of Fermo, who brought them a supply of money and arms. His object in coming was three-fold:—1. To propagate the Catholic religion: 2. To unite the old Irish and the Anglo-Irish Catholics, between whom there was still much jealousy: 3. To sustain the king against the parliament.

572. Matters were at this time in a bad way. The English parliament, contending successfully against the king, determined to put down the Catholics, and would have no peace and no dealings with the confederates. Ormond, in the service of his majesty, really sympathised with parliament. The feeble and double-faced king was trying to deceive both the Catholics and the parliament.

573. There was disunion in the confederation. The Anglo-Irish representatives would deal with Ormond (as representing the king) for

peace on the basis of a free exercise of their religion: the old Irish party, with whom was Rinuccini, would have more than that—National independence and the re-establishment of the Catholic church in all its former grandeur.

574. The Anglo-Irish party prevailed in the assembly, and in March 1646 a treaty was signed between the confederates and Ormond who professed to act for the king; in which the only concession to the Catholics was exemption from the oath of supremacy. This gave great discontent to the Nuncio and to the old Irish all over the country.

575. The disunion among the Catholics extended to the army. There was bitter rivalry between Owen Roe who was a great general, and Preston who was an indifferent one. The Anglo-Irish party was on the side of Preston, and refused support to Owen Roe; and Monro continued to plunder and devastate Ulster without opposition.

576. At length O'Neill with great effort collected an army of 5,000 foot and 500 horse; and marching north inflicted a crushing defeat on Monro and his more numerous army at Benburb on the Blackwater: an exploit quite as brilliant as that of his uncle Hugh at the Yellow Ford. This restored the influence of the old Irish party—the "Nuncionists," as they were called.

577. There was, however, increasing distrust between O'Neill and Preston, but for which they could easily have taken Dublin from Ormond. At length in July 1647 Ormond delivered up Dublin to the parliamentarians and went through England to France, and colonel Michael Jones, a parliamentary officer, became its governor.

578. The confederates now met with serious disasters. In August 1647 colonel Jones defeated Preston at Dungan Hill near Summerhill in Meath, and killed more than 5,000 of his men. And in November of the same year lord Inchiquin (formerly a royalist, now on the side of Parliament), known as "Murrogh the Burner" from his merciless ravages in Munster, inflicted quite as bad a defeat on the confederate army at Knocknanoss near Mallow, through the incompetency of their commander lord Taaffe.

579. In May 1648 Preston, against the wishes of the Nuncio and his party, signed a truce with Inchiquin in which it was agreed that the Catholics should not be molested in the practice of their religion. Quarrels and discussions and plots went on, till at length Ormond returned in 1648; and in January 1649 peace was finally signed between him and the confederation, on the main condition that the penal laws should be repealed: which ended a war that had lasted for seven years. About a fortnight after the conclusion of peace, King Charles was beheaded in England.

CROMWELL (1642-1649)

580. In England the parliament had triumphed. The death of the king

caused somewhat of a counter-movement in Ireland; and the royalist cause was now—1649—sustained by the confederates, with Ormond the lord lieutenant, and Inchiquin—now again turned royalist—at their head, and by the Scots of Ulster. They proclaimed the Prince of Wales king as Charles II.; and they were well pleased when, in February 1649, Prince Rupert on their side entered the harbour of Kinsale with sixteen frigates.

581. Rinuccini, seeing his mission a failure, returned to Rome in February 1649. O'Neill, the only great soldier now in Ireland, was at the head of a small army of old Irish; but the other confederate leaders kept him in the background through jealousy.

582. On the side of the parliament Jones still held Dublin, and Sir Charles Coote Derry. Inchiquin took from them Drogheda, Dundalk, Newry, and Trim. Ormond besieged Dublin, first encamping at Finglas and afterwards at Rathmines. He sent major-general Purcell on 25th of July to fortify the old castle of Bagot Rath near Rathmines. But colonel Jones sallied forth in the night and surprised not only Purcell but Ormond himself, and utterly routed the whole army (2nd of August 1649). This great disaster was caused by the bad generalship of Ormond.

583. Oliver Cromwell was appointed by Parliament lord lieutenant and commander of the forces in Ireland, and landed at Dublin 14th August, 1649, with 9,000 foot, 4,000 horse, military stores, and £20,000 in money, accompanied by his son-in-law, Ireton, as second in command. He issued a proclamation against plunder, ordering that all supplies taken from the natives should be paid for.

584. He first proceeded against Drogheda. It had been garrisoned by Ormond with 8,000 troops, chiefly English, under Sir Arthur Ashton. Cromwell began by battering down the steeple of St. Mary's church. Next day, the 10th September 1649, the cannonade continued, till towards evening two breaches were made. Two desperate attempts to enter were repulsed; but the third succeeded; and immediately, on Cromwell's order, the whole garrison, including the commander Sir Arthur Ashton, with many friars and townspeople, were massacred.

After this, Trim, Dundalk, Carlingford, Newry, and several other places in the North surrendered.

585. Cromwell returned to Dublin, and marching south, appeared before Wexford. It was well fortified and garrisoned with 3,000 men, under the command of David Sinnott. Cromwell began his cannonade on the 11th of October, and when some breaches had been made, Sinnott asked for a parley.

But meantime the commander of the strong castle just outside the walls treacherously delivered it up to Cromwell's troops. This enabled a party of the besiegers to get into the town and open the gates. The garrison retreated to the market place, where they found the townspeople congregated. Here they defended themselves in desperation for an hour, but were overpowered by numbers; and Cromwell's soldiers under his orders killed garrison and townspeople without distinction to the number of 2,000 (11th of October 1649).

586. The fate of Drogheda and Wexford struck the Irish with terror; and many towns now yielded on mere summons. New Ross was surrendered by Lord Taaffe; but Ireton failed in his attempt to take Duncannon. Cork, Youghal, Kinsale, and some other southern places were given up by their garrisons. Having failed to take Waterford, Cromwell marched to Dungarvan, which at once surrendered; after which he rested his troops for a month in mid-winter at Youghal.

587. At the end of January 1650 he set out to traverse Munster. Most towns he came to were given up; and where there was serious resistance he usually executed the garrison. Kilkenny, where the plague was raging, was yielded in March.

588. Clonmel was commanded by Hugh O'Neill, Owen Roe's cousin— Owen himself having died a few months before—and here, in the month of May, Cromwell met with the most determined resistance he had yet experienced, losing 2,500 of his men in the attack. But O'Neill having exhausted his ammunition, quietly withdrew during the night with his men to Waterford unknown to Cromwell; and the town surrendered on favourable terms.

589. In the North, Coote and Venables were almost equally successful, and captured town after town; and by this time the Parliamentarians had possession of the greater number of the fortresses of both North and South.

590. After the surrender of Clonmel, Cromwell, seeing the country virtually subdued, sailed for England on the 29th May 1650, leaving Ireton to finish the war. In August Preston surrendered Waterford.

591. While the confederates were loyally fighting for the young King Charles, who was at this time in Scotland, he, in order to gain the favour of the Scots, repudiated any agreement with the Irish, and declared himself against allowing them liberty to practise their religion.

592. The Irish distrusted both Ormond and Inchiquin, both of whom had mismanaged the war, and who were suspected of intriguing with the parliament; and Ormond, finding he had lost the confidence of the Catholics, sailed from Galway for St. Malo in December, leaving lord Clanrickard as his deputy.

593. Limerick, the most important place in possession of the royalists, was next to be attacked. It was commanded by Hugh O'Neill, the defender of Clonmel. By forcing the passage of the Shannon at O'Brien's Bridge, Ireton got at the Clare side of the city, which was now invested on both sides. Meantime Lord Muskerry, coming from the south to its relief, was defeated by Lord Broghill, and his troops scattered.

594. O'Neill defended the city with great bravery; but there was disunion, and he was not supported by the magistrates; and the plague was raging among the citizens. At length colonel Fennell betrayed his trust by opening the gates to Ireton, who took possession on the 27th of October 1651. The garrison of 2,500 laid down their arms and were allowed to march away unmolested.

Ireton caused several of the prominent defenders to be executed, among them Dr. O'Brien, Bishop of Emly; but he was himself killed by the plague within the same month. The traitor Fennell was hanged with the others, though for a different reason.

595. After Ireton's death, lieutenant-general Edmund Ludlow taking command, marched to the aid of Coote at Galway, which surrendered on the 12th May 1652, after a siege of nine months. The capture of a few detached castles completed the conquest of Ireland by the Parliamentarians.

596. Charles Fleetwood, Cromwell's son-in-law (he had married Ireton's widow) took command of the army in succession to Ludlow, and was afterwards appointed lord deputy. Under his direction a High Court of Justice was instituted in October 1652, to punish those who had been concerned in the rising of 1641; about 200 were sentenced and hanged, and among them Sir Phelim O'Neill.

THE CROMWELLIAN PLANTATION (1652-1658)

597. The war was now—1652—ended: but the pestilence continued; and famine came to help in the work of destruction. For two or three years these two scourges desolated the country. But worse even than all this was to come. Cromwell's soldiers were to be paid by grants of confiscated estates when the country should be conquered. The English parliament now professed to consider the whole of Ireland forfeited; and that therefore they might do as they pleased with land and people.

598. In August 1652, the Parliament passed an act to dispose of the Irish. The poorer sort of people of the three provinces of Ulster, Leinster, and Munster—small farmers, ploughmen, labourers, &c.—were not to be disturbed: the new settlers would need them. All others—the gentry of all classes—were ordered to transplant themselves and their families across the Shannon into Connaught and Clare, where they were to be given small allotments in lands that had been left waste.

They were to move by the 1st May 1654: any Catholics of those ordered away—young or old—men or women—found in any of the three provinces after that date, might be killed by whoever met them. Moreover, they were not permitted to live within four miles of the sea or of any town, or within two miles of the Shannon.

599. During this terrible migration of families mostly accustomed to a life of easy comfort, numbers perished of hardship and want; and after the

settlement most of the survivors came at once to poverty; for they had no houses, implements, stock, or capital, to start them in their new life.

600. But great numbers of the younger men, instead of migrating, formed themselves into bands to be avenged on the new settlers, like the expelled natives of Queen Mary's time. These "tories," as they were called, gave great trouble, plundering and killing at every opportunity: they were hunted down by the settlers, and neither gave nor received quarter. This terrible war went on for many years till the tories were exterminated.

601. The Irish soldiers who had fought against the Parliament were allowed to enlist in foreign service; and 34,000 emigrated and entered the service of France, Spain, Austria, and Venice.

602. There were widows and orphans everywhere, and a terrible fate awaited these: they were hunted and brought forth from their hiding places everywhere, and vast numbers of them, and many men also, were sent to the West Indian Islands to be slaves.

603. The laws against the Catholic religion and against Catholic priests were put in force with unsparing severity But the priests remained among their flocks, hiding in wild places and under various disguises; and the Catholic religion was practised as earnestly and as generally as ever.

604. A new survey of the country was made, and the lands were distributed to Cromwell's soldiers and to those who had advanced money to carry on the war.

605. This vast exodus went on from 1652 to 1654. But it was found impossible to clear the gentry completely out of the land. Many settled in wild places; many were taken as under tenants on their own lands; and in course of time many intermarried with the new settlers.

606. This dreadful Cromwellian episode must be taken as proceeding, not from the English government, but from the will of one man, who then ruled as despotically in England as in Ireland, though not with such cruelty.

RESTORATION AND COMPROMISE (1658-1665)

607. Oliver Cromwell died in 1658 and was succeeded by his son Richard as lord protector. In England there was an obvious growing desire to restore the monarchy. In Ireland the two most powerful parliamentarians, Sir Charles Coote in Ulster and Roger Boyle lord Broghill in Munster, son of the great earl of Cork, skilfully observing the signs of the times, turned round and declared for Charles II.

608. The restoration of the king in 1660 put the Catholics in high hope that they would be reinstated in their lands: for they had fought and suffered for Charles and his father. But the ungrateful king gave himself little concern about those who had befriended him either in England or Ireland; and the Catholics received a scant measure of justice.

Broghill was made earl of Ossory and Coote earl of Mountrath; and these two enemies of the Catholics and of the king were also made two of the three lords justices: Sir Maurice Eustace lord chancellor being the third.

609. On the 8th of May 1661, a parliament—the first for twenty years—was assembled in Dublin, nearly all Protestants. They voted £30,000 to the marquis—now duke—of Ormond: who was a little later on appointed lord lieutenant.

They passed the Act of settlement which confirmed the new settlers in their holdings. Those of the dispossessed Catholic owners who could prove that they were innocent of any connection with the rising of 1641, and all Protestants who had been dispossessed, were to be restored. Any of the new settlers whom this arrangement displaced were to be "reprised" by getting land elsewhere.

610. To try these numerous cases a "Court of claims" was established, which began its sittings in February 1663. The conditions for proving "innocence" were very stringent and hard to comply with. Yet of 186 Roman Catholics who came before the court during the first three months, 168 established their innocence and were to be reinstated.

611. This so alarmed the settlers that a stop was put to the proceedings; and a new act was passed, known as the "Act of explanation," under which the adventurers agreed to give up one third of their possessions. But this did not afford near enough for all those who proved themselves "innocent," and the available land was greatly diminished by immense grants to favoured individuals: the king gave 120,000 acres in Tipperary to his brother the duke of York (afterwards James II.); and large districts were given to lords Ormond and Inchiquin.

612. After much wrangling, matters were adjusted; and it came to this, that whereas before the settlement the Catholic proprietors possessed about five millions of acres, or two thirds of all the arable land (the remaining third being held by Protestants of the Plantation times of Elizabeth and James), after the time of this final arrangement they had only two-and-a-half millions or one-third, while two thirds remained with the Protestants.

613. There remained a large proportion of the Catholics who were not restored: many of these held on in their poor homes in Connaught; and many sinking into hopeless poverty, perished of privation.

614. In the three planted provinces the great preponderance of the poorer people were Catholics: besides great numbers of Catholic gentry who resisted expulsion. The highest class of Protestant settlers remained apart from and unmixed with Catholics; but the middle and lower classes—like the settlers of earlier times—became gradually absorbed by intermarriage among the old native race; and in half a century had in a great measure adopted their language, religion, and habits.

RELIGIOUS TROUBLES AFTER THE RESTORATION (1665-1685)

615. At the time of the Restoration the population of Ireland was about 1,100,000: of whom 800,000 were Roman Catholics—including the old

English who were nearly all Catholics; 200,000 Non-conformist Protestants, or Puritans, and 100,000 episcopal Protestants, belonging to the Established Church. The new Cromwellian settlers were almost all Puritans. Both sections of Protestants were alike hostile to the Roman Catholics.

During the parliamentary sway the Non-conformists had the upper hand, and the Established Church was repressed, and its clergy removed; while still stronger measures, as as we have seen, were taken against the Roman Catholics.

616. One of the first acts of Charles II. was to restore the Established Church in Ireland; and the bishops and ministers returned to their dioceses and parishes. But as the members of this church were so few, most had very small flocks, and very many none at all. Bramhall, a man so much in favour of the "divine right" and extreme prerogatives of the king, that he was called the "Irish Laud," was made archbishop of Armagh, and Jeremy Taylor bishop of Down and Connor. This restoration of the church was bitterly resented by the Puritans, who detested government by bishops.

617. The Act of uniformity was brought to bear chiefly on the Presbyterians, who now suffered a sharp, though short, persecution. Nearly all determinedly refused to comply with the requirements of the act, and the clergy were expelled from their ministry and their homes: some were fined or sent to jail; some were banished from the country. But most held their ground and secretly kept religion alive among their flocks.

A large number of the lay members—sober, industrious, and peaceful people—unwilling to bear these religious hardships, sold their property and emigrated to the Puritan colonies of New England. But by unyielding firmness the Presbyterians at length obtained toleration and justice.

618. While the Presbyterians were suffering, the Catholics were treated with some leniency by Ormond, through the interference of the king. Ormond however soon resumed his severities; whereupon the king removed him in 1669, and appointed lord Robarts, who was in his turn succeeded as lord lieutenant in 1670 by lord Berkeley. This was followed by renewed severities against the Nonconformists, and by further toleration for the Roman Catholics.

619. The Catholic cause was advocated and advanced in London by colonel Richard Talbot afterwards earl and duke of Tirconnell, and by his brother Peter Talbot Roman Catholic archbishop of Dublin.

620. But the leniency experienced by the Catholics was of short duration. It was known that the king's brother James duke of York was a Roman Catholic. The king himself was believed to be a Catholic also; and reports went abroad that he was conspiring to restore the Catholic religion over the Three Kingdoms. Matters were brought to a crisis by the Titus Oates plot in England in 1678. This was an evil turn for the Irish Roman Catholics;

for now there were all sorts of wild unfounded rumours of their wicked intentions towards Protestants.

Measures of extraordinary severity—proclamations in quick succession—were brought into play, and the Catholics now passed through a period of great suffering. Several innocent persons were arrested and imprisoned: and Dr. Oliver Plunket archbishop of Armagh was brought to London, where in 1681, he was tried and executed on false testimony.

King Charles died in 1686, a Catholic, and attended by a Catholic priest.

JAMES THE SECOND (1665-1685)

621. In 1685 James II. succeeded his brother as King of England. He was a Roman Catholic, and his accession gave great joy to the Catholics of Ireland, and corresponding alarm to the Protestants. He soon entered on the dangerous task of gradually restoring the Catholic religion in both countries. Colonel Talbot, a strict Catholic, of a disposition over-zealous and imprudent, was sent to Ireland as commander of the forces, and was created earl of Tirconnell. As a sort of set-off, the king appointed his own brother-in-law, lord Clarendon, who was a Protestant, lord lieutenant, in place of Ormond.

622. But Clarendon was a mere shadow; Tirconnell was the real ruler; and one of his first acts was to disarm the militia, who were all Protestants. He also appointed Catholic officers all through the army, as well as Roman Catholic judges on the bench; and many other important posts were filled up by Catholics. He made an attempt to have the Act of settlement repealed; but failed.

623. At length in 1687 Tirconnell was appointed lord lieutenant. This created quite a panic among the Protestants, and terrific rumours ran rife of intended massacres; so that hundreds fled from their homes to England and elsewhere.

624. In the midst of all this excitement and alarm, and while Tirconnell openly persevered in his course, William Prince of Orange landed in England in November 1688, with a fleet and an army, at the invitation of some of the leading Protestants. King James, at the first appearance of danger, fled to France (in December); and William took possession of the throne of England without opposition. But he had to fight for Ireland.

THE SIEGE OF DERRY (1688-1689)

625. Tirconnell took immediate measures to secure Ireland for King James. He raised and armed an army of Catholics, and disarmed the Protestants. He took possession of most of the important places through the country; but the people of Enniskillen refused to admit his garrison. Then began the War of the Revolution.

626. Lord Antrim marched to take possession of Derry; but while the aldermen and magistrates were hesitating, a few of the bolder young apprentices seizing the keys, locked the town gates on the 7th of December

1688, and shut out Antrim and his Jacobite forces.

627. In February 1689. lieutenant-general Richard Hamilton was sent north by Tirconnell to reduce Ulster, where the Protestants were now making preparations for defence; and having captured some places and been repulsed in others, he arrived near Derry.

628. Meantime King James sailed for Ireland from Brest with 100 French officers, 1,200 Irish refugees, arms and ammunition for 10,000 men, and a supply of money. Among the French officers were De Rosen and the French ambassador count d'Avaux. Among the Irish were Patrick Sarsfield, the two Hamiltons, and the two Luttrells. James landed at Kinsale on the 12th March 1689, and passing through Cork, proceeded to Dublin.

629. Having visited Derry in April, where he found his army engaged in the siege, he returned to Dublin and summoned a parliament. During the short sitting of this parliament, from the 7th May to the 20th of July, the following measures, among others, were passed:—Poynings' Law was repealed. There was to be full freedom of worship.

The Act of Settlement was repealed, whereby the new settlers would have to restore the lands to the old owners. A number of persons—2,445 in all—were attainted, and their lands declared confiscated, for having joined the Prince of Orange. But all this active legislation came to nothing; for before there was time to enforce it, King James and his government were superseded.

630. To meet current expenses a tax was levied on estates. But as this was not enough, the king seized some coining machines, and issued base coins, each representing £5, which all persons were obliged to take in exchange for goods, though their actual value was only about four pence. This unwise measure did great mischief and ruined hundreds of traders.

631. Meantime the siege of Derry which had been commenced on the 18th of April 1689, was carried on in good earnest by Hamilton, who was afterwards joined by De Rosen. It has been related how the gates had been shut by a few young apprentices. But there were many among the authorities who did not approve of this action; and Colonel Lundy the governor had from the beginning made himself intensely unpopular by recommending surrender, so that he had at last to make his escape over the wall by night in disguise.

632. The command then devolved on major Baker and captain Murray. The feeble-hearted town council were still for surrender; when the humbler citizens—those of the class who at first had shut the gates—with Murray at their head, took the matter into their own hands and resolved on resistance. The besiegers began their work vigorously the walls and town were battered by their cannon; many houses took fire; and people were struck down everywhere in the streets. But the greater the danger and distress the higher seemed to rise the spirits of the defenders. They were encouraged by

the clergy, among the most active of whom was the Rev. George Walker, who kept constantly exhorting the people from both pulpit and rampart.

633. During May and June the fighting went on daily; there were sallies by the besieged, and attempts to storm by the besiegers, with desperate conflicts and great loss of life. Such was the spirit of the defenders that the women sometimes assisted, handing ammunition and refreshments to the men; and armed with stones and all sorts of first-to-hand missiles, they mixed in the fights as boldly as their sons, brothers, and husbands.

634. But soon provisions began to run short; and there was no way of procuring a supply; for the town was quite surrounded except on the river side; and here the besiegers had cut off communication by a great boom composed of strong cables and logs of timber bound together, stretched tightly from bank to bank.

635. Every day watchmen took station on the church tower, anxiously looking out to sea for relief; and at length in the middle of June they shouted down the joyous news that thirty ships were sailing up Lough Foyle. But the hopes of the citizens were short-lived; for major-general Kirke the commander of the fleet, hearing of the boom and of the armed enemies and forts lining the river banks all the way up to the town, refused to proceed farther.

636. For forty-six days he lay idle in the lough, while the townspeople were famishing, driven to eat horseflesh, dogs, grease, and garbage of every kind. The garrison fared no better. Yet these brave young fellows—ragged and starving—stood resolutely to their posts, and had never a thought of yielding.

The fighting at last ceased, and it now became a question of starving the defenders into surrender.

637. On the evening of the 30th of July, when silence, gloom, and despair had settled down on the town, the watchers were startled by a bright flash down the river, followed by the roar of artillery; and a hungry multitude, rushing eagerly to the battlements, saw relief approaching. For Kirke had at last taken heart and sent three ships with provisions. In spite of the destructive fire from both sides, the ships approached full sail, crashed through the boom, and relieved the town. Next day Hamilton marched away. Thus ended, on the 31st of July 1689, a siege of 105 days, one of the most famous in Irish or British history.

638. The ancient walls of Derry are still perfect, though the town has extended far beyond them; and on the site of one of the bastions, rises a lofty pillar surmounted by a statue of the Rev. George Walker.

639. Enniskillen, the other Williamite garrison, was threatened by the approach of an Irish army; but the Enniskilleners, marching forth on the very day of the relief of Derry, intercepted and utterly defeated them at Newtownbutler. Sarsfield, who commanded a detachment at Sligo, on

hearing of these disasters, retired to Athlone; and now Ulster was nearly all in the hands of the Williamites.

THE BATTLE OF THE BOYNE

640. The siege of Derry was only the beginning of the struggle. King William had now leisure to look to Ireland and he sent over the duke of Schomberg—then over 80 years of age—who landed in August 1689, at Bangor, with an army of about 15,000 men. After a siege of eight days, Carrickfergus Castle was surrendered to him; and he settled down for some time in an entrenched camp near Dundalk, in an unhealthful position, where he lost a large part of his army by sickness.

641. In the following year King William came over to conduct the campaign in person. He landed at Carrickfergus on the 14th June 1690, and immediately joined Schomberg. About half of the united army were foreigners, excellent soldiers, a mixture of French, Dutch, Danes, Swedes, and Prussians or Brandenburghers.

642. James had advanced from Dublin to Dundalk, but fell back on the south bank of the Boyne, with his centre at the village of Oldbridge, whither William followed him and took up his position on the north bank. He had about 40,000 men; James about 26,000. The Irish army was largely composed of recruits, badly drilled and badly armed, with the unskilful and irresolute King James at their head; they were opposed by a more numerous army, well trained, well supplied with all necessaries, and commanded by William, a man of determination, and one of the best generals of the time.

643. On the evening of the 80th June, King William while reconnoitering, was slightly wounded by a cannon shot from the opposite side; and the report went round among the Irish that he was killed.

On the morning of the 1st of July 1690, William's army began to cross the river. One division of 10,000, under lieutenant-general Douglas, had marched at sunrise and crossed at Slane about five miles up the river, a passage which James though warned, had left unguarded.

644. The rest of the army attempted the passage at four different fords; and all met determined though unavailing resistance. The famous Blue Dutch guards and the French Huguenots with the veteran Schomberg at their head, dashed in, ten abreast, opposite James' centre at Oldbridge; and here Schomberg, rallying a body of Huguenots who had been broken by the Irish, was killed by a musket bullet which struck him in the neck. About the same time Walker of Derry was shot dead in the ford.

645. William himself crossed at the head of his cavalry lower down towards Drogheda. The battle raged for about a mile along the river. The Irish contested the field valiantly; but no amount of bravery could compensate for the disadvantages under which they fought; and William gained a decisive victory.

646. In the evening, the defeated Irish retreated in good order southwards through Duleek to Dublin. The pusillanimous James had shown no courage or skill or ability during the battle: at the first intimation of defeat he fled, and was the very first to reach Dublin. Sarsfield exactly pictured the situation when he exclaimed:—"Change kings and we will fight you over again."

647. Having given the chief command to Tirconnell, James embarked at Kinsale and landed at Brest, the first bearer of the news of his own defeat. The Irish army evacuated Dublin and marched to Limerick; and William arrived and took possession of the city on Sunday the 6th of July. After this, Drogheda, Kilkenny, Duncannon, and Waterford surrendered in quick succession.

648. A pillar to Schomberg's memory now rises from a rock in the Boyne near the spot where the gallant old warrior fell.

THE SIEGE OF LIMERICK (1690)

649. The Irish now took the Shannon for their line of defence and concentrated their forces at Limerick and Athlone. William marched towards Limerick. Douglas attacked Athlone with 12,000 men; but after a siege of seven days he was repulsed, and joined the king at Limerick.

650. On the 9th of August 1690, William encamped at Singland just outside the walls of the old city, with an effective army of about 26,000; the Irish army of defence numbered about 25,000, only half of them armed. The city was badly prepared for defence: the French general Lauzun said "it could be taken with roasted apples"; and deserting his post, marched to Galway and embarked for France.

651. William was deficient in artillery: but a great siege train was on its way from Dublin, with heavy cannons, plenty of ammunition, and other necessaries for a siege.

652. When general Patrick Sarsfield came to hear of this, he determined to intercept the convoy. Marching out silently at dead of night at the Clare side, with 500 picked horsemen, he rode to Killaloe, fifteen miles above Limerick, and crossed the Shannon at an unguarded ford a little above the town (Sunday night, August 10th, 1690).

653. Turning south-east, and having given his party a brief rest, he came on the convoy on the next night towards morning, beside the ruined castle of Ballyneety near the village of Oola. All were asleep except a few sentinels, and the attack was a complete surprise. When the party of horse dashed in among them there was little resistance, and in a few minutes Sarsfield had possession of the whole train. He caused the cannons to be filled with powder and their mouths buried in the earth; a fuse was laid to magazine and cannon; and the whole train was blown up in one terrific explosion. A part of William's army heard the ominous rumble in the distance, and too well divined what it meant.

Sarsfield, successfully eluding a party sent out too late to intercept him, made his way safely back to the city. This brilliant exploit greatly raised the spirits of the besieged.

654. Notwithstanding this disaster, King William, sending to Waterford for more heavy cannon, pressed the siege. The men worked at the trenches, which, in spite of the most determined opposition, were advanced within a few feet of the walls. The cannons made a great breach near St. John's Gate; and through this it was determined to make an assault.

655. In the afternoon of the 27th of August 1690, a storming party, leaping up from the trenches, entered the breach, supported in the rear by 10,000 men. They fired their muskets and threw their hand grenades among the defenders: but were met by a terrible fire from all sides, front and flanks. Nearly all the front ranks were destroyed, and the rest showed signs of wavering; but thousands of resolute men pressed on from behind, and the Limerick men, now sore pressed, began to yield in their turn.

656. From every convenient standpoint the citizens viewed the terrible fight, but could see little through the thick cloud of smoke and dust. When they became aware that the assailants were prevailing, they rushed down in crowds from their secure resting-places, and seizing every available weapon, joined eagerly in the fray. Even the women—more active still than the women of Derry—rushed to the very front, and regardless of danger, flung stones and bottles and missiles of every kind in the very faces of the assailants.

657. The Brandenburgh regiment, fighting steadily, had advanced to the Black Battery and were swarming round and over it; when suddenly the magazine was exploded, and battery and Brandenburghers were blown into the air in horrible confusion.

658. For four hours this dreadful conflict raged, and a cloud of smoke and dust, wafted by a gentle breeze, reached the whole way to the top of a high hill sixteen miles off. The assailants, unable to withstand the tremendous and unexpected resistance, at last yielded, and turning round, rushed back through the breach in headlong confusion.

King William had witnessed the conflict from Cromwell's fort; and having seen the repulse of his best troops, he returned to the camp deeply disappointed. Over 2,000 of his men were killed or wounded: the loss of the Irish was comparatively small.

659. William raised the siege, which had lasted three weeks, and returned to England, leaving general De Ginkel in command; and on the 31st of August the army marched away from the city.

The heroic defenders of Limerick had, almost without ammunition, repulsed a well—equipped veteran army directed by a great general who had never been foiled before.

660. In September 1690, Cork surrendered, after a fierce struggle, to the

Williamite general John Churchill, afterwards the celebrated duke of Marlborough; Kinsale followed; and this ended the campaign of 1690.

THE SIEGE OF ATHLONE AND THE BATTLE OF AUGHRIM (1690)

661. Tirconnell, who had gone to France to solicit aid, returned in January 1691, with some money and stores; and in May a French fleet arrived in the Shannon with lieutenant-general St. Ruth to take command of the Irish army.

662. On the 19th of June Ginkel appeared before Athlone with an army of 18,000 men. The town was divided in two by the Shannon. The Irish took their stand at the Connaught side, destroying two arches of the bridge.

663. St. Ruth was at that side with his army a short distance from the town. The English proceeded to throw planks across the broken arches; but a volunteer party of eleven Irish rushed forward to pull them down, straight in the fire of the English batteries. They were met by a tempest of grape, and when the smoke cleared away every man lay dead. Another party, eleven undaunted men, dashed in and tore down the planks; but again the grape did its work, and nine out of the eleven fell.

664. Foiled in this attempt, Ginkel adopted another plan. It was found that the river could be forded at a spot a little below the town: and partly through dissension among the officers of the Irish army, and partly through the remissness of St. Ruth, a detachment of the English crossed the river on the 30th of June. They seized the bridge; and the army, crossing, took possession of the town.

665. We learn that about this time William offered terms to Tirconnell:— To the Irish Catholics the free exercise of their religion, half the churches, half the employments, and half their ancient estates. But the Irish mistrusted the good faith of the offer and rejected it.

666. After the taking of Athlone St. Ruth fell back on the village of Aughrim in Galway, five miles from Ballinasloe, determined to give battle. He occupied a skilfully-chosen position along the ridge of Kilcommedan hill beside the village, with a morass in front. The numbers engaged might be about 20,000 each side. In Ginkel's army, besides English, Scotch, and Irish, there were Huguenots, Danes, and Dutch.

667. Skirmishing began about midday on the 12th of July 1691, and continued till about six, when a general engagement came on. The English crossed the marsh and were advancing up hill, but were charged by the Irish and driven back in confusion, so that St. Ruth exclaimed, "The day is ours!" But soon after, while riding down the slope to give some orders, a cannon ball took off his head. This lost the day. The fight was, however, still stubbornly maintained, but late in the evening the Irish gave way. A great number who had taken refuge in a bog were massacred; and they lost altogether 4,000 or 5,000 men. Only about 500 prisoners were taken.

668. Galway submitted on the 21st of July, and Sligo in September, both on favourable terms, their garrisons being allowed to march to Limerick.

THE SECOND SIEGE AND TREATY OF LIMERICK (1691-1695)

669. The Duke of Tirconnell proceeded to put Limerick in a state of defence; but he died of apoplexy in the city on the 14th of August 1691: after which the chief command devolved on Sarsfield.

670. On the 80th of August Ginkel began the bombardment with sixty cannon and nineteen mortars: and soon the city was on fire in several places. After a time he was able to occupy the Clare side, but the besieged showed no signs of yielding. The Clare end of Thomond bridge was attacked, and defended; till the Irish overpowered by numbers had to retreat across the bridge. The town-major, a Frenchman, raised the drawbridge too soon and shut out 600 of them, who were all massacred on the bridge.

671. There was now a short truce, and negotiations were entered into for capitulation. Ginkel was anxious to end the war, fearing the rainy season, and Sarsfield saw no hope in further unaided resistance. A treaty of peace was at length signed by Ginkel and the lords justices Sir Charles Porter and Thomas Coningsby on the one hand, and on the other by Sarsfield, now earl of Lucan. The stone on which it was signed is still to be seen on a pedestal beside Thomond bridge. The treaty was soon after confirmed by King William. This ended the War of the Revolution; and William and Mary were acknowledged sovereigns of Ireland.

672. A few days afterwards a French fleet sailed up the Shannon: 18 ships of the line and 20 transports, with 3,000 soldiers, 200 officers, and arms and ammunition for 10,000 men; but Sarsfield refused to receive them, and honourably stood by the treaty.

673. The Treaty of Limerick contained forty-two articles. The most important of the civil articles were:—The Irish Catholics were to have the same liberty of worship as they enjoyed in the reign of Charles II. Those in arms for King James to retain the estates they possessed in the time of Charles II., and to be permitted to freely exercise their callings and professions. The oath to be taken by the Roman Catholics who submitted, to be the oath of allegiance merely, not the oath of supremacy.

674. The principal military articles were:—The garrison to be permitted to march out of the city with arms and baggage, drums beating and colours flying. Those officers and soldiers who wished might go to any foreign country, the government to provide them with ships; those who chose might join the army of William and Mary. Ginkel was anxious to keep those fine soldiers in the king's army, but only 1,000 joined; and 2,000 got passes for their homes.

675. More than 20,000—among them Sarsfield—went to Brest and entered the French service. These formed the nucleus of the famous Irish

Brigade, who afterwards distinguished themselves in many a battlefield—Fontenoy, Ramillies, Blenheim, Landen, &c. Numbers of the gentry attained distinguished positions on the Continent. Sarsfield, after brilliant service, fell mortally wounded at the battle of Landen in 1693, where he commanded the left wing of the French army. It is stated that while lying on the ground, seeing his hand stained with his own blood, he exclaimed "Oh, that this was for Ireland!"

676. There was at this time and for long after, a vast exodus of the very flower of the Irish people; and between 1691 and 1745 it is reckoned that 450,000 Irishmen died in the service of France.

677. The war had cost the English about seven millions, representing probably fifty millions of our money, besides vast destruction of houses, cattle, and other kinds of property.

678. King William was kindly disposed towards the Irish; and taking advantage of the Treaty, he restored a good part of their estates, and granted many pardons. But he rewarded his followers with vast grants. He created Ginkel earl of Athlone, and gave him 26,000 acres; to William Bentink, son of the duke of Portland, 136,000 acres; to the countess of Orkney 96,000 acres. Altogether he made 76 land grants to his own people.

679. We shall see further on that the Treaty of Limerick was broken by the English; but for this violation King William was not to blame.

680. Lord Sydney, the lord lieutenant, summoned a parliament which met in Dublin on the 5th October 1692; it was exclusively Protestant. This was the first held since 1665, with the exception of that of King James.

It asserted the independence of the Irish parliament, and though granting a supply of money to the king, it rejected a money bill sent from England, on the ground that it had not been originated in the Irish commons. Sydney was so indignant at this refractory proceeding that he twice prorogued this parliament, which was finally dissolved on the 5th November 1698.

681. In less than a century there had been three great confiscations in Ireland, the old proprietors being in all cases dispossessed:—the first after the Geraldine and O'Neill rebellions; the second in the time of Cromwell; and the third after the conquest by King William.

These three included the whole island, except the estates of half a dozen families of English blood. Moreover, the three confiscations sometimes overlapped; so that large portions were confiscated twice, and some three times over, within that period. As the result of all, only about a seventh of the land of all Ireland was left in the hands of the Catholics.

682. The Catholics of old English blood were involved in this general ruin, so far as their numbers went, as well as those of the native Celtic race.

PART V. THE PERIOD OF THE PENAL LAWS
1695-1829.

BEFORE the year 1695 there were many penal enactments against Irish Catholics; but they were intermittent and not persistently carried out. But after that date they were, for nearly a century, systematic and continuous, and as far as possible enforced. Accordingly this Period is specially distinguished as the Period of the Penal Laws.

These laws were the work of the governing classes; the great body of the English people, whether in England or Ireland, had no hand in them. And as in 1641 Catholics saved many of the settlers from destruction, numberless instances are recorded where Catholics were protected from the operation of the laws by the pitying kindness of their Protestant neighbours. In many instances the laws could not be carried out, partly on account of their excessive severity, and partly from the passive resistance of the general body of Protestants.

Towards the close of the eighteenth century the penal code was gradually relaxed; and, except in a few particulars the Emancipation act of 1829 put an end to the penal enactments against Catholics.

THE PENAL CODE

683. The Irish Catholics were now crushed and dispirited; they were quite helpless, for their best men had gone to France; and all hope of resistance was at an end. They had however obtained tolerable conditions in the Treaty of Limerick; but here they were doomed to a bitter disappointment. The English parliament were not satisfied with the treaty, and in its most important provisions refused to carry it out. This greatly displeased King William, who would have faithfully adhered to the pledges, on the faith of which the Irish had surrendered Limerick.

684. The government of Ireland was now completely in the hands of the small Protestant minority, who also possessed almost the whole of the land of the country; and they held nearly all the offices of trust or emolument. This "Protestant Ascendancy," as it is called, was confirmed by the penal legislation, now to be described.

685. It will be convenient to bring the leading enactments of the whole penal code into this chapter, though it will oblige us to run in advance a little in point of time.

In 1695 the English parliament, going over the head of the Irish parliament, passed an act setting aside the oath of supremacy, but substituting something much worse:—Every member of parliament, bishop, holder of any government office, lawyer, and doctor, had to take an oath of allegiance (which was unobjectionable) and also an oath of "Abjuration"—abjuring the Catholic religion: which of course would exclude Catholics from all these positions.

686. In the same year lord Capel was appointed lord deputy; he

summoned a parliament which met in Dublin on the 27th August. This parliament completed what the English parliament had begun. In violation of the Treaty of Limerick, they passed a series of penal acts in the two sessions of 1695 and 1697. The principal items of this code are the following:—

687. Education. No Catholic was to teach school or teach scholars in private houses; no Catholic to send his child abroad to be educated. Penalty: forfeiture of all goods, and ineligibility to fill any office, such as guardian or executor, or to accept any legacy. These measures altogether deprived Catholics—as such—of education.

688. Arms and property. All Catholics were to deliver up their arms: magistrates might break open the houses of Catholics and search for arms. But gentlemen having the benefit of the Treaty of Limerick might keep a sword, a case of pistols, and a fowling-piece. No maker of arms could take a Catholic apprentice.

689. No Catholic to keep a horse worth more than £5 (equal about £30 of our money): if a Catholic had a valuable horse, any Protestant might take it by tendering £5.

690. Religion. The Catholic parish clergy, i.e. the existing parish priests, were not disturbed; but all had to be registered, and should give security for good behaviour. All bishops, Jesuits, friars, and monks were ordered to quit the kingdom by the 1st of May 1698. Any who returned were guilty of high treason: punishment death. For any priest landing in Ireland, imprisonment, after which transportation to the Continent. No person to harbour or relieve any such clergy. Any priest who turned Protestant to get a pension of £30. No burials in churchyards of suppressed monasteries. No Catholic chapel to have steeple or bells.

691. Social position. Catholics and Protestants were not to intermarry. If a Protestant woman married a Catholic, her property was forfeited to the next Protestant heir. A Protestant man who married a Catholic was to be treated as if he were himself a Catholic.

A Catholic could not servo on a grand jury, and an attorney could not take a Catholic clerk.

This was the first instalment of the penal code; but it was followed by much worse.

692. In 1708 the duke of Ormond came to Ireland as lord lieutenant. The house of commons petitioned him for a further extension of the penal laws, which were brought to their extreme limit of severity, chiefly in the first years of the reign of Queen Anne, and partly in the reign of George II. There was no reason for this additional legislation, for the Catholic people had been as a body quiet and submissive. The most important provisions of this "Popery act" as it was called, which became law in 1704, were these.

693. If the eldest son of a Roman Catholic father turned Protestant, he

became the owner of his father's land, and the father became merely life tenant. If any other child became Protestant, a Protestant guardian was appointed, and the father had to pay for separate maintenance and education.

694. If the sons were all Catholics, the land was equally divided among them when the father died: this was for the purpose of gradually impoverishing and weakening the old Catholic families.

695. The previous codes contained provisions to prevent Catholics practising as lawyers. The present act increased the penalty; and a subsequent act in the reign of George II. prohibited anyone from practising as a solicitor who had not been a Protestant since fourteen years of age.

696. No Catholic could purchase land, or take a lease longer than 81 years. If land came by descent to a Catholic, or was given to him, or was left him by will, he could not accept it.

697. No person could vote at an election, or could hold any office civil or military, without taking the oaths of allegiance and abjuration, and receiving the sacrament according to the English rite on Sunday. This last applied to the Presbyterians and other dissenters as well as to Catholics: but they were induced to withdraw their opposition to it by a promise that it would never be turned against them: a promise which was soon broken. The act requiring the reception of the sacrament according to the English rite is called the "Test act."

698. No Catholic in future to come to live in Limerick or Galway: those at present living in those cities were permitted to remain, but had to give security for good behaviour.

699. Rewards were offered for the discovery of Catholic bishops, Jesuits, unregistered priests or schoolmasters: the amount to be levied off the Catholics.

700. In the last year of Queen Anne's reign the English parliament passed the Schism act, drawn up by St. John lord Bolingbroke: it provided that no person could teach school without a license from the Protestant bishop, which could not be granted unless the applicant received the sacrament according to the rite of the established church; and this act was made to apply to Ireland.

701. In the reign of George II. (in 1727) an act was passed directly disfranchising all Roman Catholics—depriving them of votes at elections of every kind.

702. The Test and Schism acts were brought to bear against the Presbyterians of Ulster, who were now subjected to bitter persecution. They were expelled from Belfast and Derry, they were dismissed from the magistracy, prohibited from teaching school, their marriages were declared void, and the Regium Donum, an annual grant given by King William to their clergy, was stopped for the time. But these sturdy people never in the

least yielded.

There were many other similar provisions in the "Popery act" and in the others.

703. The earl of Wharton, who came over as lord lieutenant in 1709, attempted to have the Test act repealed —the great grievance of the Presbyterians—so as to unite all denominations of Protestants against the Catholics; but he was not able to have this done.

704. Ever since the conclusion of the war the country swarmed with bands of young men belonging to the dispossessed families, who lived among the mountains and bogs and made plundering raids on the settlers at every opportunity. These were called rapparees and tories. Numerous privateers, manned by the same classes, also hovered round the coasts with commissions from James II. and committed great havoc.

The rapparees and tories were outlawed; and in 1697 the Rapparee act was passed for their suppression. But it had little effect, and for many years the country continued to be unsettled and disturbed.

RESTRICTIONS ON IRISH TRADE AND MANUFACTURE

705. Ireland enjoys great natural advantages of soil and climate; and towards the end of the seventeenth century, in spite of wars and other troubles, several branches of manufacture, trade, and commerce were prospering.

But the English traders and merchants fancied that Irish prosperity was their loss, and in their short-sighted jealousy, persuaded the English parliament to ruin the trade of Ireland (except that in linen) by imposing restrictions.

706. This legislation was generally the work of the English parliament alone; but sometimes the Irish parliament followed in the same direction; and in obedience to orders from the other side, passed acts destroying their own trade, All this was the more to be wondered at, seeing that the blow fell almost exclusively on Irish Protestants; for at this time the Catholics were barely able to live, and could hardly attempt any industries.

707. The English "Navigation act" of 1660, as amended in 1663, prohibited all exports from Ireland to the colonies; and also, in the interest of English graziers, prohibited temporarily the import of Irish cattle into England. In 1666 this last prohibition was made to be permanent. These acts almost destroyed the Irish cattle and shipping trades; and the people, being unable to find a market for their horses and cattle, fell into great distress.

708. The Irish, driven from cattle rearing, applied themselves to other industries, especially that of wool, for which the country was well suited. We have seen that Wentworth crippled the trade: nevertheless it began to flourish again: but this also was doomed. The English cloth dealers, fancying that it injured them, petitioned in 1698 to have it suppressed: and

King William, in the speech from the throne, promised to discourage the Irish wool trade, to encourage the Irish linen trade, and to promote the trade of England.

709. Accordingly, in 1699, the Irish parliament, under directions from the other side, helped to ruin their own country by putting an export duty of four shillings in the lb. on fine woollen cloths, and two shillings on frieze and flannel. At the same time the English parliament passed an act prohibiting the Irish from exporting either wool or woollen goods to any ports in the world except Liverpool, Milford, Chester, and some ports on the Bristol Channel. Moreover no woollens were to be shipped to these from any Irish ports except Drogheda, Dublin, Waterford, Youghal, Cork, and Kinsale.

710. This was the most disastrous of all the restrictions on Irish trade. It accomplished all that the English merchants looked for: it ruined the Irish wool trade. It is stated that 40,000 of the Irish Protestants were immediately reduced to poverty by it; and 20,000 Puritans left Ireland for New England. Then began the emigration, from want of employment, that continues to this day. But the English parliament professed to encourage the linen trade; for this could do no harm to English manufacture.

711. As always happens when there are prohibitive tariffs, smuggling now increased enormously. Wool soon became a drug in the home markets: worth only five pence a lb.; while it would sell for two shillings and sixpence in France. This was an irresistible inducement to smuggle: and the smugglers brought, in return, contraband goods—brandy, wine, and silk. No one cared to interfere with this illegal trade; thousands of the Irish of all classes profited by it; and high and low, squires, clergy, and peasants, Protestants and Catholics, all were in active combination against the law.

712. The government was powerless to stop this contraband trade; and for generations it flourished all round the coasts. All this was the result of unjust and unwise legislation.

713. In subsequent times the parliament interfered with almost every branch of Irish trade and manufacture:—beer, malt, hats, cotton, silk, gunpowder, iron and ironware, &c. And the embargo in the time of the American war not only ruined the farmers, but ruined the trade in salted beef and other such commodities.

714. When, subsequently, these restrictions were removed and trade was partially relieved, the remedy came too late. Some branches of manufacture and trade had been killed downright, and others permanently injured. A trade extinguished is not easily revived. The trade in wool, a chief staple of Ireland, which was kept down for nearly a century, never recovered its former state of prosperity.

715. The consequence of all this destructive legislation is that Ireland has

at this day comparatively little manufacture and commerce; and the people have to depend for subsistence almost exclusively on land. And this again, by increasing the competition for land, has intensified the land troubles that we inherit from the older times of the plantations.

716. The king and his English parliament did not agree very well. He was tolerant; they were intolerant; and they took every opportunity to thwart and mortify him, which embittered his later life. The parliament passed an act in 1700 to take back all those estates he had granted; a measure which gave the king great annoyance.

A fall from his horse which broke his collar bone gave his shattered constitution such a shock that he sank and died on the 8th of March 1702. He was succeeded by Queen Anne. George I. succeeded Anne in 1714.

"THE SIXTH OF GEORGE I." (1703-1727)

717. The proceedings of the Irish parliament and the political history of the country during the eighteenth century have reference solely to the Protestant colony. The struggles of the Irish legislature for independence, culminating in Grattan's parliament of 1782, were the struggles of the Protestants: the Catholics had no political existence, and had no part— could have no part—in any of these contests.

718. The Irish parliament, and the people of the colony in general, fearing further interference with their prosperity on account of the commercial jealousy of the English, and despairing of being able to maintain their rights through their own parliament, petitioned in 1703 for a parliamentary union with England. But the English government rejected the proposal.

719. The hostile attitude of the English government towards Ireland produced the same result as in times of old—a feeling of distrust and aversion among the colonists, in which the Irish parliament shared.

720. These feelings were intensified by what was called the Annesley case, which brought the English and Irish houses of lords into collision, A dispute about property arose in 1719 between two Irish persons, Hester Sherlock and Maurice Annesley, which the court of exchequer decided in favour of Annesley; but the Irish house of lords, on being appealed to, reversed this and gave judgment in favour of Hester Sherlock, Annesley appealed to the English house of lords, who affirmed the exchequer decision, reversing that of the Irish lords; and they fined Burrowes the sheriff of Kildare for not putting Annesley in possession in obedience to their decree. But the Irish peers remitted the fine, and went farther by taking into custody the three barons of the court of exchequer.

721. The English parliament ended the dispute by passing, in 1719, a momentous act (known as "the Sixth of George I.") deciding that the English parliament had the right to make laws for Ireland; and depriving the Irish house of lords of the right to hear appeals.

722. Poynings' act did not give the English parliament the power of legislating for Ireland, which was now for the first time asserted. The Sixth of George I. quite took away the independence of the Irish parliament.

723. In 1719 the penal statutes against dissenters began to be relaxed. The penal laws had no effect whatever in suppressing the Catholic religion: we find the Irish parliament in 1723 complaining of the continued increase of Catholicity; and in this same year they proposed another bill of so extreme a character that it had to be suppressed on account of the indignation it caused in England.

724. The English parliament tried to keep down that of Ireland, chiefly by Poynings' act (which was an Irish act), and for a long time succeeded. The Irish parliament was in general very submissive; for all the great officials, from the lord lieutenant down, were Englishmen and in the English interest; and they generally had a majority in both houses.

725. Yet there was sometimes resistance; and we have seen that in 1692 a money bill was rejected in Dublin because it had originated in England. Within the parliament there was always a small determined opposition against dictation, "Patriots" as they came to be called, who were seconded by some very brilliant and able men outside.

726. Long before—in 1698—William Molyneux, one of the members for the University of Dublin, a friend of Locke and a man of great scientific eminence, published his famous book, "The Case of Ireland's being bound by Acts of parliament in England stated," in which he denounced the commercial injustice done to Ireland, and maintained that the Irish parliament was independent of that of England, and had a right to make its own laws. This essay was received in England with great indignation; and the parliament there, pronouncing it dangerous, ordered it to be burned publicly by the common hangman.

727. The ablest of those outside parliament was Jonathan Swift, who was appointed dean of St. Patrick's, Dublin, in 1713, having previously been vicar of Laracor in Meath. Much inconvenience had for some time been felt in Ireland from the want of a small copper coinage; and at last in 1728, the English treasury, with the minister Walpole at their head, granted a patent to one William Wood, an Englishman, to coin £108,000 in debased halfpence and farthings, for circulation in Ireland. This would put £40,000 profit into the pockets of Wood and the king's favourite the duchess of Kendal. The Irish parliament was not consulted at all in the matter.

728. This gross job created intense alarm and indignation in Ireland; and the two Irish houses addressed the king, representing that this base coinage would diminish revenue and destroy commerce. But Wood had strong support in England: the expostulation of the Irish lords and commons had little effect; and he would have succeeded but for Swift.

729. Popular excitement increased: there were multitudes of pamphlets,

songs and coarse caricatures on broadsheets circulating in Dublin; but it was Swift's "Drapier's Letters" that crushed the scheme. These were a series of five letters pretending to be written by a Dublin draper, with the signature "W. B. Drapier," attacking the scheme, and pointing out in simple, homely, vigorous language that the most ignorant could understand, the evils the dean asserted would result from the coinage.

730. He told his readers that twenty-four of these halfpence were worth no more than one good penny; that if a lady went shopping she should have to bring with her a cart loaded with the new coins; that a farmer would have to employ three horses to bring his rent to his landlord; that a poor man would have to give thirty-six of the halfpence for a quart of ale; and that it would ruin all classes, even the very beggars, for when a man gives a beggar one of these halfpence it "will do him no more service than if I should give him three pins out of my sleeve."

731. These letters increased the excitement tenfold, and the English government became alarmed. They circulated a certificate from Sir Isaac Newton, then master of the mint, that the coins were good; but to no purpose. The lord lieutenant (Lord Carteret), who was of course on the side of the king, offered a reward of £300 for the discovery of the author: but though every one knew who the writer was, no attempt was made to inform on the dean or molest him. The printer Harding was arrested and put in prison; but two grand juries in succession refused to return him for trial, and he had to be let off.

732. Meantime Dr. Hugh Boulter an Englishman, the king's chaplain, was appointed archbishop of Armagh in 1724, and was intrusted with the chief management of the English interest in Ireland. He was bitterly hostile to the Roman Catholics; but otherwise he was a good man.

733. Soon after his arrival he wrote to the duke of Newcastle that things were in a very bad state in Ireland, and recommended that the halfpence scheme should be abandoned. At length, in 1725, the patent was withdrawn: but Wood received from government an indemnity of £3,000 a-year for twelve years. This victory over the government consolidated the ranks of the patriots and greatly strengthened their hands.

734. These transactions made the dean amazingly popular in Ireland with all classes, high and low, Protestant and Catholic.

735. He wrote also in favour of Irish industry, recommending the people to use none but Irish manufactures; and, like Molyneux, he maintained that it was only the king and parliament of Ireland that had the power to make laws for the country. His writings show some sympathy for the Irish Roman Catholics. He was bitterly opposed to Lord Wharton (lord lieutenant in 1709), whose chief aim was to enrich himself.

George I. died in 1727, and was succeeded by his son George II.

STRUGGLES FOR PARLIAMENTARY INDEPENDENCE (1727-

736. On the accession of George II., lord Carteret, who was popular on account of abolishing Wood's halfpence, was retained as lord lieutenant. In 1727 the Catholics prepared an address to him expressing their loyalty, and their intention to keep peaceful. It was presented to the lords justices, one of whom was archbishop Boulter; but they never forwarded it, and no notice was taken of it.

737. It was chiefly through primate Boulter's influence that the Catholics were disfranchised in the beginning of this reign. Finding that they would not conform, his next plan was to begin with the children. He induced the government to found the "Charter schools" in 1780: free schools in which the children of poor Roman Catholics were taught, clothed, fed, and apprenticed to a trade, all free: and educated as Protestants. But these charter schools did not effect much.

738. For years there had been great distress from the general depression of trade; and this, as well as the Test and Schism acts, drove from the country vast numbers of the Ulster Presbyterians, who continued to emigrate to New England. This alarmed the Government, as it increased the relative proportion of Catholics; yet they obstinately retained these two acts, though the duke of Dorset the lord lieutenant attempted to have them repealed in 1733: failing like lord Wharton.

739. The duke of Dorset was succeeded in 1787 by the duke of Devonshire, who lived in great magnificence, and bought over men by liberal bestowal of places; so that the Patriot party found it hard to retain their influence in parliament.

740. In 1745 the Scottish rebellion broke out in favour of the Pretender; but though his army was largely composed of exiled Irishmen, the Irish Catholics at home, thoroughly crushed, took no part in it. Nevertheless the English government felt greatly alarmed about Ireland: and in that same year they sent over the earl of Chesterfield as lord lieutenant, with instructions to exercise moderation.

741. The local oligarchy of Dublin pressed for more severity against the Catholics: but be ridiculed their recommendations: and having satisfied himself by his spies that the Catholics had no hostile designs, he allowed them to worship in their chapels without molestation.

A few days after the battle of Culloden in 1746, which crushed the rebellion, he was recalled. On the day of his departure he walked through the streets to the place of embarkation with his countess on his arm, amid the acclamation of the people, Catholics and Protestants.

742. In 1747 the earl of Harrington came over as lord lieutenant. In the same year George Stone was appointed primate of Armagh; and like primate Boulter, had the chief management of English affairs in Ireland. His constant study was to maintain English ascendancy, which he did in

the most arrogant manner; so that he rendered himself intensely unpopular.

743. The duke of Dorset returned as lord lieutenant in 1751. His son lord George Sackville was secretary, and made himself quite as much detested as primate Stone, and for the same reasons. At this time there was a surplus of revenue; and the consideration of how to apply it revived the old question of privilege between the English and Irish parliaments.

744. The Patriots proposed, in 1749, that it should be applied to pay off some portion of the national debt; but the court party held that this could not be done without the sanction of the king.

745. There were two very able men on the side of the Patriotic party:— counsellor Anthony Malone their leader in parliament, a man of a high order of intellect, and a good orator; and Dr. Charles Lucas, first a Dublin apothecary, and subsequently a practising physician; a member of the town council; but not yet in parliament.

746. Primate Stone and secretary Sackville violently advocated the king's right to interfere; and they and their party were as violently resisted by the opposition headed by Malone in parliament, by Lucas outside, and by the earl of Kildare (afterwards duke of Leinster) in the house of lords.

747. In 1758 the commons, after great opposition from the party of Stone and Sackville, passed a bill by a small majority (of 6) disposing of the money without making any reference to the king or his consent. This gave great offence to the court party. At the same time the earl of Kildare presented a bold address to the king complaining Of the arrogance and corruption of Stone and Sackville.

748. The disturbances reached such a serious pass, that the English government recalled lord Dorset in 1755, and sent over the marquess of Hartington in his place. Under him matters settled down: but the Patriots had gained ground—the two parties being now nearly balanced—and the spirit of independence had greatly advanced within the last few years.

749. There was an increasing tendency to toleration; and even the Catholics began to bestir themselves to obtain relief, but with small result for the present.

The Catholic movement had its small beginnings in the efforts of three Catholic gentlemen:—Dr. Curry, a physician of Dublin, the historian of the civil wars in Ireland; Charles O'Conor of Bellanagar in Roscommon, a well-known scholar and antiquarian; and Mr. Wyse of Waterford. They endeavoured to stir up the Catholic clergy and aristocracy to agitate for their rights; and though they did not succeed, they spread enlightenment and infused some small life and hope among the Catholics.

750. They were more successful with the merchants and business men; and they founded the "Catholic Committee" to watch over the interests of Catholics, which was to hold its meetings in Dublin. In 1757, when John Russell duke of Bedford was appointed lord lieutenant in place of the

marquess of Hartington, the Catholics forwarded him an address to which lord Russell sent a kindly-worded reply. This was the first faint beginning of a movement for Catholic relief which subsequently became so formidable under O'Connell.

751. In 1759 there were rumours of a Union between England and Ireland, which caused great excitement. The people of Dublin became enraged when they heard that their parliament was to be removed to London, and that they would have to pay the same taxes as in England; and there was a terrible riot. The mob broke into the House of Lords, and seated an old woman on the throne to mock Bedford, who even before this had become very unpopular; and they tried to burn the parliamentary books.

They also made every lord and commoner they met in the streets swear to oppose the union. The military were called out, but the rioting went on, till night sent the mob home. The people who rose this time were all Protestants: the Catholics were still too crushed and timid to take part in any such movement.

THE EXPEDITION OF THUROT (1759-1760)

752. England was at this time at war with France, and a report of a projected French invasion caused great alarm. Towards the end of 1759, an army was collected at Vannes in Brittany, which was to be conveyed by a powerful fleet anchored at Brest under admiral Conflans. A smaller squadron of five vessels lay at Dunkirk under Thurot, an enterprising commander, an Irishman, whose real name was O'Farrell.

753. Admiral Hawke kept a watch on the fleet at Brest; but being forced by a storm to take refuge in Torbay, the fleet put to sea. It was intercepted by Hawke off Quiberon bay, on the French coast, on the night of the 14th November 1759, and defeated; after which the French abandoned all thoughts of an invasion.

754. Commodore Boys had been watching Thurot, who however eluded him and sailed out. But he was driven by storms to Bergen in Norway, where he remained till December. One of his vessels had disappeared in the storm; one returned to France; and with the remaining three he appeared off Carrickfergus on the 21st February 1760. Having been tossed about by storms, his crew were reduced by famine and hardships, and were now half starved. With about 1,000 men he disembarked and attacked the castle, which was defended by colonel Jennings with only 150 men of the 62nd regiment, having no cannon and hardly any ammunition.

755. After a brief defence Jennings had to surrender, and the hungry French fell on all the food they could find; but did not molest the people. As there were not sufficient provisions, they obtained some from Belfast under threat of burning that town and Carrickfergus. On the 26th of February they re-embarked, on hearing that an armed force was advancing

on them; but they were intercepted a little north of the Isle of Man by captain Elliott, who had sailed in pursuit from Kinsale with the ship Æolus and two others. There was a sharp action in which Thurot was killed; and his three vessels were captured and brought into Ramsey.

George II. died suddenly at Kensington of heart disease on the 25th October 1760, and was succeeded by his grandson George III.

IRISH SECRET SOCIETIES (1760-1762)

756. The misery and discontent prevailing all over the country at this time gave origin to various oath-bound societies, by which the country was for many years disturbed.

757. The Whiteboys who first rose up in 1761, were so called because they wore white shirts over their coats when out on their nightly excursions: and their operations were chiefly in the counties of Waterford, Cork, Limerick, and Tipperary. This combination was not political: it was not directed against the government, but against the oppressive encroachments of the local landlords: and members of different religions joined in it.

758. The landlords had everywhere begun to enclose as their private property the "commons", which belonged to the people, and without which they found it impossible to live; for the peasantry were at this time in a state of great distress. The Whiteboys levelled the fences at night, whence they first got the name of "levellers." The people suffered also from the exactions of the collectors of tithes for the ministers of the Established Church, payments which the landlords evaded: and they also complained of the excessive rents charged for bogs.

759. The Whiteboys soon passed beyond their original designs, setting themselves up as the redressers of all sorts of grievances; and they committed terrible outrages on those who became obnoxious to them. Sometimes they brought people out of their beds in winter, and immersed them naked up to the chin in a pit of water full of briars.

760. In 1762 a large force was sent against them under the marquis of Drogheda, who fixed his head-quarters at Clogheen in Tipperary. The parish priest, father Nicholas Sheehy, was accused of enrolling Whiteboys, and a reward was offered for his arrest; but he surrendered, was tried in Dublin, and was acquitted. Soon afterwards he was arrested on a charge of murdering one of the witnesses against him: he was tried this time in Clonmel, and on the evidence of the same witnesses who had been disbelieved in Dublin, he was convicted and hanged. Father Sheehy asserted his innocence to the last; the people considered him a martyr, and his execution caused fearful excitement.

761. in Ulster there were similar secret associations among the Protestant peasantry, originating in causes of much the same class as those of the south. The first ground of complaint was that every man was forced to give

six days' work in the year and six days' work of a horse, for making or repairing roads, which the gentry often turned to their own use, while they themselves contributed nothing.

762. Those who banded together against this were called "Hearts of oak." Another association, the "Hearts of steel," rose in 1769, against unjust and exorbitant rents, chiefly exacted by middlemen—speculators or "forestallers"—who took lands from absentee landlords at greatly increased rents, and made their own profit by doubling the rents on the poor tenants.

The "oak boys" and the "steel boys" were quite as merciless as their brethren of the south, and like them, set themselves to redress all sorts of agrarian abuses.

763. The oppression of the northern peasantry by the gentry caused a great emigration of the very flower of the people to New England; and when a little later the war broke out between England and the United States, the most determined and dangerous of the troops who fought against the English were the sturdy expatriated Presbyterians of Ulster, and the descendants of those who had emigrated on account of religious persecution and the destruction of the wool trade.

764. There were many other secret societies at this time and for long after, culminating in the later developments of the United Irishmen.

PROGRESS TOWARDS PARLIAMENTARY INDEPENDENCE (1762-1772)

765. In 1762 a bill was passed in the Irish parliament to enable Catholics to lend money on the security of land: but it was suppressed in England: and in the following year it was rejected in the Irish parliament on the ground that it would tend to throw land into the hands of the Catholics.

766. About this time the Patriots, under the powerful lead of Henry Flood, and aided by the growing eloquence of young Henry Grattan, attacked the pension list, which was a source of great corruption, and had grown to enormous proportions. Many thousands of pounds were given to persons who never had any connexion with Ireland. But these efforts were vain, for the pensions, so far from being abolished, grew year by year.

767. The question of most interest at this time was the duration of parliament. In England the utmost time was seven years: in Ireland parliament lasted as long as the king wished; and the preceding one had continued during the entire reign of George II.: thirty-three years.

This state of things led to great abuses; and in 1765 the Patriots introduced a Septennial bill, which was passed in Ireland but suppressed in England.

768. Lord Townsend became lord lieutenant in 1767, and was at first popular from his gay convivial manner and his lavish distribution of favours.

769. Charles Lucas had continued to issue books and pamphlets violently attacking the court party, denouncing Poynings' act, and maintaining the right of Ireland to self-government. The corporation disfranchised him; and as he heard the House of Commons were about to prosecute him he retired for a time to England, where he practised with success as a physician. He returned in 1760, and was elected member for Dublin in 1761. He was the founder of the Freeman's Journal, which advocated the rights of the people and boldly upheld liberal principles.

770. Some years after his arrival Lucas and the Patriot party re-introduced the Septennial bill and had it carried (1767); but the term was changed in England to eight years. This "Octennial" bill was accepted by the Irish parliament, and caused great joy in Ireland.

771. As a consequence of the Octennial act it was necessary to elect a new parliament, and the viceroy (Lord Townsend) used bribes and corruption everywhere in order to secure a majority for the government. He now became as odious as he was at first popular.

772. But with all his bribery he was not able to induce the individual members to relinquish the right to originate money bills in the commons. In October 1769, the privy council sent over a money bill, which was rejected by the Irish house of commons, as in 1692, "because it had not its origin in that house"; for they maintained the just doctrine that the representatives of the people had alone the right to tax the people.

773. On this, lord Townsend had the commons summoned to the bar of the house of lords, where he lectured them sharply. He then ordered the clerk to enter his protest, which was done in the journal of the lords; but the commons were firm, and would not permit it to be entered in their journals. The excitement in Dublin on this occasion was almost as great as in the time of Wood's halfpence.

774. The viceroy prorogued the parliament now and several times subsequently so as to prevent a meeting till 1771. But he employed the interval in buying over several prominent members of the opposition by places and pensions, among others Sexton Pery, Hely Hutchinson, and lord Loftus. During all this time Dublin teemed with newspapers, letters, pamphlets, ballads, squibs, and satires against Townsend and the government, and the opposition gained in strength and determination.

775. When the house met in 1771, addresses to the viceroy were adopted in both houses. Sixteen of the lords protested, with the duke of Leinster (lately earl of Kildare) at their head. In the Commons it was carried by only a small majority: for the Patriots bitterly opposed it as degrading. Among the opponents were the speaker Ponsonby, Hely Hutchinson, Henry Flood, and Sexton Pery—even though he had got a pension: and the speaker Ponsonby resigned rather than present it. Pery was appointed in his place. But it ought to be said that though Pery accepted pension and place from

the government, he always took the side of the Patriots.

776. All this time the Catholics were absolutely silent, taking no part in political questions: their only desire being to avoid the sharp fangs of the law. Yet there were signs of some faint desire to indulge them a little. In 1771 lord Townsend had an act passed—which had been previously often rejected—enabling a Catholic to take, on long lease, and reclaim 50 acres of bog; which, however, was guarded by the precaution that the bog should not be nearer than a mile to any town or city.

777. But to counterbalance this little favour, which caused great alarm to some, he increased the pension offered to priests who became Protestants from £30 to £40. The witty Dublin people called the additional £10, "Townsend's Golden Drops."

778. The viceroy had one other trial of strength with the parliament. A money bill for supplies was brought forward in 1771, and passed in the Commons, then transmitted to England, in accordance with Poynings' act, and sent back with some alterations. But the Irish commons rejected it, and passed another of their own granting the supplies.

779. Townsend at last grew tired of the sleepless opposition of the Patriots and of the everlasting deluge of hostile literature; so that he resigned in 1772, and was succeeded by Simon earl of Harcourt.

780. Townsend had, during his administration, brought to great perfection the art of corrupting parliament by pensions, places, and titles, to secure a majority for the Court or English party. But this had, on the other hand, the effect of consolidating the patriotic party, and of strengthening their determination to break down the purely English interest, and to have Irish affairs managed solely for the benefit of Ireland.

THE AMERICAN WAR AND ITS EFFECTS ON IRELAND (1772-1778)

781. Lord Harcourt, coming as lord lieutenant in 1772, was well received by the leaders of the opposition. On the assembling of parliament in October 1773, a bill was introduced at his suggestion to put a tax of two shillings in the pound on the incomes of those absentee landlords who did not reside at least six months of the year in Ireland. But through the influence of the great landed proprietors it was rejected.

782. At this time three great men began their career, and for years played an important part in Irish affairs:—Henry Flood, born near Kilkenny, 1732: died 1791: Henry Grattan, born in Dublin, 1746, the son of the recorder, died 1820; Edmund Burke, born in Dublin in 1730; died 1797.

783. Burke, who figured in the English parliament, was, perhaps, the greatest political philosopher that ever lived. He began his public life in 1765, as private secretary to lord Rockingham, the English prime minister, and in the following year he was elected member for Wendover. In 1774 he became member for Bristol. He opposed the American war; and on this

question and on those of the French revolution, and the Stamp act, he wrote powerful pamphlets, and made a series of splendid speeches. He lifted himself above the prejudices of the times, and all his life advocated the emancipation of the Catholics.

784. Grattan was, perhaps, Ireland's most brilliant orator and one of her purest and greatest patriots. He began his parliamentary life in 1775, at twenty-nine years of age, as member for Charlemont; and his very first speech was in opposition to the pensions of two absentees. In oratorical power, Flood was second only to Grattan.

785. In 1775 began the war between England and her North American colonies, which was brought on mainly by an attempt to tax the colonists without giving them any voice in the matter. Against this they revolted, and in the end succeeded in making themselves independent.

786. This war deeply affected Ireland in more ways than one. In November of the same year the Irish parliament agreed, on the king's request, to send 4,000 Irish troops for service in America, England to bear the expense. But they declined another proposition, to supply their place with 4,000 Protestant troops from Germany, which greatly mortified the government. At this time the nominal force in Ireland was only 12,000 troops; but the real available force was greatly less.

787. In order to cheapen provisions for the British army, as well as to prevent supplies reaching America, an embargo was, in 1776, laid on the exportation of provisions from Irish ports, which almost ruined the farmers, and produced wide-spread distress.

788. The Irish parliament showed such dangerous discontent at this measure, that it was dissolved, and a new election ordered; and lord Buckinghamshire was sent over as lord lieutenant. The elections were greatly corrupted by bribes to secure a majority for the government. The embargo gave rise to a flourishing smuggling trade in provisions, which was extensively carried on, especially round the intricate coasts of the south and west.

789. In Ireland the people generally sympathised with America; for they felt that the grievances from which they had so long suffered, were exactly those against which the Americans had risen in revolt. Their feelings were intensified by witnessing the distress caused by the embargo, which was forced on this country from England without their consent.

790. When the war began in 1775 there were some discussions in the English parliament about removing of the commercial restrictions on Ireland: and there were a few trifling concessions; which, however, were much more than counterbalanced by the embargo.

791. In 1777 the English general Burgoyne with 6,000 men had to surrender to the American general Gage at Saratoga. This caused great consternation in England, which was increased when France declared for

America.

792. In 1778 France acknowledged the independence of the United States, which produced greater alarm still. Soon after, in the same year, the English Catholics were partially relieved by the English parliament, and the Irish embargo on provisions was removed immediately after.

793. In May 1778, a bill was introduced in the Irish patliament by Mr. Luke Gardiner, afterwards lord Mountjoy, granting considerable relief to Irish Catholics and Dissenters, and after a long contest and determined opposition it was carried by a majority of only nine.

794. This act repealed those enactments which prohibited the purchase of freehold property by Catholics and which gave the whole property to the eldest son who became a Protestant. Instead of the right to purchase, they got what was as good, the right to lease for 999 years. In the following year the Test Act was abolished; which relieved Dissenters as well as Catholics.

THE VOLUNTEERS (1778-1779)

795. While the American war was going on, with France and Spain also hostile, the possibility of foreign invasion was in men's minds. At the same time Ireland was in a very defenceless state: for since the withdrawal of the 4,000 men for America there were very few troops.

796. The danger was brought home to the people of the three kingdoms by the great number of American privateers that swarmed around the coasts, capturing British merchant vessels and doing immense damage. Paul Jones, a Scotchman in the American service, who commanded the "Ranger," especially distinguished himself by his daring exploits. He committed great havoc on the Irish coast, and outside Carrickfergus he captured, in 1778, the English brig the "Drake," and got safely off with her to Brest.

797. The Irish saw that if they were to be protected at all they must protect themselves; and this gave origin to the volunteers. The first volunteer companies were raised in Belfast in 1779, where the people still retained a vivid memory of the descent of Thurot, nineteen years before.

798. The movement rapidly spread: the country gentlemen armed and drilled their tenants: and by May 1779 there were nearly 4,000 enrolled in the counties of Down and Antrim. The Irish government did not look upon this movement with favour; but the feeling of the country was too strong for them. The movement extended to other parts of Ireland; and before the end of 1779, 42,000 volunteers were enrolled. Lord Charlemont was in command of the northern volunteers: the duke of Leinster of those of Leinster.

799. We must remember two things in regard to these volunteers. First, the government measures for suppressing Irish trade had produced great distress and great discontent all over the country. The rank and file of the volunteers were the very people who felt the prevailing distress most, and

without being in any sense disloyal, they were bitterly hostile to the government, while their sympathies were entirely with the patrotic party. It was indeed the Patriots who originated and controlled the volunteers.

800. The government were well aware of all this: but they dared not attempt to keep down the movement. They were obliged even to go so far as to supply arms, though much against their will: but all other expenses, including uniforms, were borne by the people themselves.

801. The second matter to be borne in mind is that this was almost exclusively a Protestant movement, the Catholics not yet being permitted to take any positions of trust.

802. Parliament met in October 1779. The patriotic party had now the volunteers at their back, and assumed a bolder tone. Flood had been their leader down to 1774 when he took office from the government, having been appointed vice-treasurer with a salary of £3,500. This obliged him to keep silent on most of the great questions that agitated parliament; and he lost the confidence of the people, which was now transferred to Grattan.

803. The embargo had been removed; but all the older restrictions on Irish trade still remained, under which it was impossible for the country to prosper.

804. On the assembling of parliament, Grattan in an amendment to the address, demanded free trade. After some discussion the following motion was carried unanimously:—"That it is not by temporary expedients, but by a free trade alone, that this nation is now to be saved from impending ruin."

805. Even the members in government employment voted for this: it was proposed by Walter Hussey Burgh the prime serjeant, and was supported by Flood, Hutchinson, Ponsonby, and Gardiner, all holding offices. Dublin was in a state of great excitement, and the parliament house was surrounded by an immense crowd shouting for free trade.

806. The address, with Grattan's amendment, was borne through Dame-street by the speaker and the commons in procession, from the parliament house to the castle, to be presented to lord Buckinghamshire the lord lieutenant. The streets were lined both sides with volunteers under the duke of Leinster, and as the procession walked along they were received with acclamation by an immense multitude; and the volunteers presented arms.

807. It was in the debates on this question that Hussey Burgh made his reputation as an orator. In one of them he used a sentence that has become famous. Someone had remarked that Ireland was at peace:—"Talk not to me of peace," said he: "Ireland is not at peace; it is smothered war. England has sown her laws as dragons' teeth: they have sprung up as armed men."* This sentence produced unparalleled excitement; and when it had calmed down so that he could be heard, he announced that he resigned his office under the crown. "The gates of promotion are shut," exclaimed Grattan: "the gates of glory are opened!"

808. But to the British parliament alone, which had laid on the restrictions, belonged the task of removing them. In November 1779 the English prime minister, lord North, introduced three propositions to relieve Irish trade: the first permitted free export of Irish wool and woollen goods; the second free export of Irish glass manufactures; the third allowed free trade with the British colonies. The two first were passed; the third after a little time. The news of this was received with great joy in Dublin.

* Alluding to a well-known classical myth.

THE DAWN (1779-1782)

809. So far the popular party in Ireland had been successful all along; and their ideas grew with their success. They had obtained some relief for trade: they now resolved that their parliament, which was bound down by Poynings' law and by the Sixth of George I., should also be free.

810. On the 19th of April 1780, in a magnificent speech, Grattan moved his memorable resolutions:— That the king with the lords and commons of Ireland are the only power on earth competent to enact laws to bind Ireland.

That Great Britain and Ireland are inseparably united under one sovereign.

The question however was not put directly to a division: Flood was in favour of postponement, the parliament adjourned, and consequently the resolution was not entered on the journals. It was obvious however that the sense of the house was on the side of Grattan.

811. The next conflict was on a Mutiny bill. In England the Mutiny bill—the bill to maintain and regulate the army—is not permanent: it is passed from year to year, lest the army might be used by the king or government as an instrument of oppression. The Mutiny bill for Ireland was passed by the Irish parliament; but having been transmitted to England it was returned changed to a perpetual bill. When this was proposed by the government in the Irish parliament, it was most resolutely opposed, and created fearful irritation and excitement all over the country. But the court party carried it in spite of all expostulation.

812. Meantime the excitement and enthusiam for home government went on; and the opposition, led by Grattan, gained strength and confidence by the great increase of the volunteers, who, much against the wish of the government, continued to be enrolled in the four provinces, and at last numbered 100,000 men.

813. In December 1780, the English government, not satisfied with lord Buckinghamshire's administration, recalled him and sent over the earl of Carlisle as lord lieutenant, with Mr. Eden (afterwards lord Auckland) as secretary.

814. This new viceroy found the whole country agitated on the question of legislative independence. During the early months of 1781 innumerable

meetings were held all over Ireland; and what was more significant, there were reviews of the volunteers everywhere in the four provinces.

815. In Belfast lord Charlemont rode through the crowded streets at the head of his splendid corps, and issued an address in which he hailed the spirit of freedom that had enabled them, without help from outside, to provide against foreign invasion, and looked forward to the accomplishment of legislative independence.

816. The action of the English government appears to have been singularly short-sighted and ill-judged in irritating the Irish people at the very time of wars with America, France, Spain, and elsewhere. Their proceedings instead of suppressing the spirit now abroad through the country, or allaying excitement, intensified the discontent and spread the agitation.

817. In the session of 1781, which did not open till October, Grattan was the great leader of the popular party. He was seconded with almost equal ability by Flood, who towards the end of the preceding year, finding his position of enforced silence unendurable, had thrown up his government appointment, joined his old friends, and thereby regained much of his former popularity. They had at their back a number of able and brilliant men—Hely Hutchinson, John Fitzgibbon (afterwards lord Clare, and a bitter enemy of the cause he now advocated), Hussey Burgh, and others.

818. Barry Yelverton had given notice of motion for the 5th of December 1781 for the repeal of Poynings' act; but on that day news came of a great disaster, the surrender of lord Cornwallis and his whole army in America, which ruined the cause of England in the war. Whereupon Yelverton, abandoning his motion for the time, moved an address of loyalty and attachment to the king, which was carried.

819. On the 7th December Grattan drew attention to the rapidly increasing debt, largely due to pensions; but the government, nevertheless, carried their money bills, pensions and all.

On the 11th December, Flood took up Yelverton's motion for an inquiry into Poynings' act; but was defeated by government.

820. During all this session government were able to secure a majority by a skilful and plentiful distribution of patronage:—pensions, places, promotions, titles, and other such inducements. At last Grattan, hopeless of being able to contend successfully in parliament with the government, determined to let the empire hear the voice of even a more powerful pleader. Under the management of lord Charlemont, Flood, and himself, a convention of delegates from the volunteer corps of Ulster was summoned for the 15th of February 1782, at Dungannon, the old home of Hugh O'Neill.

821. Two hundred and forty-two delegates from 143 volunteer corps of the northern province assembled in the Dissenting Meeting House of

Dungannon, most of them men of wealth and station. They passed thirteen resolutions, of which the most important were:—

822. That the king, lords, and commons of Ireland have alone the right to legislate for the country.

That Poynings' law is unconstitutional and a grievance, and should be revoked;

That the ports of Ireland should be open to all nations not at war with the king:

That a permanent mutiny bill is unconstitutional:

And "That as men and Irishmen, as Christians and as Protestants, we rejoice in the relaxation of the penal laws against our Roman Catholic fellow-subjects." This last was inserted at the instance of Grattan.

823. The resolutions of the Dungannon Convention were adopted by all the volunteer corps of Ireland; and they formed the basis of the momentous legislation that followed.

824. These spirit-stirring proceedings were altogether the work of Protestants: the Catholics were still shut out from taking any part in them. Yet, though the volunteers were originally instituted for Protestants only, many Catholics were enrolled as time went on.

825. On the day that the Dungannon resolutions were passed. Mr. Gardiner introduced a measure for the relief of Catholics which was adopted. They were allowed to buy, sell, and otherwise dispose of lands the same as their Protestant neighbours; they could celebrate or hear Mass; Catholic schoolmasters could teach schools; the law prohibiting a Catholic from having a horse worth £5 was repealed, as well as those which made Catholics pay for losses by robberies, and which forbade them to come to live in Limerick and Galway.

LEGISLATIVE INDEPENDENCE (1782-1783)

826. In England lord North's ministry fell in 1782, and he was succeeded by the marquess of Rockingham; after which lord Carlisle retired from Ireland and the duke of Portland came over as lord lieutenant. The Irish parliament met on the 16th of April 1782, with the new viceroy present. The citizens of Dublin, knowing what was coming, were all abroad; and among them the volunteers were conspicuous with their bands, banners, and bright uniforms.

827. The usual address was moved, to which Grattan moved an amendment comprising all the chief demands of the Irish people; ending with the declaration that the king and Irish parliament alone had the right to make laws for Ireland. These were merely a repetition of the Dungannon resolutions, with the exception of Catholic emancipation which was not expressly mentioned. The amendment was unanimously agreed to. The next part of the proceedings was in the English parliament. On the 17th of May, a resolution for the repeal of the Sixth of George I was proposed in

the house of lords by the earl of Shelburne, and in the commons by Charles James Fox; to which both houses agreed.

828. This concession, known as the "Act of Repeal," was communicated by the viceroy to the Irish parliament at its meeting of the 27th of May. It was interpreted to mean that England gave Ireland an independent parliament over which it renounced all authority, annulled Poynings' law, restored to the Irish lords the right to hear appeals, abolished the right of appeal to the English lords, and in general yielded all the demands of Grattan's amendments.

829. This was Grattan's interpretation of the repeal of the 6th of George I. But Flood differed: he wished that England should be called on to go further by passing a formal act renouncing for ever the right to make laws for Ireland. Grattan's opinion prevailed in the house; and immediately the Irish parliament passed bills embodying all the above points. The news was received in Ireland with a tremendous outburst of joy, both in the house and outside among the people; and as an evidence of gratitude, the parliament voted 20,000 men and £100,000 to the British navy.

830. It was felt and acknowledged that this consummation was mainly due to Grattan; and parliament voted him a grant of £100,000. But he accepted only £50,000, and even that after much persuasion. With this he bought an estate in Queen's County; and took up his permanent residence in a beautiful spot that he loved: Tinnehinch, near Enniskerry in Wicklow, twelve miles from Dublin.

831. But although the parliament went with Grattan, Flood's view prevailed outside, both among the volunteers and among the people. As confirming his opinion, the English parliament, in January of the following year—1783—when lord Shelburne was prime minister, actually passed the "Act of Renunciation" declaring that Ireland's right to be bound only by the laws made by the king and the Irish parliament was "established for ever, and shall at no time hereafter be questioned or questionable."

832. Lord Rockingham died in July 1782, to whom succeeded as prime minister the earl of Shelburne; and in September earl Temple succeeded the duke of Portland in Ireland as lord lieutenant.

833. At the instance of the English government lord Temple established in 1783, a new order of knights, which was to be peculiarly Irish, the Knights of the Illustrious Order of St. Patrick, which still subsists. The new members, who are chiefly selected from among the Irish aristocracy, are installed with great ceremony on the 17th of March, St. Patrick's day. The Irish parliament was dissolved in July, 1783, and a new parliament was formed which was to meet in October.

PARLIAMENTARY AND COMMERCIAL REFORM (1783-1785)

834. The Irish parliament, which was now free, was unhappily, as it stood—unreformed—as bad a type of parliament as could well be

conceived: and the government resisted all reform. The house of commons consisted of 300 members, of whom only 72 were really returned by the people: all the rest were nominated, or their election was in some way influenced, by lords or other powerful people.

One noble lord commanded sixteen seats, a money making possession, for he sold them all in election times; another had fourteen, another nine, and so on. Twenty-five individuals owned about 116 seats. At one election the proprietor of Belturbet received £11,000 for the seat. The spurious boroughs fabricated in the time of the Stuarts still existed , and all sent to parliament nominees of the government. The numbers of electors in many of these were not more than a dozen, who could in most cases be easily bought off. In some places, as at Swords near Dublin, every adult Protestant had a vote: an arrangement imitated from some constituencies in England. Under these circumstances it was always easy for the government to secure a majority by merely spending money. The house was thoroughly corrupt, with of course many noble individual exceptions.

835. Lastly the Roman Catholics, who formed four fifths of the population, were totally shut out: a Catholic could neither be a member nor vote for a member. It did not represent the nation: and it did not represent even the Protestant people. It contained within itself the elements of decay and dissolution There was never a parliament more in need of reform; and reform would have saved it.

836. Two great questions now lay before the country:—Parliamentary reform and the removal of restrictions on Irish commerce. A third question was Catholic emancipation, which however was, for the present, kept much in the background. Flood was for immediate action on reform; Grattan also was for reform, but thought the time had not come for pressing it, and left the matter in Flood's hands. Grattan was for emancipation; Flood was against it.

837. Flood felt keenly the loss of his influence; and Grattan's brilliant career and unbounded popularity had thrown him into the shade Between these two great men there was gradually growing up a feeling of rivalry and estrangement.

838. The volunteers took up the question of reform. A meeting of delegates was held in Dungannon in September, and there were other meetings in other parts of Ireland. In all these the subject was discussed, and a general convention in Dublin of delegates from all the volunteer corps of Ireland was arranged for the 10th of November 1783. These proceedings were very alarming to the government, who wanted no reform.

839. The earl of Northington was appointed lord lieutenant in June 1783, in place of lord Temple. The new parliament met in October, and the government, though fearing the volunteers, had a vote of thanks passed to them, probably to conciliate the country.

Flood brought in a motion in favour of retrenchment as a beginning of reform, in which the opposition were voted down by the government. In the debates that followed occurred a bitter and very lamentable altercation between Grattan and Flood, which terminated their friendship for ever. Yet subsequently, each bore generous testimony to the greatness of the other.

840. The 10th of November came, and 160 volunteer delegates assembled, first in the royal exchange in Dublin, and this being not large enough, afterwards in the Rotunda. Their commander was James Caulfield, earl of Charlemont, a man universally respected, of refined tastes and scholarly attainments, and moderate in his views. He was elected chairman.

841. Within the volunteers were men of more extreme views, who were for Catholic emancipation, and some even for total separation from England: these found a leader in an eccentric character, Frederick Augustus Hervey, earl of Bristol and Protestant bishop of Derry. He assumed great state: dressed out in gorgeous robes, he drove through the streets of Dublin, escorted by a company of dragoons, and followed by great mobs who idolised him.

842. The delegates held their sittings during the sitting of parliament. They discussed plans of reform, and after much labour certain propositions were agreed to, which however did not include any proposals for the relief of Catholics. This omission was the result of a discreditable manoeuvre on the part of the government, by which the convention was divided, and the ultra Protestants had the consideration of Catholic relief put aside.

843. In parliament Flood introduced a bill embodying the demands of the convention, which brought on a stormy debate. Barry Yelverton, now attorney general, afterwards lord Avonmore, led the opposition to the bill, at the same time denouncing vehemently the attempt to coerce the parliament by an armed body of men; and John Fitzgibbon and others followed in the same strain.

Flood, in a powerful speech, advocated the bill and defended the action of the volunteers. The scene in parliament is described as "almost terrific." Grattan supported the bill, but not very earnestly; and John Philpot Curran who had been elected for Kilbeggan this same year—1783—made his first parliamentary speech in favour of it. But the government party were too strong, and it was rejected by 159 against 77.

844. There were now serious fears of a collision between the volunteers and the government: but the counsels of lord Charlemont prevailed; and on the 2nd of December the convention was adjourned without any day being fixed for next meeting. This was the death blow to the influence of the volunteers, and they never afterwards played any important part in the political affairs of the country. Thus the efforts of the popular party to reform a corrupt parliament ended for the present in failure, through government opposition.

845. After this defeat of his party Flood resolved to play a part elsewhere, and entered the English parliament in December 1783, still retaining his Irish seat. He was now a member of both parliaments and spoke and voted in each.

846. In the following year he made another effort in Ireland at reform, but the Irish government successfully resisted all attempts to improve the representation. Napper Tandy a prominent member of the volunteers, Flood, and some others, made an attempt to have a series of meetings convened through the country; but the movement was put down by the government.

847. The duke of Rutland succeeded lord Northington as lord lieutenant in February 1784. The volunteers, deserted by their leaders, formed democratic associations and held secret meetings. In Dublin, Belfast, and elsewhere, they began to drill men in the use of arms, Catholics as well as Protestants; whereupon the government increased the army to 15,000 men, and took measures to revive the militia, a force in the service of the crown.

But the people hated the militia, and the country became greatly disturbed. Scenes of violence occurred everywhere. Even in Dublin the mobs paraded the streets, attacked and maimed soldiers, broke into shops and ill used the shopkeepers for selling English goods It was a time of trouble and alarm.

848. The next movement was an attempt to regulate the commercial relations with England, which were all against Ireland: and here the Irish government were on the side of reform, though their ideas fell short of those of the opposition. There were enormous prohibitory duties on Irish goods exported to England, but little or none on English goods brought to Ireland: this repressed Irish commerce and manufactures, and helped to keep the country in a state of distress and poverty.

849. To remedy this state ol things—to equalise English and Irish duties—Mr. Thomas Orde chief secretary brought down from the castle, on the part of the government, eleven propositions. One of the provisions was that all Irish revenue beyond £650,000 should be applied to the support of the British navy, which drew forth considerable opposition. The whole of the propositions were however passed through parliament in the shape of resolutions, 12th February 1785.

850. The eleven propositions were transmitted to England for adoption there; for as the restrictions had been the work of the English parliament, it was only in England they could be removed. But when they were proposed in England by William Pitt, then chancellor of the exchequer, there arose violent opposition; petitions against them poured in from companies, manufacturers, and merchants, in all parts of England, who insisted on maintaining the monopoly that enriched themselves and impoverished Ireland. Whereupon Pitt, fearing to face the storm, brought down to the

English parliament twenty propositions of his own. much less favourable to Ireland—containing several injurious restrictions—and had them passed.

851. These on being transmitted to the Irish government and introduced by them to the Irish house in August 1785, were received by the opposition with an outburst of indignation. Flood led the opposition with all his old fire and energy. Grattan denounced the propositions in one of his finest speeches; and after an all-night stormy debate, the government had so small a majority—only 19—that they thought it more prudent to withdraw the bill. Thus the whole scheme of commercial reform fell through, and matters remained much as they were till the time of the Union.

MORE SECRET SOCIETIES (1785-1790)

852. The last chapter brought us down towards the end of 1785. Distress and discontent prevailed all over the country: for which there were various sufficient causes. For the Catholics there were the penal laws. The farmers were impoverished by the extortion of "middlemen," already spoken of, who leased tracts of land from absentee landlords, and sublet them at "rack-rents" that left hardly enough to sustain life.

853. All householders, Catholics and Dissenters as well as Protestants, had to pay "tithes" for the support of the clergy of the Established Church. These would no doubt have been generally paid quietly enough but for the action of persons called "tithe-proctors," or "tithe-farmers," who collected them for absentee clergymen. These men commonly received a fixed proportion of the tithes—a third or a fourth—to pay for collection, so that it was their interest to raise as much money as possible; and they extorted from the very poorest of the peasantry contributions far beyond what the law contemplated.

854. Moreover, grazing lands were exempt, so that the impost fell chiefly on poor cottiers, while the holders of extensive grazing farms were exempt; which again discouraged tillage and tended to make grass land of the whole country.

In addition to all this was the universal stagnation of business caused by the restrictions still remaining on commerce.

855. During the summer and autumn of this year—1785—the country was fearfully disturbed. The peasantry resorted to illegal secret societies. In the south there was a revival of the Whiteboys, now calling themselves "Right-boys," led by an imaginary "captain Right." These misguided men committed outrages like the Whiteboys, on agents, middlemen, tithe-proctors, and others. The proctors especially, who had rendered themselves intensely odious by their cruel extortions, were pursued mercilessly, often mutilated and sometimes killed. Another class, who were mostly blameless, the Protestant curates, always present to bear the odium, and striving to live on poor incomes of £40 or £50 a year, often suffered grievous ill-treatment. The Rightboys were denounced by the Catholic

clergy, especially by Dr. Butler archbishop of Cashel and Dr. Troy bishop of Ossory.

856. In the north—in Armagh, Tyrone and Down—another secret society had grown up among Protestants and Presbyterians, called "Peep-o'-day boys," and afterwards called "Protestant boys" and "Wreckers." These directed their hostilities against Catholics, who again in self-defence formed themselves into bands called "Defenders." These two parties, who belonged generally to the humblest class of the peasantry, did immense damage—fought, maimed and killed each other, and caused great disturbance.

857. To meet the Rightboys' disturbance the Irish government introduced a bill in 1786: but there was such opposition that it was withdrawn. As Dublin was quite as much disturbed as the north and south, a bill for the appointment of a number of constables to aid the city watchmen was passed this year after some opposition. This small body of men originated the present splendid force of the Dublin metropolitan police.

858. Early in 1787 Fitzgibbon introduced, and the government carried, a crushing insurrection bill which was to apply to the whole of Ireland. Grattan wished, instead of coercion, an inquiry into the causes of discontent and their removal, which he called the "engine of redress," but his party were overruled. In October this year—1787—the duke of Rutland died in Dublin, and was succeeded by lord Temple, marquess of Buckingham, now lord lieutenant for the second time—he who had instituted the Knights of St. Patrick.

859. A circumstance occurred at this time in England which had much influence on the ultimate fate of the Irish parliament. In the autumn of 1788 George III. had an attack of insanity, and the appointment of a regent became necessary.

The Irish parliament, by a large majority, but much against the wish of the government, offered the regency of Ireland to the Prince of Wales without limitation—he was to be in all respects king for the time being. At the instance of Pitt however, the prince, as regent for England, was to be restricted by considerable limitations. The lord lieutenant refused to forward the Irish address; on which parliament appointed a deputation to make the offer personally to the prince. But the king's recovery ended the dispute. This divergence was subsequently used as an argument by Pitt in favour of the union, on the ground of the possibility that at some future time the two kingdoms might choose two different regents, which would lead to very serious complications.

860. In order to break up the party against him the marquess of Buckingham bribed unsparingly: he gave peerages, places, pensions, and money, openly and without limit; and he dismissed all holders of government offices who had joined in the address to the Prince of Wales,

including the duke of Leinster There was probably more political corruption in the Irish government during his time than at any previous period. He added £18,000 to the pension list, which before his arrival had risen to the enormous yearly sum of £100,000. He was succeeded in January 1790 by the earl of Westmoreland; and so intense was his unpopularity that he had to steal away from Dublin by night.

AN INSTALMENT OF EMANCIPATION (1790-1793)

861. During the year 1790 the north was far more disturbed than the south; and the Peep-o'-day boys and the Defenders increased and multiplied and continued their outrages.

Among a higher class the French revolution, now in full progress, stirred people's minds profoundly. Clubs and committees were formed, partly to stem the tide of political corruption, partly to discuss theories of government. Grattan, Curran, and others of the patriotic party openly opposed the evil system of the government: but the government was inexorable and continued its courses.

862. The members of the party of progress, the leading men of the volunteers, formed themselves into clubs which greatly influenced public opinion:—the Whig club in Dublin and the Northern Whig club in Belfast. Of both clubs, the lists included many historic names—lord Charlemont, lord Moira, Napper Tandy, Hamilton Rowan, Wolfe Tone, &c.

863. In July 1791, the anniversary of the taking of the Bastile was celebrated in Belfast by the Northern Whig club in a great procession, with drums, banners, and flags on which were depicted various scenes enacted at the Revolution; ending with a banquet, where such toasts were drunk as "The national assembly of France," "The rights of man," &c. There was nothing illegal in all this, but it gave great uneasiness to the government, who, with the example of France before them, looked on all such proceedings with an unfriendly eye.

864. Theobald Wolfe Tone was born in Dublin in 1763, and became a barrister in 1789. In the year 1791 he was appointed paid secretary to the Catholic Committee in Dublin. In the same year he visited Belfast, and thinking the Northern Whig club not sufficiently bold or advanced, he founded the society of United Irishmen in October 1791. The fundamental objects of this society, which were quite legal, were:—to include all classes and religions in its body; to reform parliament so as to break down the unconstitutional influence of the government; and to remove the grievances of all Irishmen of every religious persuasion. This last mainly aimed at the repeal of the penal laws against Catholics.

865. He next formed a branch of the society in Dublin under the auspices of the Catholic Committee; James Napper Tandy, a Protestant shopkeeper of Dublin, was its secretary.

866. The Catholic Committee had been in existence in Dublin for several

years. It was formed for the purpose of looking after Catholic interests; and the main purpose it had in view was to obtain a relaxation or repeal of the penal laws. The members felt that this business gave them quite enough to do, and as a body they did not mix themselves up much in other political movements.

867. There were two parties in this Committee, the aristocratic and the democratic. The former included the Catholic nobility and hierarchy; they looked with horror on the French revolution and its excesses, and were inclined to be timid. The democratic party consisted chiefly of business men, of whom the ablest was John Keogh, a Dublin merchant. These were for pressing their claims boldly, including the right to vote at elections, which the aristocratic party wished at least for the present to postpone. On this question, and to clear themselves from the suspicion of sympathy with revolutionary principles, sixty-four of the aristocracy seceded from the Committee.

868. Notwithstanding this defection the democrats carried their point. They assembled a meeting of Catholic delegates on the 2nd of December 1792, in Back-lane, Dublin—whence it is sometimes called the "Back-lane Parliament"—at which a petition to the king was prepared asking for the franchise and some other privileges. It was signed by Dr. Troy Roman Catholic archbishop of Dublin, by Dr. Moylan bishop of Cork, and by all the county delegates. It was presented to the king on the 2nd January 1793 by five delegates, among them John Keogh, who were graciously received by his majesty.

869. On the 9th of April 1793, a bill was passed through the Irish parliament which granted the Catholics a substantial measure of relief. The franchise was restored to them, so that all who were forty-shilling freeholders had the right to vote for members of parliament. They could enter Trinity College, Dublin, and obtain degrees; almost all civil and military situations were opened to them—they could serve on juries and be justices of the peace. The higher classes of Catholics were allowed to carry arms. They might open colleges to be affiliated to Trinity College, provided they were not exclusively for the education of Catholics.

870. In order to have the benefit of the act they should take the oath of allegiance, which however any Catholic might take. But many restrictions still remained; the most serious of which was that no Catholic could sit in parliament: neither could a Catholic be lord lieutenant or lord chancellor.

871. On the other hand, in the same session two coercion acts were passed:—"the Convention act" against "unlawful assemblies" (brought in by Fitzgibbon, now lord Clare) intended to prevent meetings of delegates such as the "Back-lane parliament": the Gunpowder act to prevent the importation and sale of gunpowder and arms, and giving magistrates the power of searching for arms where-ever and whenever they pleased.

Another act was passed to raise 16,000 militia, and to increase the army from 12,000 to 17,000.

DISAPPOINTED HOPES (1793-1795)

872. The government kept a strict watch on the United Irishmen, the Catholic Committee, and all such associations, so as to be ready for prosecutions as occasions might arise. At a meeting of United Irishmen held in Dublin in February 1798, with the Hon. Simon Butler as chairman, and Oliver Bond, a Dublin merchant, as secretary, an address was adopted and circulated, animadverting on the conduct of the lords in a secret inquiry about the Defenders. For this Butler and Bond were sentenced to be imprisoned for six months and to pay a fine of £500 each.

873. Archibald Hamilton Rowan, the son of a landed proprietor of Ulster, who had been conspicuous as a volunteer, and was now a United Irishman, circulated an address to the volunteers written by Dr. Drennan. For this he was prosecuted, and was defended by Curran in one of his most brilliant speeches. He was convicted of a seditious libel, and sentenced to be imprisoned for two years, and to pay a fine of £500.

874. While Rowan was in prison, an emissary from France arrived in Ireland to sound the people about a French invasion: the Rev. William Jackson, a Protestant clergyman of Irish extraction. He had with him a London attorney named Cockayne, to whom he had confided his secret, but who was really a spy in the pay of Pitt. These two had interviews with the leading United Irishmen in Dublin—Wolfe Tone, Leonard MacNally, Hamilton Rowan then in the Dublin Newgate prison, and others.

875. MacNally was a Dublin attorney, who managed the legal business of the United Irishmen: he was trusted by them with their innermost secrets, and lived and died in their friendship and confidence. Long after his death it was discovered that he was all the time a spy in government pay. Tone drew out a report on the state of Ireland for Jackson, who kept a copy of it in Hamilton Rowan's handwriting.

876. When the government, who knew all that was going on, thought matters were sufficiently ripe, they arrested Jackson on the 28th of April 1794. Rowan, knowing that his handwriting would betray him, contrived to escape on the 1st of May by bribing a jailer: and although £1,000 were offered for his arrest he made his way to France and thence to America. On the 23rd April of the following year Jackson was tried and convicted of treason on the evidence of Cockayne. But he had managed to take a dose of arsenic before coming into court, and dropped dead in the dock.

877. Towards the end of 1794 people's minds became greatly excited in Ireland, when it became known that Pitt had determined to adopt a policy of conciliation, and to drop coercion. With this object lord Westmoreland was recalled, and the earl of Fitzwilliam, a just, liberal, and enlightened man, having large estates in Ireland, came as lord lieutenant on the 4th of

January 1795 with the firm determination, which he did not conceal, to completely emancipate the Catholics. His arrival naturally excited their hopes, and they gave him an enthusiastic reception.

878. He at once applied himself to the work intrusted to him. He removed Edward Cooke from the post of undersecretary on a pension of £1,200 a year; also John Beresford, the commissioner of customs, whose relations held most of the lucrative offices of his department, and who retired on full pay. Both of these had been identified with the system lord Fitzwilliam came to break up. In the joy of the good news, parliament voted a large sum of money for the expenses of the navy in the war now going on with France, and 20,000 men for the army.

879. As the first direct move, Grattan, having previously arranged the matter with the viceroy, brought in a bill on the 12th of February for the admission of Catholics to parliament. But an unexpected obstacle arose which disconcerted all the intended reforms, and dashed the hopes of the Catholics.

880. A bill in order to become law must have the concurrence of the three branches of the legislature:—the king, the lords, and the commons. Beresford, after his dismissal, went to England and made bitter complaints. He had a long private interview with the king and seems to have persuaded him that the Protestant religion was in danger. The king interposed his veto: and that ended the matter. All progress was stopped. Beresford was restored, ascendancy got another lease of life, and the old policy of coercion was resumed. Earl Fitzwilliam was recalled and left Ireland on the 25th of March 1795. He was escorted by sorrowing crowds to the water side, and his coach was drawn along by some of the leading citizens, while the shops were closed and the city put on the appearance of mourning.

881. The disappointment spread sorrow and indignation all over the country, not only among the Catholics, but also among the Protestants of the two parties—the moderates led by Grattan and the more advanced represented by the United Irishmen. That cruel disappointment, from whatever cause, was in a great measure answerable for the tremendous evils that followed.

The king's objections are commonly put forward as the cause of the sudden change of policy. But some suppose that the whole scheme was planned by Pitt in order to obtain large supplies from the Irish parliament.

DRIFTING TOWARDS REBELLION (1793-1795)

882. A few days after the departure of lord Fitzwilliam, the new lord lieutenant earl Camden arrived. Grattan brought in his emancipation bill, but it was rejected by more than three to one.

883. The people were exasperated and desperate; and the active spirits came to the fatal determination to attempt revolution, hoping for foreign aid and the ultimate establishment of a republic. The United Irishmen

banded themselves as a secret oath-bound — and of course illegal — society, with branches all through the country, and a central directory of five persons in Dublin. Every precaution was taken for secrecy, but the government were kept well acquainted with their proceedings through Leonard MacNally and others within their body.

884. By May this year—1795—the organisation of the new society was complete. Tone had taken an active part in it; but now he had to leave Ireland. He was compromised by some evidence that had come out on Jackson's trial; but he escaped prosecution by the interest of powerful friends, on condition that he should immediately quit the country. Before leaving Dublin he promised the leaders that he would negotiate for help in America and France. Passing on his way through Belfast he took three leading members to Mac Art's Fort on the very summit of Cave Hill overlooking the town, and there made the same promise, and got them to swear to work to the last for Irish independence. He then sailed for America.

885. In consequence of the penal code Catholic young men who wished to become priests had long been in the habit of going to France for their education. The government, in order to stop this, as they feared the introduction of revolutionary principles, founded the college of Maynooth this year—1795—for the education of the Catholic clergy, and endowed it with an annual grant of £8,000.

886. The great majority of the leaders of the United Irishmen were Protestants, who were all of course for Catholic emancipation. But, in Ulster especially, there was, all along, bitter strife between the Catholics and Protestants. Tone, himself a Protestant, had done all in his power to bring them to friendly union and co-operation, but in vain: religious animosity was too strong for him. At last the Peep-o'-day boys and the Defenders fought a regular battle on the 21st September 1795, at a village called The Diamond in Armagh: the Protestants, though inferior in number, were better armed, and the Defenders were defeated with a loss of 48 killed.

887. The Protestants next banded themselves in a new society called "Orangemen," with the openly expressed intention to expel all the Catholics from Ulster. The Catholics were now attacked and persecuted everywhere in Ulster without any distinction, and suffered ruthless cruelties in person and property. General Craddock was sent with the military to restore order, but so close a watch was kept on his movements that he found it almost impossible to arrest the bands of armed Orangemen; and outrages still went on.

888. General Henry Luttrell lord Carhampton was sent to Connaught to repress the Defenders: he seized all who were in the jails awaiting trial, and the magistrates, imitating him, seized on many of the peasants; and all,

both prisoners and peasants were, without any trial, sent off to compulsory service in the navy.

889. Meantime the society of United Irishmen spread, until finally, it numbered 500,000. There were now many Catholics, but to the last the confederacy was mainly Protestant; and the members were more numerous and active in Ulster than elsewhere.

890. In 1795 lord Edward Fitzgerald, brother of the duke of Leinster, bad joined them. As a major in the British army he had served with credit in the American war, after which he entered the Irish parliament as an ardent supporter of reform. The government dismissed him from his post in the army for openly expressed sympathy with the French revolution In 1796 the society was joined by Thomas Addis Emmet, by Arthur O'Connor formerly member of parliament for Philipstown, and by Dr. William J. MacNevin of Dublin, one of the few Catholics among the leaders.

891. Tone had been arranging in Paris for a French invasion: the object was to make Ireland an independent republic. In May 1796 lord Edward Fitzgerald and O'Connor went to Hamburg, and O'Connor had an interview with general Hoche about an invasion; for the French and English were still at war. The matter was at last arranged. On the 16th of December 1796 a fleet of 43 ships of war with 15,000 troops and 45,000 stand of arms sailed from Brest for Ireland under general Hoche. General Grouchy was second in command, and with him sailed Theobald Wolfe Tone as adjutant-general.

892. The authorities prepared to repel the attack, but it was repelled without their intervention. The ships were dispersed by foul winds and fogs, and only sixteen that had kept together entered Bantry Bay. Here they waited in vain for general Hoche, whose vessel had been separated from the fleet by the storm. But the wild weather continued—tempest and snow—and at the end of a week, Hoche not having come up, they cut their cables and returned to France.

893. Next came a stringent Insurrection act in 1796. The Habeas Corpus act was suspended, which suspension gave the magistrates the power to arrest any one they pleased. General Lake got command of the army in Ulster, and he proclaimed martial law in Down, Antrim, Tyrone, Derry, and Donegal, which placed the people entirely at the mercy of the military.

He arrested two committees of United Irishmen sitting in Belfast, seized their papers, and suppressed their journal, the Northern Star. He disarmed Ulster, seizing vast numbers of muskets, cannons, and pikes. For publishing a violent address Arthur O'Connor was arrested and imprisoned in Dublin castle.

894. The yeomanry were called out; militia regiments were sent over from England; and military, yeomanry, and militia were let loose on the people with little restraint. The soldiers were scattered through the country

in small parties, billeted and living in free quarters on the peasantry; there was no discipline; and they did what they pleased without waiting for orders. Fearful brutalities were perpetrated, and thousands of peaceable people were driven in desperation to join the ranks of the United Irishmen.

895. Grattan and his party having ascertained from the leaders of the United Irishmen what measures of reform would satisfy them, were assured that all agitation would cease if full representation for the whole people of Ireland irrespective of creed, with the admission of Catholics to parliament, were granted. George Ponsonby moved in parliament the granting of these reasonable reforms; but the government outvoted the party by 170 to 30 and refused the concessions. Whereupon Grattan and the other leading members of his party, despairing of doing any good, and as a protest against the conduct of the government, seceded from parliament.

896. There was yet another abortive attempt at invasion. A Dutch fleet with 15,000 men commanded by admiral De Winter prepared to sail for Ireland in July 1797; but again the weather proved unfavourable; they were delayed; and when at length they sailed, the fleet was utterly defeated at Camperdown by admiral Duncan. In September of the same year Hoche died.

THE REBELLION OF 1798

897. The government were kept well informed of the secret proceedings of the rebels and abided their time till things were ripe for a swoop. They knew that the 23rd of May had been fixed as the day of rising. On the 12th of March 1798, major Swan, a magistrate, acting on the information of Thomas Reynolds, arrested Oliver Bond and fourteen other delegates assembled in committee in Bond's house in Bridge-street, and seized all their papers. On the same day Thomas Addis Emmet, Dr. Mac Nevin, and others, were arrested in their homes. A fortnight before, Arthur O'Connor and a priest named O'Coigley or Quigley had been arrested at Margate on their way to France. O'Connor was sent to a Dublin prison but father O'Coigley was tried at Maidstone and hanged.

898. A reward of £1,000 was offered for the apprehension of lord Edward Fitzgerald, the moving spirit of the confederacy. He was arrested on the 19th of May in No. 158 Thomas-street, the house of Nicholas Murphy a feather merchant, on information supplied by Francis Higgins, "the Sham squire," proprietor of the Freeman's Journal.

Lord Edward was lying ill in bed, when major Swan, yeomanry captain Ryan, and a soldier, entered the room. But lord Edward drew a dagger and struggled desperately, wounding Swan and Ryan. Major Sirr who had accompanied the party now rushed in with half-a-dozen soldiers, and taking aim, shot lord Edward in the shoulder, who was then overpowered and taken prisoner. But he died of his wound on the 4th of June, at the age of thirty-two.

899. On the 21st May two brothers Henry and John Sheares, barristers, members of the Dublin directory of the United Irishmen, were arrested. They were convicted on the 12th of July, and hanged two days after. A reprieve for Henry came too late—five minutes after the execution.

900. The stoppage of the mail coaches from Dublin on the night of the 23rd of May, was to be the signal for the simultaneous rising. They were stopped about two o'clock on the morning of the 24th, and the people rose. But Dublin did not rise, for it had been placed under martial law, and almost the whole of the leaders had been arrested. The rising was only partial: confined to the counties of Kildare, Wicklow, and Wexford; and there were some slight attempts in Carlow, Meath, and Dublin. It was premature: the people were almost without arms, without discipline, plan, or leaders.

901. On the 26th of May a body of 4,000 insurgents were defeated on the hill of Tara. On the same day or rather on Whitsunday the 27th, the rising broke out in Wexford. Here the rebellion assumed a religious character which it had not elsewhere: the rebels were nearly all Roman Catholics, though many of their leaders were Protestants.

902. This Wexford rising was not the result of any concert with the Dublin directory; for the society of United Irishmen had not made much headway among the quiet industrious peasants of that county. The Wexford people were driven to rebellion simply by the terrible barbarities of the military, the yeomen, and more especially the North Cork militia; and they rose in desperation without any plan or any idea of what they were to do. In their vengeful fury they committed many terrible excesses on the Protestant loyalist inhabitants, in blind retaliation for the worse excesses of the militia.

903. Father John Murphy, parish priest of Kilcormick, finding his little chapel of Boleyvogue (five miles southeast of Ferns) burned by the yeomen, took the lead of the rebels, with another priest, father Michael Murphy, whose chapel had also been burned; and on the 27th of May they defeated and annihilated a party of the North Cork militia on the Hill of Oulart, six miles east of Enniscorthy.

904. The rebels, having captured 800 stand of arms, marched next on Enniscorthy; and by the stratagem of driving a herd of bullocks before them to break the ranks of the military, they took the town after a contest of four hours. The garrison and the Protestant inhabitants fled to Wexford. About the same time Gorey was abandoned by its garrison, who fled to Arklow.

905. About the 29th of May the rebels fixed their chief encampment on Vinegar Hill, an eminence rising over Enniscorthy, at the opposite side of the Slaney. On the 80th of May a detachment of military was attacked and

destroyed at the Three Rocks, four miles from the town of Wexford. The rebels advanced towards Wexford: but the garrison did not wait to be attacked: they marched away leaving the town to the rebels. The retreating soldiers burned and pillaged and shot the peasantry on their way. The exultant rebels having taken possession, drank and feasted and plundered, and committed many outrages on those they considered enemies. A Protestant gentleman named Bagenal Harvey who had been seized by government on suspicion and imprisoned in Wexford jail, was released by the rebels and made their general.

906. Besides the principal encampment on Vinegar Hill, the rebels had now two others; one on Carrickbyrne Hill, eight miles from New Ross on the road to Wexford: the other on Carrigroe Hill, four miles east of Ferns. General Loftus with 1,500 men marched from Gorey in two divisions to attack Carrigroe. One of these divisions under colonel Walpole was surprised at Toberanierin or Tubberneering near Gorey and defeated with great loss; Walpole himself being killed and three cannons left with the insurgents. This placed Gorey in their hands.

907. From Vinegar Hill the rebels marched on Newtownbarry on the 2nd of June and took the town: but dispersing themselves to drink and plunder, they were attacked in turn by the soldiers whom they had driven out, and routed with a loss of 400.

908. The same thing happened at New Ross, on the 5th of June. The rebels marched from Carrickbyrne, and attacking the town with great bravery in the early morning, drove the military under general Johnson from the streets out over the bridge. But there was no discipline: they fell to drink: the soldiers returned and were twice repulsed. But still the drinking went on; and late in the evening the military returned and expelled the rebels in turn. The fighting had continued with little intermission for ten hours, the troops lost 800, among whom was lord Mountjoy colonel of the Dublin Militia: the rebels lost more than 1,000.

909. Father Philip Roche, the moving spirit in this attack on New Ross, being dissatisfied with Bagenal Harvey, who had indeed no military skill, placed a man named Edward Roche in command, removing Harvey to another less active position.

910. In the evening of that day some fugitive rebels from New Ross broke into Scullabogue House at the foot of Carrickbyrne Hill, where a crowd of loyalist prisoners were confined, and pretending they had orders from Harvey, which they had not, brought forth 37 of the prisoners and murdered them. Then setting fire to a barn in which all the others were locked up—more than a hundred—they burned them all to death. This barbarous massacre was the work of an irresponsible rabble.

911. The rebels now prepared to march on Dublin. Major-general Needham with 1,600 men garrisoned Arklow on the coast, through which

the rebel army would have to pass. On the 9th of June they attacked the town, and there was a desperate fight, in which the cavalry were at first driven back But the death of father Michael Murphy who was killed by a cannon ball, so disheartened the rebels that they gave way and abandoned the march to Dublin.

912. The encampment on Vinegar Hill was now the chief rebel station, and the commander in chief, general Lake, organized an attack on it with 20,000 men, who were to approach simultaneously in several divisions from several different points.

All the divisions arrived in proper time on the morning of the 21st of June, except that of general Needham, which for some reason did not come up till the fighting was all over. A heavy fire of grape and musketry did great execution on the rebels, who though almost without ammunition, maintained the fight for an hour and a half, when they had to give way. The space intended for general Needham's division lay open to the south, and through this opening—"Needham's Gap" as they called it—they escaped with comparatively trifling loss, and made their way to Wexford.

913. This was the last considerable action of the Wexford rebellion: the rebels lost heart, and there was very little more fighting. Many of the leaders were now arrested, tried by court-martial, and hanged, among them Bagenal Harvey, Mr. Grogan of Johnstown, and father John Murphy. Wexford was evacuated and was occupied by general Lake. The rebellion here was to all intents and purposes at an end. The whole county was now at the mercy of the yeomanry and the militia, who, without any attempt being made to stop them by their leaders, perpetrated dreadful atrocities on the peasantry. Straggling bands of rebels traversed the country free of all restraint, and committed many outrages in retaliation for those of the yeomanry.

Within about two years, while the civil war was at its height, sixty-five Catholic chapels and one Protestant church were burned or destroyed in Leinster, besides a countless number of dwelling houses.

914. During the Irish occupation of Wexford, a fellow named Dixon on the rebel side, the captain of a small coasting vessel, who had never taken any part in the real fighting, collecting a rabble and plying them with whiskey, broke open the jail where numbers of the Protestant gentry and others were confined, and in spite of the expostulations of the more respectable leaders, brought a number of them to the bridge and after a mock trial began to kill them one by one.

Thirty-six had been murdered, and another batch were brought out, when a young priest, father Corrin, rushed in at the risk of his life and commanded the executioners to their knees. Down they knelt instinctively, when in a loud voice he dictated a prayer which they repeated after him—that God might show to them the same mercy that they were about to show the prisoners; which so awed and terrified them that they immediately stopped the executions. Forty years afterwards, Captain Kellett of Clonard, one of the Protestant gentlemen he had saved, followed, with sorrow and reverence, the remains of that good priest to the grave.

915. By some misunderstanding the rebellion in the north was delayed. The Antrim insurgents under Henry Joy M'Cracken attacked and took the town of Antrim on the 7th of June; but the military returning with reinforcements, recovered the town after a stubborn fight. M'Cracken was taken and hanged on the 17th of the same month.

916. In Down the rebels, under Henry Munro, captured Saintfield, and encamped in Lord Moira's demesne near Ballinahinch. On the 14th of June they were attacked by generals Nugent and Barber, and defeated after a very obstinate fight—commonly known as the battle of Ballinahinch. Munro escaped, but was soon after captured, convicted in courtmartial, and hanged at his own door.

917. Lord Cornwallis, a humane and distinguished man, was appointed lord lieutenant on the 21st of June, with supreme military command. He endeavoured to restore quiet; and his first step was to stop the dreadful cruelties now committed by the soldiers and militia all over the country. On the 29th of July he entered into an arrangement with some of the leaders now imprisoned in Dublin, over seventy in number, to tell all they knew of the internal arrangements of the United Irishmen, without implicating individuals, after which they were to be permitted to leave Ireland.

Accordingly Arthur O'Connor, Thomas Addis Emmet, Dr. MacNevin, Samuel Neilson, and several others, were examined on oath; but it was afterwards ascertained that they had hardly anything to tell that had not been already made known to the government by spies. After all they were not allowed to go away freely, for twenty of the principal men were sent to Fort George in Scotland, where they were kept confined till 1802.

918. After the rebellion had been crushed, a small French force of 1,060 men under general Humbert landed at Killala in Mayo on the 22nd of August 1798, and took possession of the town. Two Irishmen accompanied Humbert Bartholomew Teeling and Matthew Tone, brother of Theobald Wolfe Tone. General Lake proceeded against them with a large force of militia; but the militia fled in a panic on the approach of the French.

919. Humbert now marched north. Lord Cornwallis proceeded from Dublin, and came up with him at Ballinamuck in the county of Longford with an army twenty times more numerous than the French; and after some skirmishing Humbert surrendered; after which he and his men were sent back to France. Tone and Teeling were sent to Dublin, tried, and hanged: and court-martials were held and there were numerous other executions.

920. This partial expedition was followed by another under admiral

Bompart:—One 74 gun ship named the "Hoche" with eight frigates and 8,000 men under general Hardi, sailed from Brest on the 20th of September: Theobald Wolfe Tone was on board the "Hoche." The "Hoche" and three others arrived off lough Swilly, where they were encountered by a British squadron under Sir John Borlase Warren. There was a terrible fight of six hours, during which the "Hoche" sustained the chief force of the attack till she became a helpless wreck and had to surrender. Tone fought with desperation: courting but escaping death. After the surrender he was recognised, and sent, ironed, to Dublin. He was tried by courtmartial and condemned to be hanged. He vainly begged to be shot, not hanged, on the score that he was a French officer.

On the morning fixed for the execution he cut his throat with a penknife. Meantime Curran, in a masterly speech, succeeded on legal grounds in staying the execution for further argument. But Tone died from his self-inflicted wound on the 19th of November 1798 In the numerous trials during and after the rebellion, Curran was always engaged on the side of the prisoners; and though he did not often succeed, his fearless and brilliant speeches were wonderful efforts of genius.

THE IRISH ACT OF UNION (1799-1800)

921. William Pitt the great English prime minister had long resolved upon a legislative union between England and Ireland: he believed the proper time had now come; and made very careful preparations for his purpose. At the opening of 1799 the marquis of Cornwallis was lord lieutenant and lord Castlereagh was chief secretary. The Union was indirectly referred to in the Irish parliament in the speech from the throne on the 22nd January 1799. The opposition at once took the matter up, and they were joined by many who had hitherto been supporters of the government, among others John Foster the speaker, Sir John Parnell the chancellor of the exchequer, prime sergeant Fitzgerald, and Sir Jonah Barrington: all fearing the loss of their parliament. They moved "that the undoubted birthright of the people of Ireland, a resident and independent legislature, should be maintained." After an excited debate of twenty-two hours, the votes were equally divided, 106 each side. Parnell and Fitzgerald were soon afterwards dismissed from their offices.

922. In February 1799 the scheme was brought forward in the English parliament by Pitt, and approved. In Ireland elaborate preparations were made to carry it in next session. All persons holding offices who showed themselves adverse were dismissed. The Irish government had been all along corrupt—but now, still under outside orders —it went far beyond anything ever experienced before.

Those who had the disposal of seats—a money making possession in times of election—were in great alarm; for if the union were carried the 300 members would have to be reduced to a third, so that about 200 constituencies would be disfranchised. The opposition of these proprietors was bought off by large sums: about £15,000 was paid for each seat. One proprietor got £52,000: two others £45,000 each: a third £23,000; and so on. The entire sum paid for the whole of the "rotten" or "pocket" boroughs as they were called, was £1,260,000, which Ireland itself had to pay, for it was added to the Irish national debt.

923. To purchase the votes of individual members, and the favour of certain influential outsiders, 28 new peers were created, and 22 of those already peers were promoted; and there were besides, great numbers of bribes in the shape of pensions, judgeships, baronetcies, preferments, various situations, and direct cash. All this was done with scarcely an attempt at concealment. Lord Cornwallis, a high-minded man, expressed the utmost abhorrence at being obliged to take a part in these transactions.

924. The session opened on the 15th of January 1800: the last meeting of the Irish parliament. Grattan, knowing what was coming, had himself elected member for Wicklow, and though very ill, he rose from his bed and took his seat dressed in the uniform of the volunteers. Dublin was in a state of fearful excitement. The streets were filled with dismayed and sorrow-stricken crowds who had to be kept within bounds by cavalry.

925. Lord Castlereagh brought forward the motion in the commons. The anti-unionists opposed the project most determinedly; Grattan, worn with sickness, pleaded with all his old fiery eloquence; and Sir John Parnell proposed that there should be a dissolution and that a new parliament should be called to determine this great question; but the unionists carried everything. There were many motions: on the first the government had 158 against 115: and in the others there were corresponding majorities.

In the lords the bill was introduced by lord Clare (John Fitzgibbon), who had 50 votes against 25. On the 1st of August the royal assent was given; and the act of union came into force on the 1st January 1801.

926. The following are the chief provisions of the act of union:—

I. The two kingdoms to be henceforward one:—"The United Kingdom of Great Britain and Ireland": the succession to the throne to remain the same as before.

II. The Irish representation in the united parliament to be:—In the lords: 4 spiritual peers taken in rotation, from session to session, from the Irish Protestant hierarchy; and 28 temporal peers to be elected for life by the whole Irish peerage; in the commons: 100 members.

III. All subjects of the United Kingdom to be under the same regulations as to trade and commerce.

IV. The Irish Established Church to be continued for ever, and to be united with that of England.

V. All members of parliament to take an oath, framed to exclude Roman Catholics (for no Catholic could conscientiously take it).

VI. Ireland to contribute two-seventeenths to the expenditure of the United Kingdom for twenty years, when new arrangements would be made.

VII. Each of the two countries to retain its own national debt as then existing; but ail future debts contracted to be joint debts.

VIII. The courts of justice to remain as they were: final appeals to the house of lords.

927. Pitt had at first intended to include in the articles of union the emancipation of the Catholics; but to this the leading Irish Protestants gave such fierce opposition that he had to abandon it.

But in order to lessen the hostility of the Catholics to the union, a promise was conveyed to them that emancipation would immediately follow. The promise however was not carried out; and the measure was delayed for twenty-nine years, chiefly through the invincible obstinacy of the king, who had a fixed idea that to agree to such a measure would be a breach of his coronation oath.

ROBERT EMMET'S INSURRECTION (1800-1803)

928. In 1802, Robert Emmet, a gifted, earnest, noble-minded young man of twenty-four, younger brother of Thomas Addis Emmet, attempted to reorganise the United Irishmen. He had just returned from France and had hopes of aid from Napoleon. He employed all his private fortune in the secret manufacture of pikes and other arms. His plan was to attack Dublin Castle and Pigeon House fort; and he had intended to rise in August 1803, by which time he expected invasion from France; but an accidental explosion in one of his depots precipitated his plans. The 23rd of July was now fixed; on which day he expected a contingent from the celebrated Wicklow rebel, Michael Dwyer; and another from Kildare.

929. By some misunderstanding the Wicklow men did not arrive; and though the Kildare men came, there was no one to direct them. Towards evening a report was brought that the military were approaching; whereupon, in desperation, he sallied from his depot in Marshalsea-Lane, into Thomas-street and towards the castle, with about 100 men.

930. The city was soon in an uproar; the mob rose up; and some stragglers, bent on mischief and beyond all restraint, began outrages. Meeting the chief justice lord Kilwarden, a good man and a humane judge, they dragged him from his coach and murdered him. When news of this outrage and others was brought to Emmet, he was filled with horror, and attempted but in vain to quell the mob. Seeing that the attempt on the castle was hopeless, he fled to Rathfarnham.

931. He might have escaped: but he insisted on remaining to take leave of Sarah Curran, daughter of John Philpot Curran, to whom he was secretly engaged. He was arrested by major Sirr on the 25th of August at his hiding-place in Harold's Cross; and soon after was tried and convicted,

making a short speech of great power in the dock. On the next day, the 20th of September 1803, he was hanged in Thomas-street.

DANIEL O'CONNELL (1803-1822)

932. After the Union there was no appearance of the promised bill for Emancipation. The old Catholic Committee still survived, held its meetings in Dublin, and kept the claims of the Catholics before parliament and the public; but there appeared very little hope, for King George III. continued as obstinate as ever. In 1805 Grattan became a member of the United Parliament, and devoted himself almost exclusively to the cause of Irish Catholic emancipation. In 1807 the duke of Richmond came over as lord lieutenant, with Sir Arthur Wellesley—afterwards the duke of Wellington—as chief secretary.

933. Some time before this, a few of the bishops, as an inducement for the government to grant emancipation, agreed that the crown should have a veto in the appointment of Irish Catholic bishops: that is to say, when the man had been selected by the Irish ecclesiastical authorities, his name should be submitted to the king: if the king objected another was to be chosen. But the general body of Catholics, clergy and people, knew nothing of this.

934. In 1808 a petition for Catholic relief was brought to London by the Catholic lord Fingall and Dr. Milner. It was presented to Parliament by Grattan and some others, who, on the authority of lord Fingall and Dr. Milner, offered the veto. This made the matter of the veto public; the clergy and people generally repudiated it: the bishops formally condemned it at one of their meetings; and in addition to all this the government, even with the offer before them, refused to entertain the petition.

This veto question continued to be discussed for some years, and caused considerable dissension among the Catholics. The Irish aristocracy were generally in favour of it. Those who opposed it, led by O'Connell, ultimately prevailed.

935. About this time Daniel O'Connell, afterwards familiarly known as the "Liberator," began to come prominently into notice. He was the chief figure in Irish political history for half a century, and was one of the greatest popular leaders the world ever saw.

He was born, 6th of August 1775, at Carhen near Cahersiveen county Kerry—the son of Morgan O'Connell—and was adopted by his uncle Maurice O'Connell, who afterwards left him his residence, Darrynane Abbey near Gahersiveen. He was sent at thirteen to a school near Queenstown—the very first school opened in Ireland after the relaxation of the penal laws. While still a boy he spent some time at St. Omer's and at Douay in France, where he studied with distinction. Returning, he was called to the bar in 1798, and at once came to the front as a most successful advocate. His first public speech against the Union was made to a body of freeholders in 1800 in the Royal Exchange, Dublin, which was the beginning of an agitation carried on during the rest of his life.

936. It may be said that O'Connell founded the system of peaceful, persevering, popular agitation against political grievances—keeping strictly within the law. During the whole agitation, more especially for emancipation, he was ably seconded by Richard Lalor Sheil, whose oratorical powers were little inferior to his own.

937. In 1809, a new "Catholic Committee," to advance the Catholic claims, was formed in Dublin, consisting of the Catholic peers and of delegates from various parts of the country. But the government brought the Convention act to bear on it, and arrested and brought to trial some of the leaders. O'Connell was their counsel, and argued so ingeniously that he got them acquitted. The Committee was then dissolved and re-constructed, but it gradually died out.

938. In 1812 Robert Peel became chief secretary. For several years at this period the country was in a most deplorable state. The conclusion of the continental wars was followed by stagnation in trade and great distress. The people lost all hope of relief: there were secret societies: and outrages were frequent.

939. The public mind became gradually impressed with the justice and expediency of emancipation: partly by the gigantic labours of O'Connell, and to some extent by the writings of Thomas Moore.

In 1811 the Prince of Wales became regent: and succeeded as George IV. on the 29th of January 1820, when his father, George III. died, blind and insane.

940. In 1820, Grattan, then residing at Tinnehinch, sinking under disease and feeling he had not long to live, was seized with an anxious desire to attend the parliament in London, and, as he said, "to die at his post." Having made all arrangements about his funeral, he travelled by easy stages, intending to make one more appeal for his Catholic fellow-countrymen. But he did not live to do so. With a paper in his hand on which he had written his last political pronouncement, he said to his son a very short time before his death:—"I die with a love of liberty in my heart, and this declaration in favour of my country in my hand." He died in London on the 4th of June 1820, aged seventy-three, and was buried in Westminster Abbey. After his death, his friend William Plunket, member for Dublin, subsequently lord chancellor of Ireland, greatly distinguished himself as the advocate of the Catholic claims.

941. In 1821 George IV. visited Ireland, and was received with great enthusiasm. His visit was regarded as a sure harbinger of relief by the overjoyed Catholics. He spent a month in Ireland and went away expressing his gratification at his reception. But nothing ever came of it: still no indication of an emancipation bill; the country continued disturbed,

and in 1822 the Insurrection Act was renewed.

In 1822, Peel, by an act of parliament, constituted the Irish constabulary force.

CATHOLIC EMANCIPATION (1823-1829)

942. In 1823 the "Catholic Association" was founded by O'Connell and Richard Lalor Sheil; it was the chief agency by which Catholic emancipation was ultimately achieved. The expenses were defrayed chiefly by a subscription from the people of one penny a week, which was called "Catholic rent": and the association soon spread through all Ireland. O'Connell and Sheil were all through the mainsprings of the movement: and it was the means of establishing a free press and of creating healthful public opinion. The government viewed the new association with jealousy and alarm; and an act of parliament was passed in 1825 to put it down, which O'Connell called the "Algerine act" in allusion to its despotic character.

943. But O'Connell, with his usual astuteness, dissolved the association, and reconstructed it. The new act forbade meetings for longer than fourteen days: but he arranged to hold meetings for exactly fourteen days, and made some other changes: so that he completely evaded the act; the law was obeyed; and the association went on as powerfully as before.

944. In January 1828 the duke of Wellington became prime minister; and Robert Peel was home secretary. The marquis of Anglesea came to Ireland as lord lieutenant: but he was removed soon after for being in favour of emancipation; so little was the sudden coming change anticipated. In Waterford and several other places, by means of the perfect organisation of the Catholic Association, Protestant members favourable to emancipation were returned; the forty-shilling freeholders voting for them in spite of the great landlords.

945. It had been recommended by the veteran John Keogh that some Catholic should be elected member, and should present himself and be excluded; so that the absurdity of disfranchising a constituency because the chosen member refused to take an oath that his own religion was false, should be brought home to the people of the empire. Keogh believed that this would lead to emancipation. A vacancy now occurred in Clare, as the sitting member Mr. Vesey Fitzgerald, having accepted the office of president of the Board of Trade, had to seek re-election. O'Connell determined to oppose him. His address to the people of Clare aroused extraordinary enthusiasm, and he was returned by an immense majority.

946. This election aroused sympathy all through England for the Catholics. The government became alarmed; and still more so when they found that the Association were preparing to return Catholic members all through Ireland, Wellington and Peel, forced by public opinion, gave way, being now convinced that emancipation was necessary to save the country

from civil war or revolution. Peel, on account of his change of opinion, resigned his seat for the university of Oxford in order to test the opinion of his constituents; and having been defeated in seeking re-election, he was afterwards elected for Westbury. In 1829 he introduced into the commons a bill for the emancipation of the Catholics. After several days' stormy debate the third reading was carried on the 30th of March.

The debate in the lords was even more violent than in the commons. But Wellington ended the matter by declaring that they should choose either of the two alternatives, Emancipation or civil war. It passed the third reading, and received the royal assent on the 13th of April 1829.

947. After the bill had become law O'Connell presented himself at the bar of the house to claim his seat for the first time since his election; knowing well what was to come. According to the terms of the act it was only those elected after the 13th of April that came under the new oath: this was designedly inserted by Peel in order to force O'Connell to seek re-election. The old oath was put into his hand; and looking at it for a few seconds he said:—"I see here one assertion as to a matter of fact which I know to be untrue: I see a second as to a matter of opinion which I believe to be untrue. I therefore refuse to take this oath." He then withdrew; but he was afterwards allowed to make a speech of three hours. A new writ was issued for Clare, and he was returned unopposed.

948. By this Emancipation act a new oath was framed which Catholics might take. The act therefore admitted Catholics to the right of being members of parliament in either house. It admitted them also to all civil and military offices, with three exceptions:—those of regent, lord lieutenant, and lord chancellor.

A portion of the act was directed to the suppression of the Catholic Association: but this the association had anticipated by dissolving itself, after it had accomplished its main purpose.

949. The act contained one fatal provision which O'Connell had to agree to; it raised the franchise in Ireland to £10, though in England the qualification remained at the limit of forty shillings: this disfranchised all the forty-shilling freehold voters, who constituted the main strength of the Catholic party.

950. The credit of carrying emancipation is due to Daniel O'Connell; but he was very ably assisted by Richard Lalor Sheil.

THE TITHE WAR

951. I will sketch here, in a short chapter, the leading events of the reign of William IV., which are intimately connected with those of the period just concluded.

In 1830 George IV. died and was succeeded by his brother as William IV This brought on a general election; and O'Connell and several other Catholics were returned from Ireland.

952. In the end of 1830 Wellington resigned, and was succeeded as prime minister by earl Grey. The marquess of Anglesea became lord lieutenant for the second time; E. G. Stanley chief secretary; and William Plunket lord chancellor.

953. O'Connell resumed his agitation for repeal, reviving, in this same year, the Catholic Association under the name of the Society of the Friends of Ireland. This was suppressed by proclamation; and he founded the Anti-union Association, which was also suppressed. In the following year, 1831, for attending a meeting in defiance of the proclamation, he was tried and convicted: but it all went for nothing, for he was never called up for punishment.

954. In 1831 the chief secretary the Right Hon. E. G. Stanley, in a letter to the Duke of Leinster, announced the foundation of the system of National Education in Ireland. Its two fundamental principles were, and are still.—(1) Combined literary and separate religious instruction for children of different religions: (2) No interference with the religious principles of any child. Commissioners were appointed who were intrusted with government funds: and in 1832 they began to give aid to schools. From that time to the present the National System has worked with uninterrupted success.

955. In 1832 was passed the great English Reform bill. In the same year another on similar lines for Ireland was introduced by Mr Stanley and passed. Several small "rotten" or "pocket" boroughs were disfranchised; the representation was more evenly distributed; and the number of Irish members was increased to 105. Tenants of £50 a year and leaseholders of £10 a year were to have votes. O'Connell and Sheil fought hard but vainly to have the franchise restored to the forty-shilling freeholders.

956. The Catholic peasantry were still called on to pay tithes, and also the "Church-rate" or Church-cess, a tax to keep the Protestant churches in repair: and they continued to be harassed by the exactions of tithe-proctors and others, who if the money were not forthcoming seized the poor people's cows, furniture, beds, blankets, kettles, or anything else they could lay hands on.

957. At last about 1830 there arose a general movement against tithes: the people resisted all through the south of Ireland; and for many years there was a "Tithe war." The military and police were constantly called out to support the collectors in making their seizures: and almost daily there were conflicts, often with loss of life. At Newtownbarry in Wexford, in 1831, thirteen peasants were killed by the yeomanry and police; in 1832 eleven police and several peasants were killed in a tithe-conflict at Carrickshock near Knocktopher in Kilkenny: and many other such fatal encounters took place.

958. There was determined resistance everywhere; and the cost of

collection was far greater than the amount collected. Hundreds of Protestant clergy got little or nothing and were reduced to poverty. To relieve these temporarily, government advanced a million on loan. Then there was a Coercion act: but still the people resisted. All this time O'Connell, seconded by Sheil, struggled both in and out of parliament for the total abolition of tithes.

959. In 1833 government passed the "Church Temporalities Bill"; which reduced the number of Protestant bishops from eighteen to ten; and of archbishops from four to two. It also abolished Church-rates. The money saved by this Act was left with the Church. The Tithe war went on till at last, some years later (in 1838) the tithes—reduced by 25 per cent.—were put on the landlord instead of the tenant. But the tenants had to pay still; for the landlords added the tithes to the rent.

960. On the 20th of June 1837 William IV. died and was succeeded by his niece the Princess Victoria who was then just over eighteen years of age.

PART VI. The Modern Period
TO THE DEATH OF O'CONNELL

961. In 1888, the Rev. Theobald Mathew, a young priest belonging to the order of Capuchin Friars, joined a Temperance Society that had been started in Cork, by some Protestant gentlemen, chiefly Quakers. He took the total abstinence pledge, and soon became the leading spirit in the society. From that time forth he devoted himself almost exclusively to the cause of Temperance, going all through Ireland, preaching to immense congregations, and administering the total abstinence pledge to vast numbers of people of all religious denominations. A wonderful change soon came over the country; for drunkenness with its attendant evils and miseries almost disappeared. The good effects were long felt, and are to some extent felt still. For though the practice of drinking has in a great measure returned, it is not nearly so general as formerly; and drunkenness, which before Father Mathew's time was generally looked upon with a certain degree of indulgence, and by some was considered a thing to boast of, is now universally regarded as discreditable. Through the earnest exertions of individuals and societies all over the country, the cause of Temperance has been lately making great advances, and on all hands it is admitted that the evil of drink is gradually but surely growing less and less as years go by.

962. O'Connell and other Irish leaders had all along hoped to have the Act of Union repealed, that is. to get back for Ireland Grattan's parliament, with all its independence and all its privileges. But the struggle for Emancipation absorbed so much of their energies that for about thirty years after the Repeal agitation was started in 1810, it was carried on only in a faint sort of way. In 1840 it was vigorously renewed, when O'Connell founded the Repeal Association: and in 1843, he began to hold great public meetings in favour of Repeal, at which vast numbers of the people attended, eager to support the movement and to hear his magnificent addresses. At one meeting held on the Hill of Tara, the ancient seat of the Irish kings, it was computed that a quarter of a million of people were present. About thirty of these meetings—"Monster Meetings" as they came to be called—were held during 1843. At last the Government took action, and "proclaimed," i.e. forbade, the meeting that was arranged to be held at Clontarf on the 8th October. After this O'Connell and several others were arrested, tried, and convicted. But when they had spent three months in prison, they had to be released in September, 1843; because the House of Lords, before whom O'Connell brought the case, decided that the trial was not a fair one, inasmuch as the government had selected a one-sided jury. It may be said that this ended the agitation for Repeal.

963. In those days almost the whole population of Ireland subsisted on the potato. But in 1845 and 1846, the potato crop failed and there was a

great famine, the most calamitous the country had ever experienced. In 1846 and 1847 the people died by hundreds of thousands of starvation and fever. The preventive measures taken by Government, in the shape of public works, were quite inadequate: but the English people individually made noble efforts to save the starving peasantry; and money in enormous amounts came pouring in. One sad feature of this great national catastrophe was that in each of those two years Ireland produced quite enough of corn to feed the people of the whole country; but day after day it was exported in shiploads, while the peasantry were dying of hunger. Notwithstanding the great efforts of benevolent individuals and associations, one-fourth of the people of Ireland died of famine and disease during 1846 and 1847. So tremendous a calamity had probably never been experienced by any other country of Europe.

964. After O'Connell's trial and conviction, a number of the younger men among his followers, losing faith in his method of peaceful and constitutional agitation, separated from him and formed what is called the "Young Ireland Party." They were educated men of the highest character, and many of them of great literary ability. O'Connell's various organisations from the very beginning of his career, had been almost exclusively Catholic; but the Young Ireland Party included Catholics and Protestants; and one of their aims was to unite the whole people of Ireland of all religious denominations in one great organisation.

965. "The Nation" newspaper had been founded in 1842 by Charles Gavan Duffy, John Blake Dillon, and Thomas Davis; the first two Catholics, the third a Protestant; and they now used it to give expression to their views. It was very ably conducted, its pages abounding in brilliant writing, both prose and poetry: of which a large part has become permanently embodied in Irish National Literature. The writers were much less guarded than O'Connell; their articles tended towards revolutionary doctrines; and they soon came in contact with the law. Other papers with similar principles and objects were founded, with writers who were still more outspoken. Of these latter the most conspicuous, for his brilliantly written and violent articles, was John Mitchel, an Ulster Unitarian, who openly advocated rebellion and total separation from England.

966. During all this time of disruption and trouble the whole of the Catholic clergy and the great body of the people, forming collectively the "Old Ireland Party," stood by O'Connell. The secession of the young Irelanders was a cause of great grief to him; and he denounced them with unsparing bitterness; for he foresaw that they would bring trouble on themselves and on the country; which indeed came to pass soon after his death. Yet in many ways this brilliant band of young men exercised great influence for good, which remained after the trouble and the trials were all past and gone, and which remains to this day. They infused new life and

energy into Irish national literature, spread among the people a knowledge of Irish history, Irish music, and Irish lore of all kinds, and taught them to admire what was good and noble among past generations of Irishmen of every creed and party.

967. In 1846, O'Connell, worn out by labour and anxiety, began to decline in health; and he suffered intense anguish of mind at witnessing the calamities of the people he loved so well; for the famine was at this time making fearful havoc among them. In the following year his physicians, hoping that change of air and scene might benefit or restore him, advised him to go to the Continent. He set out on a journey to Rome, partly devotional and partly for health; but his strength failed on the way; and he died at Genoa on the 15th May, 1847, at the age of seventy-one. In accordance with his latest wish, his heart was carried to Rome, and his body was brought back to Ireland and buried in Glasnevin, where a stately pillar-tower, after the model of the round towers of old, now marks his resting-place.

PARNELL

968. The Young Ireland Party now determined to attempt revolution. But the government, knowing all their plans and intentions, began to take measures. Mitchel was arrested and sentenced to transportation. William Smith O'Brien, Thomas Francis Meagher, and John Blake Dillon went down to the country in 1848, and tried to raise an armed rebellion: but the people did not join them, and, after a trifling skirmish at Ballingarry in Tipperary, the rising was easily put down. The leaders—including Smith O'Brien, Meagher, and several others—were soon arrested, tried, and sentenced to death. But the sentence was commuted to transportation for life, and they were all sent to Van Diemen's Land; from which many of them afterwards escaped. These events, it may be said, brought to an end the Young Ireland movement.

969. The famine had ruined the majority of the landlords as well as of the people, and most of the estates were heavily in debt. In 1849 the Government formed a court in Dublin to sell encumbered estates. The purchasers bought the estates as they stood, and no allowance was made for the tenants' improvements, so that most of them lost the savings effected by the labour of their lives. In 1860 the government made an attempt to remedy this, but it came to nothing. The new owners generally raised the rents, and there were evictions, resistance, and outrages; while the people continued to emigrate by tens of thousands.

970. About 1862 James Stephens founded what was called the "Society of the Fenian Brotherhood," with the object of bringing about the independence of Ireland by force of arms. It was a secret oath-bound Society, but the Government were made aware of all the proceedings by spies. In 1865 Stephens and several others were arrested: but after a few

days Stephens escaped from prison by the help of the warders, who were themselves Fenians unknown to the authorities. All the others were sentenced to penal servitude.

In 1867 another rising was attempted: but it was easily suppressed. The Fenians formed a plan to seize Chester Castle, containing a great store of arms: but it was never carried out, as the authorities discovered the plot in time.

In the same year (1867) two Fenian prisoners were rescued from a prison van in Manchester: the police officer in charge was unintentionally shot dead, after which three of the rescuing party were tried and hanged. Towards the end of the year an attempt was made to blow up Clerkenwell prison in order to release a Fenian prisoner, which caused the death of several persons and grievous injury to many others.

971. Partly on account of these events, the minds of Englishmen began to be turned to the need of some reform and improvement in the condition of things in Ireland: and Mr. Gladstone, the Prime Minister at the time, directed his attention to the disestablishment of the Irish Protestant church, which had been the established church since the time of Elizabeth. It was shown in Parliament that it had not been able to carry out the intention for which it was originally established, the conversion of the Irish Catholics, who, instead of diminishing, had been relatively increasing. After much determined opposition the Protestant Church of Ireland was disestablished in 1869, so that it was no longer in connexion with the government; but due precaution was taken that none of the Protestant clergy then living should suffer any loss.

972. In 1870 Mr. Gladstone made another attempt to secure that the Irish tenantry should be compensated for their improvements in their farms in case of eviction: but the working of the Act was obstructed in various ways, and it did little good.

973. In 1878 the Intermediate Education Act was passed, providing for Intermediate Education in Ireland by payments to schools and by prizes to successful students. The funds were supplied from the money left after the disestablishment of the Church: and the system has been highly successful.

974. The condition of the Irish tenantry continued to be very bad: and about 1879 a "Land League" was formed by Michael Davitt, to agitate for reform and improvement. This League subsequently exercised great influence in the country and in parliament. In 1880 Charles Stewart Parnell was elected head of the Irish Party, and turned out the greatest Irish popular leader of modern times after O'Connell. He was a great Leader of Men, and by him the members of the Party were held together in a manner never equalled, so that they acted and voted as one man.

The land agitation became daily more intense and violent, and boycotting was very generally brought into play against those who resisted or opposed the movement. An attempt was made to put down the whole agitation by a Coercion Act passed at the instance of Mr. Forster, chief secretary for Ireland, giving the authorities power to arrest and keep in prison, without trial, all persons "reasonably suspected" of breaking the law. During the passing of this bill, Parnell and another Irish member, Joseph Biggar, obstructed and delayed the proceedings in every possible way, by taking advantage of the rules of the House of Commons, but not breaking them. In spite of all they could do, however, the bill was passed (1881).

975. By far the most important Act to reform the Irish land laws was passed by the Gladstone Government in 1881. By this law a Land Court was formed for fixing fair rents—"judicial rents," as they are called; and it was also laid down that so long as a tenant paid his rent he could not be evicted. This Act acknowledged the tenant as joint owner with the landlord. While it was passing through the Commons Mr. T. M. Healy, M.P., induced the Government to insert a clause of great importance, exempting the tenants' improvements from rent: a provision which is now known as the "Healy clause." In the cases brought before this court the rent was reduced on an average by 20 or 30 per cent. The rent once fixed by the court was to remain so for 15 years, when it would be again revised. Although the justice of the decisions of this court has often been questioned, by both tenants and landlords, it continued to do much good for the country.

976. Meantime great numbers of "suspects" were in jail all through Ireland under Mr. Forster's Act. At last matters came to a climax when Mr. Parnell and several other leaders were arrested and put into Kilmainham jail (1881). While here, Parnell and the others issued the "No rent manifesto"—advising the tenants all through Ireland to pay no more rent. It was, however, condemned everywhere by the clergy; and the people took little notice of it, but continued to pay their rent as before. After this the Government suppressed the Land League by proclamation.

977. After Parnell's imprisonment the state of the country became worse than ever, and outrages increased everywhere. The Government at last became convinced that his arrest, and Mr. Forster's Act that led to it, were a mistake. They released all the suspects and dropped the Act. It was now determined to adopt a conciliatory policy, and the government appointed Lord Frederick Cavendish chief secretary in place of Mr. Forster, who had resigned. The people of the whole country were in high hopes of better times; but these hopes were all dashed by a terrible crime. On the 8th of May, 1882, Lord Frederick Cavendish and Mr. Thomas Burke, under secretary, were murdered in open day in the Phoenix Park by some members of a gang calling themselves "Invincibles," whose chief means of carrying out their plans was assassination. The news of this crime was received with horror all through Ireland as well as in England. This was

followed by a severe Coercion Act, and all conciliatory measures were ended. In a little time the murderers were all brought to justice; five of them were hanged, and others of the Invincibles were sent to penal servitude.

In the autumn of 1882 Mr. Parnell founded the "Irish National League" to help in advancing the cause of Home Rule, and to advocate further reform in the Irish land laws. In 1888, 1884, and 1885 there were a number of dynamite outrages in London which had been plotted in America: but after a time the outrages ceased, and the Coercion Act was allowed to drop out of use.

978. In 1885 an Act was introduced and passed at the instance of Lord Ashbourne, then lord chancellor of Ireland, setting apart £5,000,000 to lend to the tenants of small holdings to enable them to buy out their farms when they could come to an agreement with their landlords; and thus become their own landlords. The tenants were to pay back the loan by annual instalments. After purchase, too, the amount the tenant had to pay yearly was less than the rent he had to pay the landlord. A few years afterwards another Act of the same kind, with the same amount of money, was passed.

These two Acts—so far as the money can go—have done great good: a large number of tenants are taking advantage of them: and they are remarkably punctual in paying back their instalments. After a certain number of years, when the purchase-money has been all paid back, the land will be quite free, with nothing to pay except rates and taxes. When a man owns his farm for ever, he has every inducement to improve it by draining, fencing, subsoiling, and so forth: and, as a matter of fact, nearly all those who have purchased their land work with great heart and spirit, and are every year becoming more comfortable and independent.

979. A dozen years before this time the Home Rule movement was set on foot by Isaac Butt (in 1874) to agitate for an Irish Parliament in Dublin: but he and his party were outvoted in the House of Commons, and the movement came to nothing. Mr. Gladstone now became convinced that it was necessary to give Ireland Home Rule; and for that purpose he introduced a bill in 1886, which was received with great favour by the Irish Nationalist party. But a considerable number of the Liberal members of parliament—hitherto Mr. Gladstone's followers—were opposed to the bill. They did not want to give a Parliament to Ireland, and they severed themselves from Mr. Gladstone's policy, forming a separate party who were, and are still, known as "Liberal Unionists," meaning that they still remained Liberals, but insisted on a single united Parliament for England and Ireland. When the question came on in the House of Commons, these voted with the Conservatives against the Home Rule bill, the Government were defeated, and the bill was thrown out. The rejection of the Home Rule bill caused intense disappointment to the great majority of the Irish people,

and gave great satisfaction to the Irish Conservative minority.

980. The land troubles continued, and evictions went on increasing, till at last some tenants adopted what was called the "Plan of Campaign." This meant that on any estate where the landlord insisted on what were considered impossible rents, the tenants in a body agreed to retain all the rents in their hands till some settlement was arrived at. Many landlords were forced to give reductions; but as time went on the Plan was often greatly abused, by being brought to bear on landlords that deserved well of their tenants, who now found it impossible to obtain their rents, and were, in many cases, reduced to poverty. Sometimes also dishonest persons, pretending to act in accordance with the Plan, refused to pay ordinary debts, such as those incurred for goods got on credit. Boycotting also was often practised against individuals; and what with all these causes of disquietude the country became very much disturbed.

981. In 1887 a Crimes Act for Ireland was passed, giving the authorities greater powers to arrest and prosecute persons for various specified offences. There were frequent collisions between the police and people; and in a scuffle at Mitchelstown, Co. Cork, the police fired a volley by which two persons were killed and several wounded. A proclamation was issued suppressing the National League in a large part of the south and west of Ireland. The state of disquietude continued: meetings were proclaimed, but were held in spite of the proclamations; the police and people often came into collision. Several of the leaders were imprisoned, among them Mr. William O'Brien, and Mr. T. D. Sullivan, then Lord Mayor of Dublin.

But with all this weary state of unrest there are a few pleasanter features to be recorded. Considerable numbers of small farmers continued to buy out their farms under the Ashbourne Acts; and hundreds of tenants applied to the Land Court to have judicial rents fixed, so that the Land Commissioners had much more business on hands than they could get through.

TO THE DEATH OF PARNELL

982. The London "Times" now (1888) brought a terrible charge against Mr. Parnell. It accused him of having written letters encouraging persons to commit crimes and outrages, and of saying that Mr. Burke, who was murdered in the Park, got only what he deserved. The writer went on to state that the letters, in Parnell's handwriting, were in the "Times" office. Parnell at once declared these accusations false, and brought an action for slander against the "Times." After a long trial it was found that all the letters had been carefully forged, in imitation of Parnell's handwriting, by an Irish newspaper editor named Pigott, who sold them for a good sum to the editor of the "Times." Pigott fled, but was pursued: and when he found himself overtaken, committed suicide. The "Times" had to acknowledge

the forgery, and by agreement of both sides, handed Parnell £5000 as damages, besides paying all the enormous expenses.

983. The Plan of Campaign still went on, though it—as well as boycotting—had been condemned by a rescript from Rome, and by the Catholic ecclesiastical authorities in Ireland. While many landlords were forced by it to reduce their rents, a large proportion of them resisted it with great determination; and large numbers of the tenants who held back their rents were evicted from their farms. These farms were, in many instances, given by the landlords to others—often persons brought from a distance. But the position of these new settlers was generally a very unpleasant one: for they were absolutely boycotted by the people of the neighbourhood, so that they often found it hard to obtain the necessaries of life; and in many cases they had to be protected by the police. Towards the close of the year (1889), however, the country became more tranquil; the Plan of Campaign failed on many estates, and there was much less boycotting.

984. At this time a circumstance occurred that led to the disruption of the Nationalist party. For a considerable period, very unfavourable rumours affecting Mr. Parnell's personal character had been going about: but he persisted in declaring them false, and that when the proper time came he would prove them so. But when the proper time did come, it was found that they were all true. On this, the Irish Catholic bishops and the majority of his followers declared that they would no longer have him as leader (1890); but a section of the Nationalists took his part, and determined that they would still follow him. So the Nationalist party became broken up into two sections, Parnellites and anti-Parnellites, who were bitterly opposed to each other. The hierarchy and Catholic clergy in general were all through, to the very end of this dispute, on the side of the anti-Parnellite party; and later on the bishops issued a manifesto declaring Parnell unworthy to be leader, and appealing to the people to sever themselves from him.

985. One of the most extensive and influential landlords in the south of Ireland was Mr. Smith Barry: and, so far, he and his tenants had agreed very well. But it happened that he gave aid to a neighbouring landlord who was trying to resist the Plan of Campaign; and for doing this, Smith Barry's tenants—urged on by some of the Nationalist leaders—quarrelled with him, though having little or no fault to find with his manner of dealing with themselves. Then commenced a bitter struggle. The tenants resorted to the Plan of Campaign on his estates, and he evicted them wholesale for non-payment of rent. He was the owner of a great part of the town of Tipperary—a town then very prosperous, and having a large number of well-to-do shopkeepers, his tenants. Following the advice of one or more of the leaders, they now resolved to abandon their dwellings and shops wholesale, so as to cut off the supply of rent from the landlord. They built

up a temporary town in the neighbourhood, which they called "New Tipperary," to which most of them removed; while others, who thought the matter unadvisable and foolish, and who did not wish to remove, were forced to do so. But after a considerable interval the shopkeepers, getting tired of their new abodes, and finding themselves not prospering, settled matters with their landlord, who treated them very well on the occasion; they went back to their old homes; and so this business came to an end.

986. During 1890, and far into 1891, Parnell went through the country, holding meetings of his followers and making speeches; and there were many violent scenes, quarrels, and collisions, between the two parties. At last he became ill: yet with extraordinary energy he still persisted in attending and speaking at meetings in all sorts of weather, when he ought to have been in his bed. But human nature could not stand this strain: and at last he broke down utterly, and died on the 7th of October, 1891. His death, instead of ending the dissension, as many thought it would, only made matters worse: and though the majority of the anti-Parnellites were anxious for reconciliation, the Parnellites bitterly rejected all advances. The leader of the Parnellites was Mr. John Redmond, M.P., while Mr. Justin M'Carthy, M.P., was at the head of the anti-Parnellites, and, after his resignation, Mr. John Dillon, M.P. Some years later on, both parties were united under the leadership of Mr. John Redmond, M.P.: a union brought about mainly by Mr. T. Harrington, M.P., one of the Parnellite members.

Another Home Rule Bill for Ireland was brought forward by Mr. Gladstone in 1893; while Mr. John Morley was Chief Secretary for Ireland. It was passed in the Commons, though not with a very large majority—43 in a house of 651: but the House of Lords rejected it, 419 of them voting against it, and only 41 in favour of it. The news was received this time in Ireland with little surprise or excitement; for everyone foresaw that the Lords would throw it out, as the majority in the Commons was so small.

INDUSTRIAL PROGRESS

987. About this time the farmers all through the country, under the encouragement and guidance of Sir Horace Plunkett, began to form themselves into "Co-operative Societies" for the improvement of home industries, and especially of agriculture: one general association, founded by Sir H. Plunkett, being at the head of all—the "Irish Agricultural Organisation Society." These associations have effected great good by spreading enlightenment and introducing improved methods. Among other benefits many "Credit Banks" have been established, in which farmers and others can borrow small sums of money at a reasonable rate of interest, instead of having recourse to private money-lenders, who generally charged enormous and ruinous rates for their loans.

988. Another good result of this co-operative movement is the spread of "Creameries," which began to be formed in many districts about this time.

Hitherto each farmer who kept cows had his butter made in his own home. But in most cases there were bad appliances, and many of the women were more or less unskilled in making butter; so that it was not as good as it might be, and brought low prices. Instead of following this plan, the farmers of a district combined together to form a company, each paying for a number of shares according to his means: or a company for the purpose was formed in some other way. They had a Creamery erected, where butter is made on a large scale by special machinery, and under the management of skilful persons. To this all the farmers around send their milk, for which they are paid a good price, and after the butter is made they get back the buttermilk, which they use chiefly in feeding calves. In the Creamery, the very best butter is made from the milk; the manager sells it at a high price; and the proceeds are divided among the members of the company according to the number of their several shares, giving a good profit. By these Creameries, moreover, the credit of Irish butter is kept up—a very important matter. The farmers find this plan of disposing of their milk and butter far more profitable than making the butter in their own homes: and accordingly Creameries are spreading more and more over the whole country.

989. In various parts of Ireland, especially in the west, certain districts have become greatly overcrowded or "Congested"—i.e., the people are clustered closely in particular spots, living in poor cabins, each family with a little bit of land quite insufficient for support. They pay the rents as best they can, partly by industries outside their farms, such as fishing, gathering sea-weed, &c.; and in a great many cases the able-bodied men go to England every autumn, where they get work, and return home with their earnings after the harvest. In all cases, the people of these congested districts are miserably poor, and live in a very wretched, comfortless way, hardly able to support life.

To help to remedy this state of things, the "Congested Districts Board" was established at the instance of the Chief Secretary, Mr. Arthur Balfour. The Board were empowered to adopt various means to carry out their good work, for which they were furnished with funds by the Government, the money being advanced as a loan at a small rate of interest. In great numbers of cases the Board purchased farms sufficiently large for the support of the several families, to which the cottiers removed, and for which they were to pay reasonable rents.

The Board also encourage local industries among the people, such as fishing, rearing poultry, pig-feeding, and the production of bacon tor home use and for exportation, cattle-breeding and such like; and it has made money grants to schools for Technical Instruction in certain Industries suitable to the districts. Most of their enterprises, or those undertaken under their auspices, have been attended with very satisfactory results, such, for instance, as the

Woollen Industry, established by the nuns at Foxford in the county Mayo. This gives employment to the cottagers, both young and old, in all that neighbourhood, so that the whole district has been altered: instead of half-idle, listless poverty, there is now to be seen everywhere cheerful work, life, and prosperity, Under this Board also, and aided by the generosity of the Baroness Burdett-Coutts, a fishery school was established at Baltimore, county Cork, by the parish priest, the Rev. Father Davis, which did, and continues to do, immense good. A year or so later on, the Board purchased the whole of Clare Island, outside Clew Bay in Mayo, which they divided among a number of people, each family having a good-sized comfortable farm at a moderate rent. These are only a few examples of the great good done by this Board; and they are still working on with great energy and success.

990. The "Light Railways Bill," which was passed at the instance of Mr. Balfour, in 1895, for constructing narrow-gauge and moderately cheap railways through remote districts, besides giving employment daring construction, is doing much service by opening up those places, so that the farmers are now able to send their produce to markets—a thing they could not do before for want of means of conveyance.

991. A great advance has been gradually making in recent times to improve the condition of the labouring class. Formerly nearly all the labourers in the country places lived in wretched cabins, which were often dirty, comfortless, and unhealthy, and hardly afforded shelter. In most cases, too, they paid as much rent as if the houses were good. Now the custom has grown up, under the provisions of the law, for the County Authorities to erect "Labourers' Cottages"—neat, comfortable little houses, built of brick and stone, with slated or tiled roofs, and having a sufficient number of apartments. Attached to each cottage is a small plot of land for a kitchen-garden. These cottages and garden plots are given to the labourers of the place at very low rents, barely sufficient to pay off in time the expenses of erecting the buildings. So, while the counties are at no loss, the labourers are great gainers, for they have clean, pretty cottages, and good gardens, generally at lower rents than they had to pay for their poor cabins. In some parts of the country, "Labourers' Cottages" are to be seen everywhere, and the old cabins have almost completely disappeared.

992. On one question which came under public notice about this time, all parties in the country were united in opinion—a very rare circumstance in Ireland. For some time past, a Commission appointed by the Government had been inquiring whether Ireland's contribution of taxes to the support of the empire was the proper amount; for many persons in Ireland had long maintained that the country paid too much. The Commission was composed of a number of Englishmen and Irishmen, specially selected on

account of their skill in matters of that kind. After a long and most careful investigation, they issued their Report in 1896; and their verdict was that Ireland paid nearly £3,000,000 every year more than was just or right in proportion to her means. On this "Financial Relations Question," as it is called, meetings began to be held all over the country, which were attended by the most influential men of all parties and religions alike—men of the most extreme and opposite opinions joining in friendly union on the same platform, and making vigorous speeches, calling on the imperial parliament to relieve Ireland from this excessive taxation. Up to the present, however, nothing has been done; but many in Ireland are in hopes that parliament will deal with this important question in the near future.

993. Another Land Bill was passed this year (1896), by which many changes and improvements were made in former Acts, and which made it easier for tenants to purchase out their farms. One general effect of all the Land Acts is that, except where tenants have bought out their farms, the land belongs partly to the landlord and partly to the tenant, as already remarked. For the landlord has a right to rent, while, on the other hand, the tenant generally owns whatever improvements he has made, and cannot be disturbed so long as he pays his rent. This is what is called "Dual Ownership"; and it is on all hands considered an undesirable arrangement. Among other evils, it gives rise to many disputes and lawsuits between landlord and tenant. The Government are trying to put an end to this state of things, by encouraging the tenants to buy out their holdings if they can come to an agreement with the landlord as to terms. Many are doing so, as we have already seen, and year by year the numbers of "Peasant Proprietors," as they are called, are increasing. But many leading men, especially Mr. T. W. Russell, M.P., consider the process too slow, and are in favour of "Compulsory Purchase," i.e., that the landlords should be forced by law to sell, or the tenants to buy, in all cases at a fair valuation; while others again dislike compulsion, and prefer to let the voluntary system of purchase take its course.

994. There have been two Universities in Ireland for a considerable time past, namely, the Dublin University—or Trinity College, as it is commonly called—and the Royal University (which latter was established in place of the older Queen's University); but in neither of them is any provision for religious instruction for Catholic students: so that the Catholics have long demanded a University at which they can conscientiously attend. About twenty years before the time we have now arrived at, Mr. Gladstone attempted to remedy this grievance by bringing in a bill to have one University for all Ireland, which should include Trinity College, the three Queen's Colleges (of the Queen's University) and a new College, to be founded, in which there would be full opportunity for Catholic religious teaching: but the attempt failed, for the bill was thrown out by Parliament.

This question continued to be agitated and discussed very earnestly, and most of the leading statesmen of both England and Ireland were in favour of establishing such a University, notably Mr. Arthur Balfour and Mr. John Morley; but up to the present (i.e. to 1905, when this was written) no practical steps have been taken in the matter.

995. The most important event for Ireland towards the close of the century was the passing of the Irish "Local Government Act," in 1898, which made a complete change in the home administration of the country. By this Act nearly all local affairs, such as the fixing, collecting, and expenditure of rates, poor law management, roads, bridges, labourers' cottages, sanitation, schools for Technical Education, and such matters, instead of being in the hands of persons directly appointed by Government, are now managed by several kinds of Councils, whose members are elected by the free votes of the people. The Act came into operation in 1899.

996. The Government also established a "Department of Agriculture and Technical Instruction," with Mr. Horace Plunkett as Vice-President and chief manager. One of its functions is to provide for what is badly wanted, "Technical Education" for the instruction and improvement of workers in the various trades and industries, especially Agriculture. It also applies itself to the establishment of new industries, and to the revival of others that are either decaying or have died out altogether. Already this new Board has done a great deal of good, and there is every prospect that it will effect much more. It ought to be remarked here that the Commissioners of National Education in Ireland have greatly helped the cause of Technical and Industrial Education by issuing a new Programme encouraging managers and teachers of National Schools to teach the pupils various simple handicrafts suitable for children, so far as it can be done witnout interfering with the necessary literary education.

997. In 1900, the last year of the century, Her Majesty Queen Victoria—then in the eighty-first year of her age—visited Ireland after an absence from the country of nearly forty years. She received a most cordial and respectful welcome by the immense crowds that thronged the streets of Dublin: and the whole city was decorated and illuminated in a manner that had no parallel within living memory. After a stay of three weeks Her Majesty returned, highly gratified with her reception.

998. Wyndham's Land Act.—We have seen the attempts made to settle the Irish Land Question down to 1896. But by far the most important of all the Irish Land Acts was passed in 1908, at the instance of Mr. Wyndham, Chief Secretary, aided all through by skilled advice. Down to this year the great majority of the farms still remained unpurchased, for there was generally a gap between what the tenant was willing to give and what the landlord was willing to sell for. By this Act a free grant (or "Bonus," as it is usually called) of twelve millions was given by Government to enable

the two parties to come to an agreement, so that when the tenant offered so much for his farm, a sum was added to it—a part of the twelve millions—that brought it high enough for the landlord to accept. A vast sum was also set apart for lending to tenants, to enable them to buy, which they are to pay back in instalments, as in the Ashbourne Acts. This Act is working very successfully. Great numbers of tenants are buying out their farms, so that in a few years most of the land of the country will belong to "Peasant Proprietors." Provision is also made to enable the landlords to keep their own homes and demesnes, and live in Ireland—a thing much to be desired. So far (i.e. to 1905, when this was written) nearly all the landlords who have sold out have elected to remain.

999. In 1908 an Irish University Bill was introduced by Mr. Birrell, Chief Secretary for Ireland, and passed through Parliament, after much discussion, but with little opposition. By this Act, Trinity College continues unchanged, remaining, as before, the University of Dublin. The Royal University is to be dissolved, and two new Universities have been created. One—which will be called The National University of Ireland—will be in Dublin, with three constituent Colleges—Queen's College Cork, Queen's College Galway, and a new College to be founded in Dublin. In Belfast the Queen's College has been constituted a University which will be known as the Queen's University of Ireland. The arrangements laid down for the new University in Dublin have met with the approval of the Roman Catholic ecclesiastical authorities, so that Catholic students are quite free to avail themselves of it: and thus Mr. Birrell's Irish Universities Act of 1908 has removed a long-standing and most serious Roman Catholic educational grievance.

1000. From this brief narrative of the events of the last forty years or so, it will be seen that much has been done to remedy the evil effects of the unjust and ruinous laws. But much remains to be done, both by the Government and by the people themselves. On the part of the people, what they need most of all is to avoid intemperance, and to help the cause of Temperance by every means in their power. Another most necessary thing is that those of all parties and religions, throughout the four provinces, should unite for the common good, and should pay more attention to the encouragement and development of industries, so as to give increased opportunities of employment to the working classes, and induce them to remain at home. This desirable state of things is slowly but surely coming about: matters are gradually improving year by year; and those who have the welfare of the country at heart entertain strong hopes that the time is not far off when the people of Ireland will at last be prosperous and contented.

NOTE ON THE FORMATION OF COUNTIES

THE division of Ireland into shires or counties is of Anglo-Norman and

English origin. The counties generally represent the older native territories and sub-kingdoms.

King John, as has been already stated, formed twelve counties in 1210, namely Dublin, Kildare, Meath, Uriel (or Louth), Carlow, Kilkenny, Wexford, Waterford, Cork, Kerry, Limerick, and Tipperary. King's County and Queen's County were formed in the time of Queen Mary. Sir Henry Sidney, about 1565, formed the county Longford from the ancient district of Annaly. He also divided Connaught into six counties:—Galway, Sligo, Mayo, Roscommon, Leitrim, and Clare (but Clare was subsequently annexed to Munster, to which it had anciently belonged). Sir John Perrott, about 1584, formed the following seven counties of Ulster:—Armagh, Monaghan, Tyrone, Coleraine (now the county Derry), Donegal, Fermanagh, and Cavan: the other two Ulster counties, Antrim and Down, had been constituted some time before. This makes thirty, so far. In the time of Henry VIII, Meath was divided into two: Meath proper, and Westmeath. At first the county Dublin included Wicklow; but in 1605, under Sir Arthur Chichester, Wicklow was formed into a separate county. This makes the present number thirty-two.

Made in the USA
Middletown, DE
15 November 2019